STUDIES IN

SOCIAL INEQUALITY

THE POLITICAL SOCIOLOGY
OF THE WELFARE STATE

THE POLITICAL SOCIOLOGY OF THE WELFARE STATE

Institutions, Social Cleavages, and Orientations

Edited by Stefan Svallfors

STANFORD UNIVERSITY PRESS
STANFORD, CALIFORNIA

Printed in the United States of America on acid-free,
archival-quality paper

Library of Congress Cataloging-in-Publication Data

The political sociology of the welfare state : institutions,
social cleavages, and orientations / edited by Stefan
Svallfors.
    p. cm.
  Includes bibliographical references and index.
  ISBN 978-0-8047-5435-4 (cloth : alk. paper)
  1. Welfare state. 2. Political sociology. I. Svallfors,
Stefan.

JC479.P62 2007
306.2—dc22

2006035449

Typeset by Newgen in 10/14 Sabon

CONTENTS

Tables

Figures

Stefan Svallfors is professor of sociology at Umeå University, Sweden. His research deals mainly with the comparative study of attitudes and values and their links to social structure and institutions. His current research focuses on class differences in attitudes in comparative perspective. He is the editor of *Analyzing Inequality: Life Chances and Social Mobility in Comparative Perspective* (Stanford University Press, 2005) and author of *The Moral Economy of Class: Class and Attitudes in Comparative Perspective* (Stanford University Press, 2006).

Jonas Edlund is assistant professor of sociology at Umeå University. He is head of the Swedish part of the International Social Survey Program (ISSP). Edlund's current research focuses on the associations between "varieties of capitalism" and job-characteristics and their links to gender and class.

Mikael Hjerm is assistant professor of sociology at Umeå University. His research focuses mainly on attitudes of nationalism, racism, and questions of integration in different institutional contexts. He is currently interested in how national identities relate to perceptions of the welfare state. Hjerm is head of the Swedish part of the European Social Survey.

Staffan Kumlin is Hans Meijer Pro Futura Fellow at the Department of Political Science, Göteborg University. He studies comparative political behavior and public opinion, and his work has previously appeared in journals such as *Comparative Political Studies, Journal of Public Policy,* and *European Journal of Political Research*. He is the author of *The Personal and the Political: How Personal Welfare State Experiences Affect Political Trust and Ideology* (Palgrave-Macmillan 2004).

Maria Oskarson is assistant professor of political science at Göteborg University. Her research deals mainly with different aspects of the relation between social and political cleavages and attitudes, both from a comparative and national (Swedish) perspective. Her current work is an analysis of political exclusion in Sweden over the last decades.

Maria Pettersson is a Ph.D. candidate at the Department of Political Science, Göteborg University. Her dissertation focuses on the relationship between public service dissatisfaction and political action, with special attention paid to the institutional features of public service areas and how this could affect the extent to which citizens voice their grievances. She will finish her dissertation in 2008.

PREFACE

This volume emanates from the research program "The Political Sociology of the Welfare State," financed by the Swedish Council for Social and Working Life Research (FAS 2002-0811; 2005-1694) and the Bank of Sweden Tercentenary Foundation (K2002-0058). The editor has also enjoyed a Research Professor Grant from the Swedish Research Council (421-2003-1977). These grants have made it possible for us to concentrate on our work in a concerted and sustained manner. As sociologists and political scientists working together we have found collaborating across disciplinary boundaries not just intellectually rewarding but genuinely fun. So the grants are proof that governments can make (at least some) people happy (at least some of the time).

A draft version of the volume was discussed at a seminar with invited commentators at the Konrad Adenauer Centre in Cadenabbia, Italy, May 2005. Martin Rhodes, Edeltraud Roller, Michael Shalev, and Erik Olin Wright gave us the most delightful trashing anyone of us has ever experienced. Supporters of academic politeness would probably have found the seminar unbearably straightforward, but to us it was an intellectual delight. The three weeks or so we had expected to use for revisions of the manuscript turned out to be six months—including a complete overhaul of some of the chapters and substantial revisions of most of them. The quality of the volume has benefited immensely from their comments and we are deeply grateful for their time and effort. And it was great fun—not least the unforgettable hike along the slopes around Lago di Como.

We have also benefited from other comments on individual chapters. Among commentators we still remember are Linda Berg, Stefan Dahlberg, Ingid Esser, Walter Korpi, Johannes Lindvall, Knud Knudsen, Kenneth

Nelson, Joakim Palme, Christina Ribbhagen, Jan Teorell, and the participants in the seminar, "Elections, Public Opinion, and Democracy," at the Department of Political Science, Göteborg University. Our apologies to anyone we may have forgotten—your comments were so excellent that we now imagine we came up with them ourselves!

Jonas Pontusson and John Stephens provided wonderful encouragement and helpful comments in reading the final manuscript. Finally, the editor wants to thank David Grusky for his outstanding ability to dissolve all doubts and for never taking no for an answer. He is simply the most persuasive person found in academia, and Stanford University Press is truly blessed to have a series editor like him.

Stefan Svallfors
Umeå, May 2006

THE POLITICAL SOCIOLOGY
OF THE WELFARE STATE

CHAPTER ONE

Introduction

Stefan Svallfors

Political sociology seeks to understand the relation between social and political life. Its aim is to map variations in the relationship between social structure, political orientations, and political action, and to explain the patterns that arise. Thus broadly conceived, the field will include analyses of issues as different as the rise and fall of political parties, the development and effects of political institutions, or the orientations and action patterns of mass publics. In this volume, a group of political scientists and sociologists, in various ways, try to describe variations and untangle mechanisms in the links between political institutions, social cleavages, and orientations among citizens in the advanced industrial societies.

Political and societal developments over the course of the last few decades highly warrant a return to the classic questions within political sociology. As will be described in this chapter, welfare states in Western capitalist societies have undergone considerable change since their "maturation" a quarter of a century ago. Public policies have been restructured, decision-making structures have become increasingly complex, and the level and patterns of inequality have changed to a considerable extent. Such processes of change have varied considerably across countries and different types of political economies. However, none of the countries in the Western hemisphere have entered the twenty-first century with institutions and social cleavages intact from the 1970s.

The many reasons behind these changes are intertwined in complex patterns. Comparative research has revealed that the simplistic picture of state regulation and welfare state provisions undergoing a "race to the bottom," as a result of increased international competition and "globalization," is simply false (Scharpf and Schmidt 2000; Huber and Stephens 2001a; Pierson 2001b; Swank 2002). There are no signs of convergence among Western political economies; if anything, the reverse is true. We may therefore speak of "diverse responses to common challenges" (Scharpf and Schmidt 2000).

Nevertheless, as pointed out by Pierson, the mature welfare states have entered a stage of "permanent austerity" in which it has become increasingly difficult to sustain levels of provision (Pierson 2001a). In this process, "globalization" is actually a less important driving force than factors found within the advanced industrial nation-states themselves. Aging populations, post-industrialism, and the problems of financing welfare services are considerably more important than international economic competition or financial deregulation in explaining the rise of a more austere environment for welfare policies.

The aim of this volume is not to add still more analyses that attempt to chart and explain changes in welfare states and decision-making arrangements. Rather, these developments motivate and form the backdrop to our own attempts to grapple with variations of and mechanisms behind individual-level political orientations and identity formation. In what ways have various sociopolitical orientations changed in recent years in the advanced capitalist political economies? How do national institutions impact the ways in which such orientations are formed? What attitudinal correlates are found in the wake of changing stratification patterns? How do attitudes become translated into action under various institutional arrangements? How does "permanent austerity" impinge on views about government and policies? What impact do new supranational institutions have on the orientations of mass publics?

These are themes that have received less attention than many other aspects of welfare states in comparative perspective.[1] In spite of considerable progress over the last few years, comparative research on orientations, values, and attitudes has still not reached the status of a mature research field. If we take as a point of comparison the sophisticated comparative research on the determinants of welfare state development (for example, Scharpf and Schmidt 2000; Pierson 2001b; Huber and Stephens 2001a; Korpi and Palme 2003), or comparative studies of electoral behavior (for example, van der Eijk et al. 1996; Evans 1999; Norris 2004; Thomassen 2005; see summaries in Brooks et al. 2003; Manza et al. 2005), it is obvious that comparative research on orientations and attitudes still has some way to go. The extensive high-quality databases that have been created over the last decade or so are still underutilized. One aim of the present volume is to make a contribution to the growing literature that uses such databases in order to conduct theoretically informed comparative work.

My purpose in this chapter is to set the scene for the empirical contributions that follow. First, I provide an outline of the basic parameters of change. What are the current main patterns of change in welfare states and decision-making structures, which form the backdrop to our analyses? Next, I present our conceptual framework of analysis, including key concepts such as *orientations, social cleavages, institutions, moral economy, feedback effects*, and *political articulation*. This is followed by a discussion of our methodological strategies and the data materials on which our analyses build. As the analyses are mainly based on large-scale comparative survey data, I consider the possibilities and limitations of such data. The chapter concludes with a chapter-by-chapter overview of the contributions of the six authors in relation to the main issues of the volume.

CHANGING WELFARE STATES

It seems there are several main components in the ways welfare states have shifted over the last decades—some relating to changes in decision-making structures, others to changes in stratification patterns. The first tendency is summarized in the catch-word "governance" (Pierre 2000; Pierre and Peters 2000). The concept of governance is "notoriously slippery" (Pierre and Peters 2000: 7), but what we intend to focus upon are the ways in which the complexity of political decision making and political steering has increased over time. It seems there are at least three interconnected aspects of these changes in democratic polities. The first is the drive toward decentralization of the welfare state, which has been clearly present in most Western countries. It has become a widespread belief among political decision makers that democratic accountability and efficiency in service delivery are enhanced by delegating authority to subnational levels.

Furthermore, the so-called new public management school, whose advice has been widely adopted by implementing bodies, argues that efficiency in the public sector is enhanced by delegating budgetary responsibility to the lowest possible level and by creating "internal markets" through which organizational subunits interact (Lawson and Taylor-Gooby 1993;

Hood 1995; Pierre 1995). We may therefore speak of a double decentralization of the implementation of welfare policies, from the national to the subnational level and from central to peripheral units within organizations (Peters and Pierre 2000).

Second, at the same time the central state has shifted responsibilities downward, competencies have also been shifted upward to political bodies at a higher level than the nation-state. The most important development in this respect is, of course, the establishment and expansion of the European Union (EU). The expansion of the EU has taken place both in a geographical sense, with the incorporation first of a number of smaller countries on the periphery of Western Europe and then the enlargement eastward, and in a policy sense, with the influence of the European political level growing slowly but steadily.

Third, more informal and issue-specific forms of policy making and attempts to influence politics have been growing. These forms are many and variegated, ranging from poor people's grassroots organizations, to highly professionalized issue interest groups with a middle-class basis, to elite networks manifested, for example, in the World Economic Forum (www.weforum.org) or the European Round Table of Industrialists (www.ert.be). Furthermore, lobby groups constantly attempt to influence decision making through informal contacts with political elites, both at the national and international level (Naurin 2001, 2004). The decline in political party memberships and the partial demise of formalized cooperation between trade unions, employers, and the state is a concomitant to this growing informalization of politics. More politics is now conducted within loose networks of power and is less evident at the bargaining table than was the case 20 years ago. This development might well be particularly pronounced within the political institutions of the European Union (Jachtenfuchs 2001: 253–5), something that makes a growing Europeanization a driving force for a further informalization of politics.

What are the implications for political preferences, attitudes, and values of these combined changes in welfare state governance? One thing we should expect is that when the system for decision making becomes more complex, politics will become less visible and political accountability more diffuse (Hirst 2000). It has become harder and harder for the ordinary citizen to decide exactly who is to praise or blame for various political outcomes (Kumlin 2003). Responsibility is shifted between various levels (subnational, national, international) and between various agencies (legislatures, implementing bodies, subunits of organizations) in ways that are not easily traced, even for highly sophisticated observers.

This development is particularly interesting to analyze since it coincides with a general rise in educational levels and ensuing political efficacy among the population of Western nations (Inglehart 1997: Ch. 10; Goul Andersen and Hoff 2001: Ch 2). More people nowadays feel competent about their own political abilities, but the political landscape they try to make sense of has become more complex and diffuse.

A particularly important question in this respect is what kinds of institutional arrangements are particularly conducive to citizens' "empowerment"—that is, their autonomy of power and their ability to affect decisions taken by public authorities (Hoff 1993; Kumlin 2004). Some institutional arrangements are likely to increase efficacy and participation while others are likely to decrease them.

We might also expect conceptions of *demos* to change as a result of changes in governance, but the direction of this change is very hard to predict. On the one hand, we could expect a widening conception of *demos* to result from increasing supranational political integration. The slowly emerging European public resulting from European political integration is a case in point, as are also the borderless social movements sometimes transcending boundaries even between the rich North and the poor South.

On the other hand, we could also in some groups expect a shrinking of the conception of *demos*, as a defensive reaction against perceived (cultural and economic) threats from the "outside." Reactionary attempts to draw sharp boundaries against "others" of various kinds are present not only among the extreme right-wing movements but also among mainstream political parties. Furthermore, tendencies toward decentralization of decision making and devolution might nurture a narrower and geographically more circumscribed conception of *demos*. This is clearly evident in several attempts to create larger local or regional autonomy or even national independence for subunits of the current European nation-states (Keating and Loughlin 1997; Keating 1998).

The implications of changes in governance might be given a pessimistic or optimistic interpretation, depending on assumptions and point of departure. The pessimistic scenario is that we are moving into a "post-democratic" stage, where all the formally democratic institutions are still in place but where democracy has become an empty shell with decisions being taken in other places than in democratically elected bodies, and witnessed by an increasingly apathetic public. The optimistic scenario is that we are moving into a more diversified democracy, with a plethora of possibilities for democratic participation emerging in local, national, and supranational arenas (Held and McGrew 2002; Held 2002, 2004: Part II).

Regarding the output side of politics, new market-emulating reforms may at the same time increase choice and empower citizens; this must be judged as a positive democratic development, and make political account-ability harder to assess—which is quite problematic from a democratic point of view.

Comparative politico-sociological research can hardly be expected to judge how far the real world of democracy resembles a dystopia or utopia. Where it can make a contribution, however, is in saying something about which institutional arrangements are likely to have which democratic ef-fects. What kinds of institutional arrangements are likely to increase par-ticipation, trust, and inclusion? Which ones are likely to have the opposite effects? How do people make sense of the increased political complexity and what effects does that action have on political participation and trust?

Changing stratification is the second main aspect of recent welfare state changes. Stratification patterns have gone through considerable changes in recent times, partly as a result of welfare state restructuring. Such changes in stratification are likely to affect the maintenance of social cleavages and thereby the formation of identities and interests.

Recent changes in this respect may be summarized under the head-ing "recommodification." Recommodification is a process through which individuals become more dependent on market forces for their life chances and living conditions (Breen 1997). It is therefore a process that reverses the trend toward "decommodification," which Esping-Andersen (1990) and others have seen as a fundamental achievement of the welfare state. The weakening of "risk-hedging" institutions such as the family and the welfare state has meant that individuals in the Western world are now more ex-posed to the play of market forces than they were a couple of decades ago.

Recommodification is clearly visible both in markets and in public policies; it takes expression both in the restructuring of institutions and in effects among individuals. Among the key factors we find a stronger domi-nance of global financial markets at the expense of national labor market regulation and welfare policies. Even if no "race to the bottom" can be detected, it is nevertheless the case that public policies have become more circumscribed by the need to pay attention to volatile financial markets, and that this has made some of the measures used for enhancing growth and welfare more or less obsolete (Huber and Stephens 2001b).

Recommodification is also apparent in the form of more precarious employment relationships. This is due both to the increased and persistent unemployment levels in the Western world from the 1970s onward and to more irregular and temporary forms of employment that have proliferated in many Western economies in the last decades (Korpi 2002; Gallie and Paugam 2000).

Also, in terms of industrial relations, recommodification is clearly discernible in the decline of union membership, institutions for collective wage bargaining, and corporatist settlements (Western 1997). However, this development has been highly uneven in the Western world and has not implied any institutional convergence since the breakup of collective bargaining and corporatist structures have been most pronounced in the liberal market countries such as the United States and Britain (Wallerstein and Western 2000; Traxler 2003). The combined effect of increasing market exposure and decline of collective institutions for wage setting has been a clear increase in wage and income inequality in virtually all Western countries since the 1980s (Rueda and Pontusson 2000; Smeeding 2002). Scattered evidence suggests that for the liberal market economies this has been combined with sharply increased volatility of earnings and incomes (Gustavsson 2004; Hacker et al. 2005).

Turning to public policies, we have witnessed at least some level of retrenchment of welfare state programs, making them less effective in countering market inequalities. Social rights are more circumscribed now than was the case in the 1980s in that replacement levels in the social insurances have declined, exposing individuals more strongly to the vagaries of the market (Korpi and Palme 2003; Allan and Scruggs 2004).

Finally, recommodification is not only visible in the distribution of incomes and benefits, but also in the very production of goods and services. This is typified by the increased roles for "internal markets" and "outsourcing" within both the public sector and private corporations, making employees more directly exposed to market forces than a quarter-century ago (Lawson and Taylor-Gooby 1993; Pierre 1995; Coriat 1997).

While the major aspects of this recommodification are common to Western capitalist countries, national variations have nevertheless been substantial. In general, there are no clear signs of any institutional convergence between different policy regimes, since the impact of market-driven reforms has been greatest in those countries that were the most market-oriented to begin with, such as the UK and the United States (Huber and Stephens 2001a; Pierson 2001b; Scharpf and Schmidt 2000; Swank 2002). In short, the trend toward recommodification has been uneven and varied, yet common among Western countries.

Recommodifying processes might result in the strengthening of social cleavages, rooted in the division of labor and ensuing market situations. Hence, we could expect class and gender patterns of distribution to strengthen. There is, however, considerable disagreement about whether increased exposure to market forces leads to a hardening of class structuration or to a gradual dissolution of class relations and their replacement by an individualized inequality (Goldthorpe 2000; Sørensen 2000). A similar argument might be made for gender relations. On the one hand, recommodification might increase differences between men and women, recognizing that men often have better market positions than women. We could then expect gender to become a more important social cleavage. On the other hand, recommodification is likely to increase heterogeneity *among* women and men, thus making gender a less clear-cut dividing line.

Recommodification might also result in the rise or rebirth of social cleavages grounded outside the division of labor. For example, nationality and ethnicity might—almost paradoxically in a presumed "age of globalization"—become more important markers of belonging and identity for groups as they become more exposed to market forces, in particular if such exposure has very different consequences for different ethnic populations within the same polity (Smith 2001: 137–9; Chua 2003).

The themes of changes in governance and changes in stratification patterns are addressed in various ways and to different extents in the empirical chapters that follow. Some of them focus on changes in stratification and ensuing patterns of attitudes and identities; others are mainly concerned with the mechanisms behind political accountability and political action. Although some of the empirical chapters do include comparisons over time, our main aim is not to chart change, but to analyze variations and mechanisms behind the formation of orientations and their consequences. What unites the chapters is thus not a focus on attitudinal change and persistence but a joint conceptual framework that is presented in the next section.

ORIENTATIONS, SOCIAL CLEAVAGES, AND INSTITUTIONS—THE ANALYTICAL FRAMEWORK

The three main concepts of our analytical framework are *orientations*, *social cleavages*, and *political institutions*. We use *orientations* as an "umbrella concept" that covers a broad set of attitudinal and political components. Orientations refer to attitudes and identities directed toward any aspect of social or political issues. The contributors to this volume tend to focus on different aspects of orientations: sociopolitical attitudes (normative orientations toward social arrangements), social and political identities (sense of belonging and allegiance), and political trust and efficacy (beliefs about the honesty and integrity of political actors and about the opportunities to influence politics) are among the key indicators.

Cleavages should be understood as borders between social categories of various kinds. Examples of such categories are different classes, different ethnic groups, men and women, young and old. Orientations may vary among groups either because such groups may be more or less endowed with crucial resources and more or less exposed to risks, or because groups are differently placed in networks of interaction and communication. The first set of factors tends to give rise to different *interests* while the second set of factors tends to create different *norms* about what is proper, just, and acceptable (Svallfors 2006: Ch. 2). Such interests and norms may, in turn, give rise to different orientations toward social and political issues.

Some authors argue that the concept of cleavage can be applied only where such cleavages exist not only at the level of social structure but also as bases for group identification and conflict, and where cleavages have taken political organizational form (Manza and Brooks 1999: 33–5; see also Bartolini and Mair 1990). We tend to take a more circumscribed view of the cleavage concept and restrict it to socially significant differences in material circumstances between different social categories. The extent to which such cleavages form the basis for identification, conflict, and organization is, in our view, an issue to be settled at the empirical rather than definitional level.

One of the issues we raise in this volume, therefore, is in what ways such cleavages have formed the bases for different orientations among the populations of different Western countries. In this regard, we assume that the relation between social cleavages and their correlates in the form of orientations is a contingent one, a relation affected both by the institutional frameworks in which people are embedded and by the forms of political articulation prevalent in different polities. Political institutions and political articulation function to establish, strengthen, or dissolve the links between social cleavages and orientations (Svallfors 2006: Ch. 2).

Political institutions may be defined as "the formal rules, compliance procedures, and standard operating practices that structure the relationship between individuals in various units of the polity and economy" (Hall 1992: 96). They are systems of rules and procedures that are embodied in, for example, social insurance systems, electoral systems, or family law. Political institutions are the result of human design in the form of political decisions and their implementation (Rothstein 1996; Rothstein and Steinmo 2002).

Political institutions affect human action in a number of ways. First, institutions modify the structure of rewards and costs. For example, welfare state intervention and labor market legislation modify the structure of rewards and costs. Second, institutions structure possibilities and incentives. Competition, recruitment, and social mobility are structured by political institutions, which therefore impinge on the incentives of social actors. Institutions also affect perceptions and norms in a more direct way: (a) they affect the *visibility* of social phenomena; (b) they affect what is considered politically *possible* to achieve in a given setting; and (c) they embody, and hence create, *norms* about what is fair and just (Rothstein 1998: 134–43; Svallfors 2003; Mau 2003: Ch. 3–4; Mettler and Soss 2004).

To assume that there is a relation between institutions and orientations does not imply that institutions determine orientations. Within some boundary limits, the relationship is instead a probabilistic one as well as one of mutual dependency and development. Certain institutions tend to make some orientations more likely than others; given a certain set of orientations, some institutions are more easily implemented or changed than others.

Institutions tend to be "bundled" into configurations, or "regimes." This is because there is a degree of internal logic by which some institutions are highly compatible with other institutions while others are less easily combined. These institutional configurations have been conceptualized as "production regimes" and "welfare regimes." The first denotes "the organization of production through markets and market-related institutions" (Soskice 1999: 101). An important distinction in this respect is between "liberal market economies" (such as those of the UK and the United States) on the one hand and "coordinated market economies" (such as those of Germany and Sweden) on the other (Soskice 1999; see also Hall and Soskice 2001: Ch. 1).

The second categorization indicates different types of institutional configurations related to welfare policies in the broad sense, the most famous one being Esping-Andersen's distinction between "three worlds of welfare capitalism" (Esping-Andersen 1990; see also Castles and Mitchell 1992; Korpi and Palme 1998). The welfare regimes distinguished by Esping-Andersen are characterized by the ways in which welfare policies, and in particular social insurance, have been organized in different countries. As noted by Huber and Stephens, "the same welfare regime is compatible with different—but not any—labour market institutions and policies" (Huber and Stephens 2001b: 109). The liberal market economies, due to the imperative to keep labor costs down and sustain managerial prerogatives, tend to have less extensive welfare policies. The welfare state is rudimentary and leaves most of the safeguarding against labor market and life cycle risks to private or company-based insurance (Esping-Andersen 1990: 26–7; Huber and Stephens 2001b). The coordinated market economies are more dependent on welfare state arrangements that may keep the social partnership going and allow the reproduction of a skilled work force. The welfare state is extensive and seeks to safeguard (at least) the working population from various risks connected to market dependency and the life course (Huber and Stephens 2001b).

The interaction between institutions, cleavages, and orientations is of fundamental importance in forging a particular "moral economy," in which the mutual rights and obligations in a society are condensed (Svallfors 1996b; Mau 2003). The notion of a "moral economy" is useful for complementing a purely self-interest perspective on preferences and attitudes, in that people's notions of social relations are guided by normative ideas of reciprocity, obligation, and responsibility, which cannot be reduced to merely a question about who is benefiting in different processes of distribution.

In forging this moral economy, the role of public policies in the broad sense is paramount. Public policies may be seen as concrete manifestations

of political institutions, and they "influence the ways individuals understand their rights and responsibilities as members of a political community"
(Mettler and Soss 2004: 61). Our particular focus is on the feedback effects
of public policies on mass publics, something that "policy-feedback scholarship still pays insufficient attention to" (Mettler and Soss 2004: 60; see
also Pierson 1993).

Political institutions are not only significant for their modifying effect
on orientations. Their role in the translation of such orientations into social
and political action is perhaps of even greater significance. By modifying
the opportunity structure, political institutions are paramount in making
or breaking the link between attitudes and action. Simply put, the available choices determine what may be chosen. Even short of actually limiting
the range of available choices, the institutional framework may render some
choices harder to make than others and thus affect the link between orientations and social/political action (Mettler and Soss 2004: 63). Also in
this respect we may speak of feedback effects from public policies on mass
publics. As noted by Manza et al. (2005: 208), not only does political participation influence the political process, but the outcomes of the political
process affect who participates and how they participate.

A final complication to consider is the importance of political articulation for forging the link between specific cleavages, institutions, and orientations. To "articulate" something is to link it to something else—in this
case, particular social cleavages to politics. Such articulation, as conducted
by political parties and other organized interests and often played out in
the mass media, is by its very nature an attempt to change the orientations
of target populations. It aims at connecting and disconnecting interpretive frameworks and distributive outcomes. The importance of political
articulation arises because "actors may have trouble identifying their interests clearly" so that "those interests have to be derived via a process of
interpretation" (Hall 1997: 197). Hence, political articulation is a source
of contingency in the relation between institutions, cleavages, and orientations. By using various forms of "symbolic politics," political actors hope
to change or even create perceptions and attitudes (Edelman 1964; 1971;
Svallfors 1996b: Ch. 3). Such "symbolic politics" always has to be conducted in particular institutional settings, which may make some forms of
articulation harder and others easier to accomplish.

Political articulation also plays an important role in modifying the link between attitudes and action. One of the simplest and most widespread forms of social action is voting. As has been repeatedly stressed, voting is not only determined by values, attitudes, and preferences but also by the options available to voters. If parties do not present themselves in their manifestos and policies as representing particular groups, there is no reason to expect the association between social cleavages and voting behavior to be strong, regardless of how strongly such cleavages impinge on the orientations of mass publics.

THE COMPARATIVE FRAMEWORK

Why do we compare the public's orientations across countries? What might be achieved by getting involved in the notoriously difficult task of conducting cross-national research? The purpose of comparative research is sometimes stated as that of finding sociological "laws" or, more modestly, "rules." If one sticks to such notions, we contend, comparative research is likely to be an eternal disappointment. The "laws" or "rules" we could find that would be both timeless and context-free are most likely to be sociologically trivial. In relation to our analytic framework, the fruitfulness of comparative research should be sought elsewhere, in an analysis of the way in which time- and space-bound institutions influence orientations and action among mass publics. In our particular case we attempt to analyze how the institutional framework affects orientations in a broad sense, and since the most important institutional variation is still found between countries, we conjecture that a cross-national comparative framework will allow us to elicit our research questions in a particularly pertinent way.

It is important, however, to keep in mind that the most relevant explanatory unit may not always be the nation-state. Important work has shown that considerable institutional variation is found within the same nation-state, and that this has considerable impact on the beliefs and behavior of the public (Soss 2004; Kumlin 2004). Nevertheless, for our purposes it seems essential to apply a country-comparative framework.

Although comparative research is thus potentially very fruitful, comparative research on orientations is fraught with difficulties that may make results and interpretations fragile (Kuechler 1987, 1998; Jowell 1998).

There is an immanent danger of creating research design artifacts instead of comparing and explaining substantive findings. Comparing is never easy, and comparative attitude research may well be particularly afflicted by methodological problems.

Several issues are of interest here. The most important problem is probably how to establish the cross-national validity of indicators. By their very nature, attitudes are context-dependent, which is why we want to compare them across nations in the first place. Of course, this is not a problem in itself. A problem arises if we find that it is not values and attitudes that vary across nations but the meaning and connotations of various concepts.

It is, of course, interesting in itself to analyze why different concepts have become loaded with different meanings in different contexts. But such differences also put strict demands on comparative attitude research regarding the design and translation of questionnaires so that we do not mistake pure research design artifacts for social facts.

The second problem in comparing attitudes, which links to the first one, is about framing. Depending on how attitude questions are framed, one may receive widely differing answers to virtually the same set of questions. For example, if issues about welfare state support are framed as issues of incentives and productivity, you will receive different answers from when they are framed as issues of redistribution. And if they are framed with concepts that have different connotations across national contexts you run the risk of creating difference where none exists.

Neither the problem of context-dependency nor the problem of framing has any ready and easy solution. But the problems do point to some considerations that should wherever possible be applied when doing comparative attitude research. The most important is that such studies must be genuinely international in creating the questionnaires or any other research instruments (Kuechler 1987; Jowell 1998). Only in this way is it possible to lessen the impact of national idiosyncrasies and prejudices in the construction of the measurement instrument itself.

Other sound methodological advice that we try to adhere to (adapted from Jowell 1998) is to use only countries that are similar enough to allow meaningful comparisons, and only countries of which we have some degree of knowledge. Furthermore, we use data only from strictly comparative surveys, where questions have been designed multinationally and implemented in a uniform way across countries. We also try not to put too much importance on differences among countries in gross percentage distributions on single questions. Our emphasis is instead on larger patterns, both in how different attitude items relate to each other, and how they are structured by social cleavages. Furthermore, whenever possible, we use compounded indexes, comprising several individual items, instead of single indicators as one possible way of lessening the impact of single semantic idiosyncrasies on results.

The two main data sets that we use, one stemming from the *International Social Survey Program (ISSP)* and one collected within the *European Social Survey (ESS)*, both have elaborate procedures to ensure that cross-national comparability is as good as possible.

The International Social Survey Program (www.issp.org; see also Smith 2005) is a comparative attitude survey that was inaugurated in the mid-1980s, and as of 2005 incorporated 40 countries across six continents. The ISSP is an attempt to create a truly comparative dataset with which to analyze attitudes and values in industrialized countries (Davis and Jowell 1989; Becker et al. 1990; Svallfors 1996a). A variety of topics have been surveyed, and from 1990, previous modules have been replicated allowing comparison both among nations and over time. The samples are nationally representative of the adult population. In addition to attitude items, the ISSP database contains standardized comparable information on respondents' characteristics such as age, sex, occupation, income, education, household composition, and so on.

The European Social Survey is a comparative survey of attitudes, behavior, and living conditions in Europe. It was conducted for the first time in 2002 in 22 European countries (www.europeansocialsurvey.org). ESS will be fielded biannually; it consists of an encompassing base module that includes standardized background variables as well as several central attitudinal and value dimensions. In addition, ESS has two thematic modules that will be rotated between the survey periods. In the 2002 survey used here, these two modules deal with "Immigration and Citizenship" and "Involvement and Democracy."

The ISSP and the ESS have used similar but different techniques in order to ensure cross-national comparability. The ISSP is a network-based enterprise, which applies a "bottom-up" strategy in that all important initiatives come from individual members of the group. There is substantial input from individual members into the questionnaire design and other decisions, for example, through the "drafting groups" appointed for each module. The process is a very democratic one, with the rule of one-member-one-vote for all decisions. The loose structure of the ISSP leads to one unfortunate situation: the degree of implementation of joint decisions varies, leading to differing data quality across countries. The expansion of the ISSP is limitless and unplanned, in that any country that applies for membership and fulfills the requirements in terms of infrastructure and implementation of the fieldwork is allowed to join. One might ask whether the ISSP membership has grown too heterogeneous to allow for meaningful comparisons. It should be emphasized, however, that the country data sets used in this book all come from European and Western industrial societies, thus making comparisons less fragile, and all have a reasonably high quality in terms of fieldwork procedures and outcomes.

In contrast, the ESS is a much more centrally coordinated enterprise, which applies a "top-down" strategy, in that all important decisions are made in a small group and then implemented by national coordinators in each country. The ESS has an extremely elaborate process for developing the questionnaire. Preparation for the first ESS round was rigorous, involving invited expert papers on all the topics the survey intended to cover and several rounds of validity checks and field tests. The structure for designing new rotating modules is also set up in a way to ensure multinational input and thorough test procedures. The ESS has a very elaborate regulatory framework, in terms of how fieldwork is conducted, samples constructed, and translations made (see further www.europeansocialsurvey.org). This should lead to a higher degree of uniform implementation than what has sometimes been the case in the ISSP. The ESS is also conducted as personal interviews, leading to overall better data quality in terms of response rates and in minimizing error.

OUTLINE OF THE EMPIRICAL ANALYSES

The changes in welfare states that have been outlined to this point form the backdrop to the empirical analyses that follow, using data from the ISSP and the ESS. A common element in all the chapters is that they widen the spectrum beyond the debate on comparative welfare regimes. In some chapters, this is accomplished by bringing in a wider set of institutions and orientations than those immediately connected to welfare policies. The institutional framework extends beyond the welfare state as narrowly conceived, and it is important to take this wider institutional environment into consideration when trying to explain national variations in orientations.

In other chapters, the contributors take a more "intensive" approach by trying to untangle in more detail what it is about institutions that matters. In other words, they try to specify the mechanisms through which particular institutions work in connecting cleavages and orientations.

Another common thread in the chapters is that the authors aim to study the feedback effects from policies on cleavages and orientations. In contrast to many previous studies, which have been mainly concerned about feedback effects on the elite level, our aim is to study the effects of orientations among mass publics. In doing this, we apply a much broader conception of feedback effects than has often been the case. Not only direct experiences of public policies are included but the whole gamut of effects from living in a particular institutional environment, as broadly conceived.

In Chapter 2, Jonas Edlund tackles an important issue within political sociology: the role of institutions and political articulation in forging the link between class and its attitudinal correlates. He takes as his point of departure arguments by Esping-Andersen and others, according to which the magnitude of class conflicts will differ across countries. This argument rests on several assumptions: The first is that differences among classes in material conditions form the base for class action. In countries where material inequality is relatively low among classes, the likelihood that class conflicts will occur is smaller than in countries characterized by pronounced material inequality. A second assumption is that the scope and organization of the welfare state structure interests and patterns of political coalition formation to a significant extent. The characteristics of the liberal welfare state are likely to discourage coalitions between poor and better-off citizens. Targeted and means-tested programs tend to drive a wedge between better-off classes and worse-off classes, thereby reducing social solidarity and increasing welfare policy class conflict. In the social democratic regime, the institutionalized encompassing programs are supposed to dampen class conflicts.

The alternative hypothesis formulated in Edlund's chapter challenges this argument on several counts. While it seems reasonable to assume that patterns of sociopolitical class conflicts share many similarities across Western countries, it is less clear whether the magnitude of class conflict varies positively with material inequality across countries. Other sources of attitude and interest formation can potentially be more important and override the effects of material inequality. Furthermore, Edlund questions whether the basic understanding of welfare state institutional impact should principally be an issue of "universal versus selective" coverage. He suggests that a more fruitful understanding of institutional feedback effects should focus on other measures of welfare state performance, such as income redistribution via taxes and transfers, and the profile of risk-reduction in social spending priorities. It is hypothesized that the redistributive character of the tax and transfer system, and the distributive profile of public spending and risk protection influence class relations and sociopolitical attitudes. The stronger the class character of risk protection and redistribution, the higher will be the probability of sociopolitical class conflict.

Moreover, Edlund maintains, institutions are not only relevant for understanding attitude formation in the sense of policy feedbacks in a "technical-legalistic" rules-of-the-game sense. Institutions may also be understood as institutionalized compromises/conflicts between different social groups. Once a particular institution has been created, the central political actors can be expected to behave as institutional guardians and institutional challengers. These collective actors are important for underpinning collective memories and worldviews. In social democratic regimes, these actors tend to be grouped chiefly along the social class axis, contributing to the salience of welfare and redistributive politics in public and political debates. In liberal welfare regimes, the labor movement is weaker and collective actors are therefore not grouped along the Left–Right axis to the same extent.

The alternative hypothesis thus suggests that class conflict will be more pronounced in the social democratic welfare regime compared to the liberal welfare regime. In addition to social class, class identity is brought into the analysis. It is hypothesized that institutional characteristics influence how important class identity is for sociopolitical attitudes, so that class identity should be particularly important in social democratic regimes.

In the empirical analysis of the chapter, six Western countries are compared: the United States, Canada, Australia, New Zealand, Sweden, and Norway. The results support the alternative hypothesis. Preferences regarding welfare state and redistributive politics are clearly more linked to social class and class identity in the social democratic regimes than in the liberal regimes.

In Chapter 3, Staffan Kumlin argues that there is some consensus that the challenges and pressures faced by mature welfare states are becoming more severe. Equally accepted, however, is the contention that the political responses will hardly involve an apocalyptic neoliberal "race to the bottom." Piecemeal cost containment reforms within existing welfare systems are more likely and have been under way for some time in many countries. Moreover, Kumlin maintains, experience tells us that even seemingly small changes in institutions and policies may instigate widespread public dissatisfaction with the performance of the welfare state. He then probes the effects of such dissatisfaction on citizens' political orientations and behavior. The analysis includes 17 West European welfare states.

Empirically, Kumlin tries to answer the following questions: Does dismay with performance undermine normative support for government intervention and welfare spending? Or does poor performance lead to exactly the opposite: to new demands for even more spending and intervention, thus potentially overloading already constrained welfare states? Moreover, what are the effects on government support, and on general support for the political system? Finally, how do these effects vary across political and welfare state–related institutional settings, and across different groups of individuals?

The results show that welfare state dissatisfaction has a (weak) negative impact on general support for state intervention, and tends to drive respondents toward the political Right when placement in the Left–Right continuum is analyzed. Disaffection also has a certain potential for undermining incumbent government support. These effects, however, are strongly conditioned by both political institutions and welfare state institutions: one finds a major impact only in social democratic welfare states with little institutional power dispersion. Finally, there is a strong and consistent negative impact of dissatisfaction on general political trust. This latter impact can be found in all investigated countries and is not affected by their institutional configuration. In the concluding section of Chapter 3, Kumlin discusses the development of welfare state politics in an era of resource scarcity and popular dissatisfaction.

In Chapter 4, Maria Oskarson analyzes the relationship between social position and political alienation, understood as the combination of low political interest and low political trust. An important issue in the chapter is whether this relationship looks different in different types of welfare states and whether it is affected by different degrees of welfare state retrenchment. Oskarson observes that although the norm-building capacity of welfare states is often referred to, less is discussed about what the consequences are if welfare states do not live up to their own norms about safeguarding citizens from sustenance problems. Are differences between social groups regarding political alienation larger in countries that have experienced more substantial cutbacks of welfare policies? Are these group differences larger in more generous welfare states where there are high expectations of the welfare state?

The selection of countries for comparison is guided by their policies on income redistribution and the degree of retrenchment in social insurance systems; they include Belgium, Germany, Great Britain, the Netherlands, Norway, and Sweden. The countries are chosen to represent one with strong retrenchment and one with little or no retrenchment within each of three pairs of different types of social insurance systems.

Oskarson's analysis shows that social risk exposure is a strong factor behind political alienation in all of the countries. This is something that other analyses have failed to notice because of their restrictive understanding of the phenomenon of political alienation. Furthermore, the effect of social risk on political alienation is particularly large in countries that have experienced substantial cutbacks, a finding that indicates welfare state retrenchment may act to further marginalize politically weak groups. Moreover, there are no signs that the political integration of weaker social groups is better in the more "encompassing" welfare states. For example, differences regarding political alienation between different social risk categories are particularly large in Sweden, the most encompassing welfare state in the sample. It might even be speculated that the moral economy of the welfare state in such circumstances is conducive to a particularly intense disappointment among those with a weak market position, and therefore tends to push people out of politics rather than including them.

In Chapter 5, Maria Pettersson explores the relationship between citizens' evaluations of public service output and political action, and specifically how this relationship differs among institutional arrangements. To compare institutions, she uses two theoretical tools: the welfare state regime typology and the concept of institutionalized citizen empowerment. The first research question asks whether welfare regime typology can help us understand possible differences among countries concerning the relation between welfare state dissatisfaction and general political action. The main findings indicate that the relationship between welfare state dissatisfaction and general political action not only is weak but also that no regime patterns can be traced. Effects are found, but they differ across countries in patterns that defy easy classification. However, these results may arise because the questions about political action are not ideally framed to study the effects of policy dissatisfaction, since the different forms of action were not linked to the policy field in question.

In the second part of Pettersson's chapter, she therefore turns our attention to a comparison of health care and schooling within a particular welfare state, Sweden. The theoretical focus here is on "institutionalized citizen empowerment," which refers to the power balance between the two parties when the individual encounters the institution. The second question raised in this chapter explores the effects of the variation in empowerment between welfare state institutions on the relation between dissatisfaction and political action, thus shifting the analysis from regimes to concrete public service institutions. In this regard, interesting differences are present between the Swedish schools and health care systems. While institutionalized channels of user-influence are relatively well established within public schools, they are almost nonexistent in health care. At the same time, the law regulating schools puts more emphasis on individual rights, but the notion of universality is more strongly emphasized within the health care sector due to its more clear-cut character of being a public good.

Pettersson's conclusion from the analysis is that dissatisfaction with schools is not related to political action aimed at schools, but that this relationship is found regarding health care services, so that citizens dissatisfied with health care take political action to a higher extent than citizens satisfied with health care. The immediate interpretation of these results is that fewer voice-opportunities in the health care system tend to make citizens more inclined to take political action, while the voice-opportunities within public schools deal directly with parents' grievances. It is also possible that citizens tend to think differently about these two institutions. While contact with public school is usually limited to one's own schooling and that of one's children, health care is something most people have contact with on a more regular basis during the course of life. It is plausible that this difference between school and health care makes health care a more clear-cut public good, and that this feature may produce different feedback mechanisms compared to the public school area. The more general conclusion that may be drawn from the chapter is that different kinds of empowerment features seem to have different effects on the relationship between dissatisfaction and political action. This finding implies further need to explore the institutional design of welfare state institutions, not only to clarify the operating mechanisms, but also to better understand the different mechanisms at work.

In Chapter 6, Stefan Svallfors broadens the empirical focus from issues related to the welfare state to include attitudes toward the market. Svallfors compares attitudes to market inequality in different classes in four Western countries. He takes as his point of departure Robert Lane's argument that market distributions in general tend to generate little dissatisfaction. Applying a perspective in which the institutional characteristics of the four countries are in focus, the chapter analyzes whether larger class differences in attitudes to various aspects of market inequality are found in the coordinated market economies of Sweden and Germany, or in the liberal market economies of Great Britain and the United States. A special emphasis is put on analyzing the extent to which attitudes to inequality are internally integrated, and different classes and countries are compared in this respect.

Svallfors indicates that the results obtained are sometimes unexpected, such as the small class differences in attitudes toward legitimate income differentials and the finding that workers stress the value of such pecuniary inequality for generating incentives to acquire responsibility and qualifications to a *greater* degree than do the higher nonmanuals. What is also surprising is the widespread acceptance and class homogeneity in Britain regarding the fairness of the system whereby money can buy better health care and schooling. Conversely, class differences are salient and more in line with expected patterns regarding attitudes toward the importance of income redistribution, whereby the workers are much stronger advocates of redistribution than the higher nonmanuals. In general, it is shown that the coordinated market economies of Sweden and Germany evince greater, in some cases much greater, class differences in attitudes than Great Britain and the United States. Differences are also noted on how well integrated different attitudes are toward equality. The Swedish attitudinal pattern is clearly the most highly integrated, as the internal consistency of attitudes is greater there than elsewhere.

At a theoretical level, Svallfors argues that the link between class and attitudes is affected not only by the actual class differences in living conditions. More important is the way in which class issues have been articulated politically. Class-redistributive institutions function not only to lessen actual class differences—something that would make class differences smaller in more egalitarian countries. They also work to make class articulation more pronounced—a factor that makes class differences in attitudes more distinct.

In Chapter 7, Mikael Hjerm asks whether national sentiments have changed in a set of countries over the course of the last decade. Hjerm argues that the nation is the primary collective identity for the legitimization of political and social institutions. The necessity of the nation as the sole provider of collective identity is questionable, he maintains, but the need for a minimum form of collective identity for the sustaining of *demos* is not. This means that diminishing collective identities can be a problem for democracy, since it is mainly based on the nation-state. There are theoretical arguments that support increase or decrease, as well as changes in the substance of such identities. However, it is clear that the factors that are assumed to affect people's identities toward the nation-state are changing. These factors are to be found in horizontal and vertical shifts in the decision-making structure as well as increasing diversity within the nation-state.

In his analysis, Hjerm sets out to examine possible changes in collective identities in different countries. Two forms of collective identities are analyzed: nationalist sentiments and patriotism. The analysis examines the three possibilities that national sentiments have changed in strength, substance, or effect. Five European countries (Britain, Germany, Sweden, the Czech Republic, and Hungary) are contrasted with three non-European countries (Australia, Canada, and the United States).

Hjerm's overall conclusion is that very little has changed. National sentiments have not increased or decreased in strength, nor have they changed in substance or effect during the period of examination. There are some country deviations, but they do not change the overall pattern. The proponents of "post"-theories are perhaps correct in arguing that the political landscape is changing in certain ways, Hjerm concludes, but from this to argue that communities of faith are evaporating and that government is rapidly being replaced by governance is a long step with little empirical backing.

In the concluding chapter, Stefan Svallfors considers the results presented in this volume in relation to the development of the field of political sociology. He argues that the papers together represent a "fourth generation" of scholarship in the field, where feedback effects of the institutional framework in general, and public policies in particular, are analyzed in a comparative perspective.

NOTE

1. This is not to say, of course, that it has received *no* attention. A selection of book-length studies includes Roller 1992; Anderson 1995; Scarbrough and Borre 1995; Svallfors 1996b; Norris 1999; Svallfors and Taylor-Gooby 1999; Mau 2003.

REFERENCES

Allan, J. P., and Scruggs, L. (2004). Political Partisanship and Welfare State Reform in Advanced Industrial Societies. *American Journal of Political Science*, 48, 496–512.

Anderson, C. (1995). *Blaming the Government: Citizens and the Economy in Five European Democracies*. Armonk, N.Y.: M.E. Sharpe.

Bartolini, S., and Mair, P. (1990). *Identity, Competition and Electoral Availability: The Stabilisation of European Electorates 1885–1985*. Cambridge: Cambridge University Press.

Becker, J. W., Davies, J. A., Ester, P., and Mohler, P. P. (Eds.). (1990). *Attitudes to Inequality and the Role of Government*. Rijswiik: Sociaal en Cultureel Planbureau.

Breen, R. (1997). Risk, Recommodification and Stratification. *Sociology*, 31, 473–489.

Brooks, C., Manza, J., and Bolzendahl, C. (2003). Voting Behaviour and Political Sociology: Theories, Debates, and Future Directions. *Research in Political Sociology*, 12, 137–173.

Castles, F. G., and Mitchell, D. (1992). Identifying Welfare State Regimes: The Links between Politics, Instruments and Outcomes. *Governance*, 5, 1–26.

Chua, A. (2003). *World on Fire: How Exporting Free Market Democracy Breeds Ethnic Hatred and Global Instability*. London: Heinemann.

Coriat, B. (1997). Globalization, Variety and Mass Production: The Metamorphosis of Mass Production in the New Competitive Age. In *Contemporary*

Capitalism: The Embeddedness of Institutions, Eds. J. R. Hollingsworth and R. Boyer. Cambridge: Cambridge University Press.

Davis, J. A., and Jowell, R. (1989). Measuring National Differences. An Introduction to the International Social Survey Programme (ISSP). In *British Social Attitudes. Special International Report*, Eds. R. Jowell, S. Witherspoon, and L. Brook. Aldershot: Gower, pp. 1–13.

Edelman, M. (1964). *The Symbolic Uses of Politics*. Chicago: University of Illinois Press.

Edelman, M. (1971). *Politics as Symbolic Action: Mass Arousal and Quiescence*. Chicago: Markham.

Esping-Andersen, G. (1990). *The Three Worlds of Welfare Capitalism*. Cambridge: Polity Press.

Evans, G. (Ed.). (1999). *The End of Class Politics? Class Voting in Comparative Context*. Oxford: Oxford University Press.

Gallie, D., and Paugam, S. (2000). *Welfare Regimes and the Experience of Unemployment in Europe*. Oxford: Oxford University Press.

Goldthorpe, J. H. (2000). Rent, Class Conflict, and Class Structure: A Commentary on Sorensen. *American Journal of Sociology*, 105, 1572–1582.

Goul Andersen, J., and Hoff, J. (2001). *Democracy and Citizenship in Scandinavia*. Basingstoke, UK: Palgrave.

Gustavsson, M. (2004). *Trends in the Transistory Variance of Earnings: Evidence from Sweden 1960–90 and a Comparison with the United States*. Working Paper 2004:11. Uppsala: Department of Economics, Uppsala University.

Hacker, J. S., Mettler, S., and Pinderhughes, D. (2005). Inequality and Public Policy. In *Inequality and American Democracy: What We Know and What We Need to Learn*, Eds. L. Jacobs and T. Skocpol. New York: Russell Sage Foundation, forthcoming.

Hall, P. A. (1992). The Movement from Keynesianism to Monetarism: Institutional Analysis and British Economic Policy in the 1970s. In *Structuring Politics. Historical Institutionalism in Comparative Analyses*, Eds. S. Steinmo, K. Thelen, and F. Longstreth. Cambridge: Cambridge University Press, pp. 90–113.

Hall, P. A. (1997). The Role of Interests, Institutions, and Ideas in the Comparative Political Economy of the Industrialized Nations. In *Comparative Politics: Rationality, Culture and Structure*, Eds. M. I. Lichbach and A. S. Zuckerman. Cambridge: Cambridge University Press, pp. 174–207.

Hall, P. A., and Soskice, D. W. (2001). *Varieties of Capitalism: The Institutional Foundations of Comparative Advantage*. Oxford: Oxford University Press.

Held, D. (2002). Cosmopolitanism: Ideas, Realities and Deficits. In *Governing Globalization: Power, Authority and Global Governance*, Eds. D. Held and A. G. McGrew. Malden, Mass.: Polity Press, pp. 305–324.

Held, D. (2004). *Global Covenant: The Democratic Alternative to the Washington Consensus*. Cambridge: Polity.

Held, D., and McGrew, A. G. (2002). Introduction. In *Governing Globalization: Power, Authority and Global Governance*, Eds. D. Held and A. G. McGrew. Malden, Mass.: Polity Press, pp. 1–21.

Hirst, P. (2000). Democracy and Governance. In *Debating Governance: Authority, Steering, and Democracy*, Ed. J. Pierre. Oxford: Oxford University Press, pp. 12–35.

Hoff, J. (1993). Medborgerskab, brukerrolle og makt. In *Medborgerskab—Demokrati og politisk deltagelse*, Eds. J. Andersen, A-D. Christensen, K. Langberg, B. Siim, and L. Torpe. Viborg: Systeme.

Hood, C. (1995). The New Public Management in the 1980s—Variations on a Theme. *Accounting Organizations and Society*, 20, 93–109.

Huber, E., and Stephens, J. D. (2001a). *Development and Crisis of the Welfare State: Parties and Policies in Global Markets*: Chicago: University of Chicago Press.

Huber, E., and Stephens, J. D. (2001b). Welfare State and Production Regimes in the Era of Retrenchment. In *The New Politics of the Welfare State*, Ed. P. Pierson. Oxford: Oxford University Press.

Inglehart, R. (1997). *Modernization and Postmodernization: Cultural, Economic, and Political Change in 43 Societies*. Princeton, N.J.: Princeton University Press.

Jachtenfuchs, M. (2001). The Governance Approach to European Integration. *Journal of Common Market Studies*, 39, 245–264.

Jowell, R. (1998). How Comparative Is Comparative Research? *American Behavioral Scientist*, 42, 168–177.

Keating, M. (1998). *The New Regionalism in Western Europe: Territorial Restructuring and Political Change*. Cheltenham: Edward Elgar.

Keating, M., and Loughlin, J. (1997). *The Political Economy of Regionalism*. London: Frank Cass.

Korpi, W. (2002). The Great Trough in Unemployment: A Long-term View of Unemployment, Inflation, Strikes, and the Profit/Wage Ratio. *Politics & Society*, 30, 365–426.

Korpi, W., and Palme, J. (1998). The Paradox of Redistribution and Strategies of Equality: Welfare State Institutions, Inequality, and Poverty in the Western Countries. *American Sociological Review*, 63, 661–687.

Korpi, W., and Palme, J. (2003). New Politics and Class Politics in the Context of Austerity and Globalization: Welfare State Regress in 18 Countries 1975–1995. *American Political Science Review*, 97, 425–446.

Kuechler, M. (1987). The Utility of Surveys for Cross-National Research. *Social Science Research*, 16, 229–244.

Kuechler, M. (1998). The Survey Method—An Indispensable Tool for Social Science Research Everywhere? *American Behavioral Scientist*, 42, 178–200.

Kumlin, S. (2003). Snedvridet ansvarsutkrävande? In *Demokratitrender*, Ed. H. Oscarsson. Göteborg: SOM-institutet Göteborgs universitet, pp. 31–53.

Kumlin, S. (2004). *The Personal and the Political: How Personal Welfare State Experiences Affect Political Trust and Ideology*. New York: Palgrave Macmillan.

Lawson, R., and Taylor-Gooby, P. (1993). *Markets and Managers: New Issues in the Delivery of Welfare*. Buckingham: Open University Press.

Manza, J., and Brooks, C. (1999). *Social Cleavages and Political Change: Voter Alignments and U.S. Party Coalitions*. Oxford: Oxford University Press.

Manza, J., Brooks, C., and Sauder, M. (2005). Money, Participation, and Votes: Social Cleavages and Electoral Politics. In *Handbook of Political Sociology*, Ed. T. Janoski et al. Cambridge: Cambridge University Press, pp. 201–226.

Mau, S. (2003). *The Moral Economy of Welfare States. Britain and Germany Compared*. London: Routledge.

Mettler, S., and Soss, J. (2004). The Consequences of Public Policy for Democratic Citizenship: Bridging Policy Studies and Mass Politics. *Perspectives on Politics*, 2, 55–73.

Naurin, D. (2001). *Den demokratiske lobbyisten*. Umeå: Boréa.

Naurin, D. (2004) *Dressed for Politics: Why Increasing Transparency in the European Union Will Not Make Lobbyists Behave Any Better Than They Already Do*. Göteborg: Department of Political Science, Göteborg University.

Norris, P. (Ed.). (1999). *Critical Citizens. Global Support for Democratic Governance*. Oxford: Oxford University Press.

Norris, P. (2004). *Electoral Engineering: Voting Rules and Political Behavior*. Cambridge: Cambridge University Press.

Peters, B. G., and Pierre, J. (2000). Citizens versus the New Public Manager— The Problem of Mutual Empowerment. *Administration & Society*, 32, 9–28.

Pierre, J. (1995). The Marketization of the State: Citizens, Consumers, and the Emergence of the Public Market. In *Governance in a Changing Environment*, Eds. B. G. Peters and D. J. Savoie. Montreal: McGill-Queens University Press, pp. 55–81.

Pierre, J. (2000). *Debating Governance: Authority, Steering, and Democracy*. Oxford: Oxford University Press.

Pierre, J., and Peters, B. G. (2000). *Governance, Politics and the State*. New York: Macmillan & St. Martin's.

Pierson, P. (1993). When Effect Becomes Cause: Policy Feedback and Political Change. *World Politics*, 45, 595–628.

Pierson, P. (2001a). Coping with Permanent Austerity: Welfare State Restructuring in Affluent Democracies. In *The New Politics of the Welfare State*, Ed. P. Pierson. Oxford: Oxford University Press, pp. 410–456.

Pierson, P. (2001b). *The New Politics of the Welfare State*. Oxford: Oxford University Press.

Roller, E. (1992). *Einstellungen der Bürger zum Wohlfahrtsstaat der Bundesrepublik Deutschland*. Opladen: Westdeutscher Vlg.

Rothstein, B. (1996). Political Institutions—An Overview. In *A New Handbook of Political Science*, Eds. R. E Goodin and H.-D Klingemann. Cambridge: Cambridge University Press, pp. 133–166.

Rothstein, B. (1998). *Just Institutions Matters: The Moral and Political Logic of the Universal Welfare State*. Cambridge: Cambridge University Press.

Rothstein, B., and Steinmo, S. (2002). *Restructuring the Welfare State: Political Institutions and Policy Change*. New York: Palgrave/Macmillan.

Rueda, D., and Pontusson, J. (2000). Wage Inequality and Varieties of Capitalism. *World Politics*, 52, 350–583.

Scarbrough, E., and Borre, O. (1995). *The Scope of Government*. Oxford: Oxford University Press.

Scharpf, F. W., and Schmidt, V. A. (2000). *Welfare and Work in the Open Economy*. Oxford: Oxford University Press.

Smeeding, T. M. (2002). Globalization, Inequality and the Rich Countries of the G-20: Evidence from the Luxembourg Income Study (LIS). In *Globalisation, Living Standards, and Inequality: Recent Progresses and Continuing Challenges*, Eds. D. Gruen, T. O'Brien, and J. Lawson. Sydney: MacMillan, pp. 179–206.

Smith, A. D. (2001). *Nationalism: Theory, Ideology, History*. Cambridge: Polity.

Smith, T. W. (2005). *The International Social Survey Program Research*. Chicago: National Opinion Research Centre.

Soskice, D. W. (1999). Divergent Production Regimes: Coordinated and Uncoordinated Market Economies in the 1980s and 1990s. In *Continuity and Change in Contemporary Capitalism*, Eds. H. Kitschelt, P. Lange, G. Marks, and J. D. Stephens. Cambridge: Cambridge University Press, pp. 101–134.

Soss, J. (2004). Making Clients and Citizens: Welfare Policy as a Source of Status, Belief and Action. In *Deserving and Entitled: Social Constructions and Public Policy*, Eds. A. Schneider and H. Ingram. Stony Brook: State University of New York Press.

Svallfors, S. (1996a). National Differences in National Identities? An Introduction to the International Social Survey Program. *New Community*, 22, 127–134.

Svallfors, S. (1996b). *Välfärdsstatens moraliska ekonomi: välfärdsopinionen i 90-talets Sverige*. Umeå: Boréa.

Svallfors, S. (2003). Welfare Regimes and Welfare Opinions: A Comparison of Eight Western Countries. *Social Indicators Research*, 64, 495–520.

Svallfors, S. (2006). *The Moral Economy of Class. Class and Attitudes in Comparative Perspective*. Stanford, Calif.: Stanford University Press.

Svallfors, S., and Taylor-Gooby, P. (1999). *The End of the Welfare State? Responses to State Retrenchment*. London: Routledge.

Swank, D. (2002). *Global Capital, Political Institutions, and Policy Change in Developed Welfare States*. Cambridge: Cambridge University Press.

Sørensen, A. B. (2000). Toward a Sounder Basis for Class Analysis. *American Journal of Sociology*, 105, 1523–1558.

Thomassen, J. (2005). *The European Voter. A Comparative Study of Modern Democracies*. Oxford: Oxford University Press.

Traxler, F. (2003). Bargaining, State Regulation and the Trajectories of Industrial Relations. *European Journal of Industrial Relations*, 9, 141–161.

Wallerstein, M., and Western, B. (2000). Unions in Decline? What Has Changed and Why. *Annual Review of Political Science*, 3, 355–377.

van der Eijk, C., Franklin, M. N., and Ackaert, J. (1996). *Choosing Europe? The European Electorate and National Politics in the Face of Union*. Ann Arbor: University of Michigan Press.

Western, B. (1997). *Between Class and Market: Postwar Unionization in the Capitalist Democracies*. Princeton, N.J.: Princeton University Press.

CHAPTER TWO

Class Conflicts and Institutional Feedback Effects in Liberal and Social Democratic Welfare Regimes

Attitudes toward State Redistribution and
Welfare Policy in Six Western Countries

Jonas Edlund

The leading theme in Esping-Andersen's (1990) modern classic, *The Three Worlds of Welfare Capitalism*, is to offer explanations accounting for the emergence and variation of welfare states. Here, the role of organized actors and the patterns of political coalition building are central to the theory. A less recognized theme, and further developed in *Changing Classes* (1993), is the claim that the rise of modern institutions has significantly influenced patterns of social stratification, implying a possible change in the social bases of electoral support. The backbone in this process is the welfare state; its configuration determines the structure of post-industrial employment as well as the risk-reducing capacity and coverage profile of social policy.

While the role of organized interests, such as political parties, unions, employer organizations, and churches, forms an integral part of Esping-Andersen's theoretical framework for understanding the formative years of the welfare state, the status of these entities for explaining contemporary mass-political conflicts around issues of social protection is less clear. In a projective, and admittedly speculative, passage on the political conflicts associated with the welfare state, Esping-Andersen suggests that the welfare state is in itself a powerful force that has the capacity to transform patterns of social stratification. Changing patterns of social stratification signal that the social bases for political alliance building may take new forms (Esping-Andersen 1990: 226–229). According to this *phase II* of the regime theory, different types of welfare state institutions, employment structures, and, thus, social stratification patterns tend to cluster into specific configurations, each promoting a distinct conflict scenario related to welfare policy.

The political conflict scenarios envisaged by the *phase II* argument are described with reference to three countries, each representing a distinct welfare regime type: Sweden (social democratic), United States (liberal), and Germany (conservative). Since the argument, which will be further developed later in this chapter, focuses primarily on the politics-markets nexus, it is sufficient to limit the center of attention to the social democratic and the liberal welfare regime types.

The implications of the argument on class stratification and welfare politics are the following. While the organizational strength of the labor movement, executed through social democracy, was the driving force behind the formation of the Swedish welfare state, the institutional setup of this particular welfare state promotes a sociopolitical landscape in which class is becoming increasingly less relevant. Universalistic and high-quality social security systems, income equality, and employment protection—all basic characteristics of the social democratic welfare state—suggest that class-based stratification loses its significance. The large public sector and the associated gender-segregated labor market promote new patterns of stratification, and thus new axes of political conflict, based on gender and sector of employment.

In the United States, on the other hand, the residual character of the welfare state, combined with modest employment protection and substantial income inequality, suggests that the principal system of stratification is class. Increased social mobility among minorities and converging employment patterns between men and women reduce the likelihood of sociopolitical conflict rooted in gender and ethnicity.

Thus, when it comes to contemporary *class* politics over the welfare state, at least two interpretations are available. The soft interpretation of the *phase II* argument suggests that changing patterns of stratification are likely to lead to changing strategies and rhetoric among organized interests. The hard version of the argument would suggest that the role of organized interests—the engines during the formative years of the welfare state—in forming contemporary mass attitudes is deemphasized, while experiences emanating from positions in the social stratification system are more central to the argument. In a similar vein, the principal institutional feedback effect in the *phase II* argument—social policy universalism (i.e., encompassing nonmarket solutions)[1]—is judged and interpreted more in terms of its effect on social stratification than by its relation to particular organized interests.

In this chapter, the *phase II* argument is confronted with an alternative hypothesis in which the path dependency of the institutionally embedded organized interests' strategies and rhetoric is central. Moreover, it is argued that the institutional feedback effect specified by the *phase II* argument is of minor importance compared to the feedback effects propelled by the welfare state in terms of size, risk profile, and redistributive capacity. Hence, the alternative approach is an argument about path dependency and inertia. Institutionally embedded forces may successfully prevent the changing patterns of social stratification from transforming the landscape of sociopolitical conflict.

As mentioned, organized interests are believed to play a key role in the process within which identities and interests are formed. Of major theoretical interest, then, is to specify how the institutional setup of the welfare state affects the links between class, class identity, and welfare state preferences. This is dealt with at length in a later section. Suffice it to say at this point that in contrast to the *phase II* argument, the alternative institutional feedback approach suggests that class is a major axis of welfare policy conflict in the Swedish social democratic regime, while in the U.S. liberal regime, class as a political cleavage is of minor importance.

The suggested implications of both approaches can easily be transformed to testable hypotheses for which aspirations of generalization travel well beyond the national borders of Sweden and the United States. The hypotheses highlight the role of social class in contemporary Western politics and societies as well as institutional feedback processes and effects. As such, this chapter is situated within the field of class analysis and research on policy feedback and mass political behavior (Mettler & Soss 2004).

As far as social stratification and political conflict are concerned, class is given analytical primacy in this chapter. The labor market is the hub of society and is, as such, the major distributor of material rewards and opportunities for self-sustenance. The welfare state can be understood as a configuration of institutions aiming to reduce risks and redistribute market-generated inequality. By applying a perspective of rational actors, it is expected that welfare policy preferences vary according to the distribution of risks and marketable resources among social strata. In market situations, insurance costs are related to calculated risks. Higher risks involve higher premiums. It is therefore expected that low-risk categories are less interested in encompassing state-financed schemes of social protection and more inclined to favor market solutions. In a similar vein, high-risk groups have an obvious interest in encompassing strategies to reduce costs. The attendance to risks and marketable resources is not evenly distributed among social strata. Some groups are in more precarious situations than others. They tend to be subjected to higher risks attached to unemployment and other conditions that severely reduce possibilities for self-support. The main system of stratification in these respects is the labor market. It is, therefore, suggested that one major determinant of welfare policy preferences is class. Individuals in class positions characterized by extensive resources and less exposure to risks (e.g., professionals, managers, and large proprietors) are supposed to be less in favor of redistributive policy and state-organized social security than those in manual occupations.

In this general theory of the relationships between class and welfare policy preferences, the distribution of resources and risks is central. In any advanced democracy, it is expected that state-financed social policy receives stronger support from the working class than from the middle classes. In a comparative perspective, however, it is expected that the strength of the relationship between class and welfare state preferences differs considerably across countries. According to the *phase II* argument, it is expected that the link is more pronounced in countries belonging to the liberal regime than in social democratic regime countries. The alternative approach predicts the opposite pattern.

It should also be noted that the concept of *class conflict* as employed in this chapter refers to class-based differences in "the attitudes . . . towards state intervention in economic and social life with the effect of overriding the distribution of resources via market mechanisms, especially that of the labour market" (Matheson 1993: 57). Behavioral expressions of class conflict such as strikes and lockouts are not included in the concept.

The attitudinal data were collected within the framework of the International Social Survey Program (ISSP), and analyzed by means of the Latent Class Analysis method. Data describing relevant country characteristics were collected from various sources. Six countries were selected for analysis. Four of them belong more or less to the liberal regime: the United States, Canada, Australia, and New Zealand. The other two are social democratic regimes: Sweden and Norway.

The chapter is organized as follows. In the next section, the chosen concept of class as well as the critique against it are described and reviewed.

In the following section, the argument of the regime theory and the story behind it are spelled out in detail. Thereafter, the alternative approach to institutional feedback effects is reviewed. Then, the key macro-variables of both approaches are operationalized and quantified. This is followed by a presentation of the microdata and methods. Then, the empirical results of the analysis are presented and commented on. In the final section, the predictive power of each hypothesis is valued and discussed in the light of the main empirical results.

THE EGP CLASS CONCEPT: CRITIQUE AND JUSTIFICATION

The principal conceptual building blocks in this chapter are *class* and *institution*. The institutional concept is covered in Chapter 1, and therefore this chapter will allocate comparatively more space to the concept of class.

In recent years, the number of works criticizing the usefulness of class as an analytical tool has increased significantly. Within some circles of the social sciences, and perhaps sociology in particular, the former universally prevailing view that class is key in social analysis seems to be under threat of extinction, a development ardently welcomed and propelled by anticlass proponents. It is widely believed that contemporary social stratification is fragmented to such an extent that the analytic categories in conventional aggregate class schemas are simply useless. Identities and interests, it is argued, are reflexively self-composed rather than rooted in structural conditions (Clark & Lipset 1996, 2001; Pakulski & Waters 1996). As pointed out by Grusky and Sørensen (1998: 1188), "This development constitutes a striking repudiation of our disciplinary heritage; in fact, it was not so long ago that commentators as mainstream as Stinchcombe . . . could allege, without generating much in the way of controversy, that social class was the one and only independent variable of sociological interest."[2] However, as this chapter will show, it is a mistake to subscribe to the assertion that the concept of class is "ceasing to do any useful work for sociology" (Pahl 1996: 89). And to proclaim *The Death of Class* (Pakulski & Waters 1996) will most certainly not qualify for entrance into the top 10 chart of imaginable responses to the results presented in this chapter.

The concept of class adopted in this chapter is an aggregated class model developed and refined within the CASMIN project (Goldthorpe 2000;

Erikson & Goldthorpe 1992a), hereafter EGP.[3] The theoretical basis for the classification of occupations within the EGP concept is to differentiate positions within labor markets and production units. A basic class distinction is made between employers and employees. To differentiate class positions among employees, the EGP approach is the following. Employers face contractual hazards in the labor market. This is analytically dealt with as problems of work monitoring and human asset specificity. The type of work that is supposed to be executed by the employee determines the significance of these problems. The differences in hazard rates are reflected in the type of contract offered to the employee. Two ideal types of employment regulations, or contract forms, are specified: the labor contract and the service relationship.

Employment relations within the labor contract entail a rather short-term and specific exchange between labor effort and wage, often under some form of supervision. Work monitoring is a relatively easy task by the means of external control, and human asset specificity is relatively low. In contrast, occupations entailing the service relationship are those in which "it is required of employees that they exercise delegated authority or specialized knowledge and expertise in the interests of their employing organization" (Erikson & Goldthorpe 1992a: 42). Typically, in a service relationship, human asset specificity is relatively high and work monitoring has to be accomplished by means other than traditional supervision. Deeply embedded within the service relationship is the principal–agent problem: the asymmetry of information that exists between the employer and the employee when assessing whether the employee acts in the interests of the employer or rather in his or her own interests when they are in conflict with those of the employer. By offering incentives—salary increments on an established scale, various sorts of fringe benefits, and prospective elements such as career opportunities—the employer attempts to reduce the risks by strengthening the reciprocal ties of affiliation between the employee and the employing organization.

The classes of employees distinguished by the schema are variants or combinations of these two ideal types of employment contract, as empirically they both appear in pure and mixed forms.

The EGP is a weak class idiom. The approach explicitly rejects the idea of incorporating notions of consciousness, action, and group belonging as well as antagonism and exploitation as class conceptual building blocks. The objective of class analysis, as understood by EGP, is to explore "the interconnections between positions defined by employment relations in labour markets and production units in different sectors of national economies; the processes through which individuals and their families are distributed and redistributed among these positions over time; and the consequences thereof for their life chances and for the social identities that they adopt and the social values and interests that they pursue" (Goldthorpe & Marshall 1996: 98–99).

The principal critique against the EGP deals with the minimalist idea of class. In order to speak about classes and class structures, according to the critics, it is simply not sufficient to build a class concept solely on employment relations. The emphasis on identifying classes with occupational positions, while not paying proper attention to "wider dimensions of economic power and social action," seriously reduces class "to a statistical aggregate with only indeterminate relations to actual consciousness or action" (Holton 1996:41). The reluctance of the approach to incorporate any "strong" components in the class concept, it is argued, leads to an overly minimalist version of class, which is neither desirable nor necessary. By resorting to a weak class idiom, the concept is deprived of certain key *gemeinschaftlich* components, that is, aspects relating to group belonging with a degree of demographic closure and identity.[4]

Now, in response to that critique the first point is to separate *economic* aspects of class from *social* aspects. Economic classes are said to exist if material or other structural inequality is shown to be systematically linked to class positions. The extent to which class-based structural inequality gives rise to class-specific worldviews, lifestyles, feelings of group belonging, values, cultures, and so on determines the degree of transformation from economic classes to social classes (Scott 2002).

As a theory of class based on employment relations, its kernel relates, of course, to the economic consequences of class (Goldthorpe & McKnight 2004). This is, however, not to say that social aspects of class are of no interest. Contrary to the image held by critics, a careful reading regarding the "imprecise" linkages between structural locations, interests, and action suggests that the EGP approach does not deny that individuals located in similar class positions may have shared identities and interests, and that these in turn may take the form of collective action. However, whether identities and interests are structured along the axis of class or by other structural locations, and whether these interests transform into political mobilization, is foremost an empirical question (Goldthorpe & Marshall 1996: 101f). Thus, whether *economic* classes are *social* should be addressed empirically.

Although the EGP approach is a minimalist version of the class concept, the conceptual clarity and consistency is a true advantage (Erikson & Goldthorpe 1992a; Goldthorpe 2000). The class concept has straightforward lines of demarcation, it is theoretically informed, and finally, it has been empirically validated (Evans 1992, 1996; Evans & Mills 1998a, 1998b). By incorporating alternative aspects of class within the concept, the consistency of the concept may be undermined. In this chapter, the chosen strategy of class measurement is a type of compromise. In an attempt to bridge the gap between the strong and weak class idioms, the EGP approach is complemented with a communal aspect of class—namely, class identity. There are three reasons for bringing in class identity in the analysis. First, class identity adds to the class concept a sense of belonging to a wider collective. Second, from a class-analytical point of view, the assertion of the anticlass critics that aggregate class identities do not matter in present society is empirically addressed. Third, in relation to the alternative hypothesis on institutional effects, class identity plays a significant role.

When analyzing the relevance of class in contemporary society, there are thus good reasons to separate economic aspects from social aspects of class. The topic of the following section is the regime theory's arguments concerning the consequences of social policy on both the social and economic aspects of class formation in comparative perspective. Thereafter, the alternative approach to these issues is discussed.

SOCIAL STRATIFICATION AND SOCIAL POLICY

The point of departure for the *phase II* argument of the regime theory is the following. The emergence of large-scale institutions, such as the welfare state, mass education, and wage bargaining institutions, have fundamentally reshaped class relations characterizing industrial society. Similar to traditional class theory, processes of social stratification are rooted within structures of employment. However, these stratification processes are heavily influenced by institutions, the welfare state in particular. The welfare state not only influences class relations in terms of the configuration of welfare benefits (e.g., universal or targeted benefits); it is a key determinant in structuring employment (Esping-Andersen 1990, 1993).

The welfare regime concept focuses foremost on the organization of social protection in terms of arrangements among the state, the market, and the family. Although different or modified classification criteria have been suggested, there seems to be little disagreement that Scandinavian countries, Sweden in particular, fit the social democratic welfare state regime-type, while the United States is considered the prime example of a liberal welfare state regime.

In the Swedish social democratic welfare regime, social protection is linked to citizenship. The core programs of the welfare state cover most of the population. Benefits are either income-related, together with a rather high basic security level for those with low or no income, or provided as citizens' rights. Social spending levels are comparatively high and are financed mainly by tax revenues. The institutional setup of the core welfare programs and industrial relations are conducive to full employment. Key factors are the strong commitment of the welfare state to provide extensive and subsidized social services, encompassing social insurance schemes linked to previous earnings, and labor market training. The high taxes on paid labor, it may also be added, do not encourage couples to view the single breadwinner alternative as an available option. The growth of post-industrial employment is intimately linked with the emergence of state-provided social services. This has resulted in an extremely gender-segregated labor market; men are primarily employed in the private sector, while the public sector employs mainly women. Moreover, women dominate the comparatively large stratum of unskilled service jobs. However, strong unions and a sophisticated system of labor law have ensured that the share of insecure and low-paid jobs is kept at a minimum level. A long tradition of collective and centralized wage bargaining has resulted in a comparatively compressed income distribution (Esping-Andersen 1990, 1993; Tåhlin 1993).

The liberal welfare regime observed in the United States is characterized by the limited role of an active state and the high reliance on market solutions. Social spending and tax revenue levels are relatively low. It should, however, be acknowledged that the U.S. system distributes a significant share of its financial resources in the form of tax deductions—a rather invisible form of regressive fiscal welfare (Hacker 2002). When it comes to public social protection, the state offers a basic security net for those with low incomes, while others who are better off are supposed to protect themselves via various private forms of insurance, often subsidized by the tax system. Public social benefits are generally means-tested or provided at a low flat rate. The liberal regime has a weak state-led commitment to social services and benefits, a passive approach to full employment, and a weak and fragmented union system. The high employment rate among both men and women is shaped by market forces rather than by an active welfare state. The U.S. trajectory has resulted in a large post-industrial sector in which low-paid and insecure service jobs constitute a prominent but not rapidly growing segment of the labor force. Lock-in effects are not prominent. On the contrary, upward social mobility is relatively open for women and minorities. Compared to Sweden, post-industrial employment in the United States is less gender-segregated and more evenly distributed across different sectors of the economy (Esping-Andersen 1990, 1993; Jacobs 1993).

Welfare outcomes produced by these institutional designs differ substantially. Almost regardless of which measurements are used for classification, countries labeled social democratic regimes are located in the top bracket of welfare effort scales, while the liberal welfare states are placed at the lower end of the scales (Esping-Andersen 1990; Kangas 1991; Palme 1990; Castles & Mitchell 1993; Korpi & Palme 1998; McFate et al. 1995a; Huber & Stephens 2001; Siaroff 1994).

It is against this background that the *phase II* argument claims that the relevance of class for explaining material differences in living conditions, as well as ideological differences manifested in voting behavior and other sociopolitical attitudes, differs considerably across countries belonging to different welfare regimes. Let us examine the argument in this respect in more detail.

CLASS CONFLICTS IN COMPARATIVE PERSPECTIVE: THE *PHASE II* ARGUMENT

The *phase II* argument can be decomposed into four assumptions. The first assumption is a somewhat softer variant of the structure-consciousness-action (SCA) model, that differences between classes in material conditions form the base for class action.[5] While the fundamental difference in political views between the working and the middle classes is supposed to exist in all advanced industrial democracies, the strength of sociopolitical class conflict is supposed to vary across countries. In countries where material inequality is relatively low between classes, the likelihood that class conflicts will occur is much smaller than in countries characterized by pronounced material inequality.

The second assumption of the *phase II* argument is closely related to material inequality as it refers to employment security. The higher the degree of employment security, the lower will be the probability that issues related to social protection enter the political agenda.

The third assumption concerns institutional feedback effects. The scope and organization of welfare policy structure interests and patterns of political coalition formation to a significant extent (Korpi 1980; Korpi & Palme 1998). The characteristics of the liberal welfare state are likely to discourage coalitions between poor and better-off citizens. Targeted and means-tested programs tend to drive a wedge between better-off classes and worse-off classes, thereby reducing social solidarity and increasing class conflict related to social policy. Issues of social protection within this regime type, the argument goes, are framed as political conflicts between "us" (the majority paying taxes) and "them" (others, often equipped with fewer political resources, receiving benefits without paying). In the social democratic regime, the institutionalized encompassing programs are supposed to dampen class conflicts, since the working as well as the middle classes are included and covered by the same insurance programs and social service facilities. The high taxes required by the social democratic regime type are not seen as a major obstacle for social solidarity. "All benefit; all are dependent; and all will presumably feel obliged to pay" (Esping-Andersen 1990: 28).

The fourth assumption is that social stratification influences the content of the political agenda and that the welfare state is the main arena for political struggles over inequality in contemporary Western societies—an assumption that is shared by others as well (Matheson 1993: 57, Svallfors 1999a; Korpi & Palme 2003). Cross-national variation in this respect is not anticipated.

By extending the argument beyond the Swedish and American cases in generic terms, it is suggested that class conflict over welfare policy is nurtured by (a) a high degree of material inequality between classes, (b) a low degree of employment security, and (c) a low degree of welfare policy universalism.

CLASS CONFLICTS IN COMPARATIVE PERSPECTIVE:
THE ALTERNATIVE APPROACH

The assumption that material inequality forms a base for class-specific interests and action is a realistic starting point. It also seems reasonable to assume that the basic rank order of classes in terms of welfare state support shares many similarities across welfare regimes. However, the *phase II* argument places too much emphasis on the political impact of changing stratification patterns and, concerning the institutional feedback effects of the welfare state, it will be argued that the issue of universal versus selective coverage is of minor importance. The claim here is that the different shapes of class conflict over social policy in social democratic and liberal regimes have less to do with material inequality and social policy universalism than with the distinctively different experiences and interpretations of the tax system and government spending priorities, which the social democratic and the liberal types of welfare regime tend to encourage. These institutional feedback effects will now be elaborated.

As pointed out, the *phase II* argument emphasizes the selective-universalism dimension as the main institutional feedback effect. The alternative approach suggests that a more fruitful understanding of institutional feedback effects is given if the focus is changed toward other measures of welfare state performance, such as income redistribution via taxes and transfers, and the profile of risk-reduction in social spending priorities.

Contrary to the idea that experienced inequalities tend to be addressed politically, irrespective of welfare regime type, it is assumed that the salience of the welfare state in the political sphere varies among different welfare regimes. In the social democratic regime, the systems of taxation, social spending, and redistribution involve a comparatively larger proportion of taxpayers and benefit receivers than in the liberal welfare regime. The size of the welfare state, as well as the risk profile, is indicative of the extent to which the welfare state can be considered to have a major influence on citizens' everyday life, and furthermore, to what extent the welfare state attracts attention from organized interests. A major source of class conflict is therefore the redistributive capacity of the welfare state.

Thus, the main argument is that the configuration of the welfare state determines certain outcomes in terms of risk protection and redistribution. Public experiences and interpretations of these outcomes shape interests and preferences regarding spending and taxing. In this process of attitude formation, the role of institutional translators—i.e., organizations with embodied interests in welfare state institutions, such as unions, employer organizations, and political parties—in framing public debate is decisive.[6] A comparison of the social democratic and liberal welfare regimes, represented by Sweden and the United States, may clarify the argument.

While the three components are interrelated, we can analytically distinguish among them: the redistributive character of the tax and transfer systems, the distributive profile of public spending and risk protection, and the institutional translators in the form of institutional guardians and challengers.

Beginning with the first component, empirical evidence clearly shows that the redistributive impact of taxation on income distribution is substantially more pronounced in Sweden than in the United States. This has less to do with income tax progression—which tends to be more pronounced in liberal low-tax countries than in social democratic high-tax countries—and more to do with the average tax rate (Edlund 1999, 2003b; OECD 1990). It is the size of the tax revenue rather than its distributive profile that determines the redistributive capacity of the welfare state (Åberg 1989; Edlund & Åberg 2002). The American tendency to use tax deductions for financing private welfare policy should also be recognized. The distributive profile of tax deductions is regressive, as many deductions pertain to activities exercised more commonly by those in the upper brackets of the income ladder (Hacker 2002). Now, as pointed out previously, the institutional properties of the tax system are likely to influence public perceptions of taxes. Among available images, perceptions of the tax system as a tool of redistribution are likely to be far more common in Sweden than in the United States. This tendency might be reinforced by the structure of the American tax system, which, when compared to the Swedish system, appears to be highly complicated and particularistic (Steinmo 1993).

Similar to the different redistributive effects achieved via taxes found in liberal and social democratic regimes, there is solid evidence suggesting that reduction of poverty and economic inequality is accomplished more effectively within transfer systems of social democratic type than in those dominant in liberal regimes. This is known as the "paradox of redistribution," which means that countries fighting poverty by flat-rate benefits along with targeting benefits to the poor have been less successful than countries relying on encompassing welfare programs (Korpi & Palme 1998). Recent research shows that the tax and transfer systems in the Nordic countries on average lift about 76 percent of the poor pre-tax/transfer households out of poverty. The corresponding figure for the liberal countries is 46 percent (Pontusson 2005: 171; cf. McFate et al. 1995b: 53). It is therefore hypothesized that public interpretations of tax-financed welfare programs as engines of redistribution are less likely to appear among Americans than among Swedes.

The second component refers to public spending priorities. Examining how governments spend their taxes helps us to understand which risks governments attempt to neutralize. The distributive profile of the risks recognized in a "night-watchman" state devoted to maintaining public order and national security is fundamentally different from the profile of an advanced welfare state attempting to reduce risks attached to unemployment, retirement, and sickness. Government spending priorities reflect the class character of risk protection. It is misleading to reduce the scope of public policy to social welfare programs, since a substantial part of public spending is addressed to non–social welfare programs. The American government allocates a larger share of its resources to non–social welfare programs than most European governments (Rose 1991; Peters 1991). It is perhaps redundant to mention that the Swedish public policy profile, with a much stronger emphasis on social welfare, offers a striking contrast to the American. Although the applied aggregate measures are admittedly crude, it is suggested that due to spending priorities, the risks to be protected against are more evenly distributed among social strata in the United States and do not take on a class character as distinct as in Sweden.

On the basis of measures of redistribution and equalization of incomes and risks, it may be concluded that the institutional setup of the social democratic welfare regime has a much sharper class profile than the liberal welfare regime. This is, again, of relevance for the widely held assumption that the welfare state is the main arena for class conflict in contemporary Western societies. The argument here is rather that welfare state–related class politics are more likely to appear in the social democratic regime than in the liberal, principally because of the combinatory effect stemming from the scope of the welfare state and its redistributive profile. It is likely that a substantially broader set of issues is considered and framed as *political and class relevant* rather than purely *private* in the social democratic compared to the liberal welfare regime. Simply put, in issues of social protection, why should we assume that Americans would turn to the political sphere advocating that the state should provide social insurance and services when the state seems to prioritize issues other than social policy?

The third component is the role of institutional translators—the rhetoric and strategies undertaken by political parties, unions, employer organizations, and other organized interests in matters of taxation and social policy. Institutions are not only relevant for understanding attitude formation in the sense of policy feedbacks in a "technical-legalistic" rules-of-the-game sense. As pointed out by Korpi and Palme (1998), institutions reflect causal factors such as actions taken by different social groupings. Institutions may be understood as institutionalized compromises/conflicts between different social groups or collective actors (Hanson 1994). Once a particular institution has been created, the central political actors involved in the process—defined here in a broad sense—can be characterized as either institutional guardians or institutional challengers. Irrespective of whether the actors are guardians or challengers, they have an interest in attempting to win public support for their ideas. Collective interests are, in other words, embodied within institutions. The institutional translators are thus important for underpinning collective memories and worldviews (cf. Rothstein 2000). By framing public debate and by offering citizens mental tools and guidelines for interpretations of "problems" and "solutions" to any given issue, institutional translators attempt to gain public acceptance of and support for needed action and are, therefore, powerful forces in the processes of attitude formation.

Obviously, the relationship between material conditions and welfare policy preferences is here differently understood in comparison to the SCA model where conditions "cause" political preferences. Far from all recognized socioeconomic inequalities are being dealt with through the translation of individualized, nonorganized inequality into lasting organizational structures such as political parties or institutions. In our understanding, material inequality is a facilitating condition, not the engine, in the process of transforming political messages into lasting sociopolitical cleavages.

A dedicated proponent of this perspective is Giovanni Sartori: "Class is an ideology. Classes materialize in the real world in close correspondence with belief systems in which 'class' becomes the central idea-element; and it is the ideology of class that obtains 'class action'. If so the question becomes how ideologies take hold. And to this effect I would subscribe to the statement that 'no idea has ever made much headway without an organization behind it . . . Wherever ideologies seem to be important in politics they have a firm organizational basis' (Barnes 1966: 522). . . . Ideological persuasion requires a powerfully organized network of communications" (Sartori 1990: 170).[7]

To summarize the argument: The extent to which welfare state politics is characterized by class conflict depends heavily on whether institutional translators are rooted in class organizations or not. A well-pronounced class conflict over welfare policy is thus understood as a successful translation handling of structural cleavages rooted in material inequality into robust sets of welfare policy preferences. In this translation process, economic classes evolve into social classes with conflicting welfare policy ideologies.

With respect to welfare state politics, one arena where successful translation processes are particularly difficult to achieve is tax policy. It is commonly suggested that strategies calling for new or increased taxes are extremely difficult to master successfully. While it may be true that political actors attempt to win public appeal by claiming tax cuts, rather than the reverse, there are reasons to believe that tax policy is articulated and debated somewhat differently in the liberal regime compared to the social democratic regime. Scattered evidence referring to Anglo-Saxon countries suggests that a message such as George H. W. Bush's "Read my lips—No new taxes," at the 1988 Republican National Convention may be representative, regardless of the political residency of the messenger. Peters (1991: 10) even suggests that "any statement about more taxes is likely to be political suicide." In the social democratic regime, the institutional translators are chiefly grouped along the social class axis, contributing to the salience of redistributive politics in public and political debates. Strategies pursued by institutional challengers—for example, business interests and right-wing parties—aiming at cutting taxes and decreasing redistribution are routinely confronted by institutional guardians, that is, the labor movement, defending the current state of affairs by arguing the necessity of taxes to secure the quality of welfare policies and to achieve redistributive goals. In the liberal welfare regime, collective actors are not grouped along the left–right axis to the same extent. Considering the residual character of the welfare system, it is doubtful whether welfare policy–related institutional guardians could be distinguished at all in the archetypical liberal welfare regime. Thus, the prerequisites for class conflict over taxation appear to be more favorable in the Swedish polarized environment of prosecutors and defenders when compared to the United States, where virtually all organized interests appear to act as prosecutors (cf. Lipset 1996; Steinmo 1993).[8]

In matters of social policy, a similar framing phenomenon can be distinguished. It is well known that targeted programs receive less public support than encompassing programs. Coughlin's (1980) distinction between "conferral of benefit" (universal vs. selective) and "perceptions of origins of risk" (beyond individual control vs. related to individual behavior) points to the problem of gaining legitimacy for programs in which the need can be questioned. Recipients of selective programs often face the accusation that their need is not beyond individual control but rather an effect of their own behavior. Now the proportion of these selective programs is much larger in the total social spending budget of liberal regimes than in social democratic regimes. The institutional setup in the liberal regime attracts institutional translators to frame social policy in the language of "us" and "them" (where no one wants to be part of "them"). In the social democratic regime, such articulations are more difficult. Power relations between institutional guardians and challengers are more evenly distributed. Universal welfare policy and social stigma rhetoric is a difficult equation to solve successfully.

And here class identity enters the discussion. Class identity is one among many ways (e.g., religion, race) that people "define what is salient about their lives and what differentiates them from others" (Wright 1997: 495). As such, class identity has a cognitive meaning (class membership) as well as an affective meaning (class-driven worldviews). While anticlass proponents argue that class identity is a truly unimportant concept with only loose connections to class positions and political preferences, others suggest that class identity is an important feature that guides individuals in their everyday life (Karlsson 2005). Both of these views are perhaps too static. It seems more fruitful to assume that the links between class, class identity, and political preferences are dynamic in character. The extent to which class identity is linked to specific welfare state preferences depends heavily on the institutional translators' past behavioral and rhetorical record.

In a similar vein, the strength of the link between class and class identity is determined by the rhetoric and past behavioral record of class organizations. Workers in social democratic regimes, characterized by a well-organized labor movement with a past record of being the main architect behind the welfare state, are thus more likely to identify themselves as belonging to the working class than are workers in liberal regimes, where working-class organizations are much weaker and have little or no past record of successfully implemented welfare policies.

Therefore, it makes a difference whether the provided social policies are regarded as excellent or insufficient, or if they are not provided at all. Perhaps more important for the working class than for the middle class, a robust class identity linked to specific welfare policy preferences requires *positive nutrition*. This is offered by institutional translators. In line with the argument, it is expected that class identity is more strongly correlated with both class and welfare policy preferences in social democratic regimes than in liberal regimes.

SUMMARY OF THE KEY VARIABLES IN THE HYPOTHESES AND OPERATIONAL PROCEDURES

Instead of in-depth descriptions of each country's institutional configuration, the key variables specified by the regime theory *phase II* and the alternative institutional feedback approach are operationalized and quantified (see Table 2.1 and Appendix Table 2.A1). These variables pertain to different aspects of political institutions and industrial relations. An inspection of the variables indicates that the United States and Canada show the closest fit to the liberal regime type. Australia and New Zealand, often pointed out in the literature as belonging to a wage earners' welfare state regime, show somewhat different scores. These scores are, however, indisputably more similar to the truly liberal countries than to the social democratic ones—perhaps an indication of the significant drift during the last decades of the antipodean countries toward the liberal regime model (Castles 1996; Huber & Stephens 2001).

In summary, the main reasons the *phase II* argument anticipates that class-based sociopolitical conflicts are not well pronounced within the Swedish social democratic regime are as follows: the gender- and sector-segregated labor market; the small proportion of low-paid jobs; the strong emphasis on employment security; a compressed income distribution; and universal social services and insurance programs. The main reasons sociopolitical conflicts are principally structured by class within the liberal U.S. regime are the following: the strong element of market solutions in the welfare system manifested in unequal access to social protection; a large proportion of badly paid and insecure jobs; large income differences;

and a comparatively nondiscriminatory labor market in terms of gender and ethnicity. The key factors in the *phase II* hypothesis, hereafter HEA (hypothesis: Esping-Andersen), are the following:

- Material equality
- Employment security
- Welfare policy universalism

In contrast, the alternative institutional feedback approach, hereafter HSE (hypothesis: Sartori-Edlund), suggests that whether or not welfare politics are characterized by class conflict depends to a significant extent on the class character of risk protection and redistribution inherent in the tax system and public policy, and on the strategies and articulations in these matters pursued by institutional translators. The size of the welfare state, as well as its redistributive capacity, and articulations of institutional translators tend to be grouped in clusters, each promoting a regime-specific degree of class conflict. Class conflict related to the welfare state is more likely to occur in social democratic welfare regimes than in liberal welfare regimes. The key factors in the HSE are the following:

- Welfare state performance: the size and the redistributive capacity of the welfare state
- Institutional translators: the political branch
- Institutional translators: the industrial relations branch

Table 2.1 lists the factors and the operationalized indicators. It should immediately be pointed out that the strategy for using levels of taxation and social expenditure as indicators for factors related to both hypotheses is, of course, not an ideal situation. However, empirically it is shown that social policy universalism, taxation, social expenditure, and redistributive capacity are strongly interrelated. Countries with universal programs are those with the highest levels of taxation, social spending, and redistribution (Åberg 1989; Edlund & Åberg 2002; Korpi & Palme 1998). The issue of substantive interest is that the predicted effects of these indicators are distinctively different. According to the HEA, in the social democratic regime, the overall effect of these indicators is interpreted in terms of universal social solidarity by the public. The HSE, on the other hand, assumes that in the social democratic regime, the effect is mainly conceived of as a struggle over the distribution of societal resources.

T A B L E   2 . 1
Macro-level indicators of material and institutional characteristics.

HEA (HYPOTHESIS: ESPING-ANDERSEN)	
Material equality	
A Income equality	Income distribution. 100 − Gini × 100. 1995 (ca). (a)
Employment security	
B Employment security index	Composite measure constructed by the ILO. 1999 (ca). (b)
Welfare policy universalism	
C Taxation	Total tax revenue in percentage of GDP. 1999. (c)
D Social expenditure	Public social expenditures in percentage of GDP. 1998. (d)
HSE (HYPOTHESIS: SARTORI-EDLUND)	
Welfare state size and redistributive performance	
C Taxation	Total tax revenue in percentage of GDP. 1999. (c)
D Social expenditure	Public social expenditures in percentage of GDP. 1998. (d)
E Redistributive capacity	Change in Gini coefficients between pre- and post-tax/transfer income distributions. 1985 (ca). (e)
Institutional translators: the political branch	
F Ideological legacy of government	Left-right ideology of cabinet. 100 × mean 1945–2000. (f)
G Strength of class-articulated conflicts between political parties	Variance of the position of political parties on a left–right scale. Mean 1950–1995. Parties classified according to CMP98. (g)
Institutional translators: the industrial relations branch	
H Union density	Mean of nonagricultural labor force and wage and salary earners. 1995 (ca). (h)
I Integration of main actors in the economy	Indicators of social partnership, industry-level coordination, and national policy-making patterns. Siaroff's Integration Index. Mean 1968–1995. (i)
J Union centrality	Wage bargaining level. Mean 1950–2000. (j)

SOURCES: (a) World Bank (Internet database); (b) ILO (2004); (c) OECD (Internet database); (d) OECD (Internet database); (e) Korpi & Palme (1998); (f) Ersson 2001; (g) McDonald & Mendes (2002), Budge et al. 2001; (h) ILO (Internet database); (i) Siaroff (1999), Armingeon et al. (2004); (j) Golden & Wallerstein (2004).

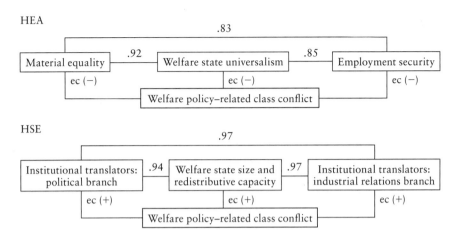

Figure 2.1. Correlations (Pearson's r) between factors related to HEA and HSE, respectively, and their expected correlations with the size of welfare policy–related conflict. (ec = expected correlation).

The indicators in Table 2.1 that refer to the HEA are A through D. As pointed out previously, welfare universalism is measured with levels of taxation and social expenditure. The indicators C through J pertain to the HSE. Taxation and social expenditure are direct measures of the size of the welfare state but also good proxies for the redistributive capacity of the welfare state. The direct measure of redistributive capacity (E) is perhaps at face value the best measure as it compares the distribution of incomes pre- and post-transfers/taxes.

When it comes to institutional translators, the idea is that the power of capital is omnipresent in capitalistic societies. Whether the power of capital is visible in the form of political action, defined broadly, depends on the strength of the labor movement. Therefore, the intensity of political rhetoric made by institutional guardians and challengers is likely to co-vary with indicators such as the ideological legacy of government, union density, integration between the main actors in the economy— including factors related to social partnership between the state, capital, and unions, as well as economic system coordination and bargaining levels (F, H, I, J). A somewhat more direct measure of the visibility of institutional translators is the degree of class politics at the level of political parties (G).

In the empirical analysis that follows, indicators E and J have been excluded, as data for them are not available in New Zealand. This is, however, not a major problem since both items are strongly related to the other items measuring the respective factor—for example, the correlation between redistributive capacity (E) and taxation (C) is 0.99. The raw data and the correlation matrix of the macro-level indicators are shown in Appendix Tables 2.A1 and 2.A2.

There are reasons to believe that the factors in each model are strongly interrelated. As discussed in the introductory chapter, welfare regimes and so-called production regimes tend to cluster.[9] Figure 2.1 shows that the HEA and HSE factors, respectively, are strongly interrelated.[10] Again, it should be pointed out that the strong correlations between the indicators do not pose a problem analytically. The major difference between the HEA and the HSE is not an argument about the true character of a "big" or "small" welfare state, respectively. The difference is, rather, that they emphasize different theoretically derived components as important predictors of class conflict over welfare policy. Before turning to the empirical analysis in order to fill the empty coefficient spaces in Figure 2.1, we need to devote some attention to the dependent variables.

DATA, VARIABLES, AND THE MEASUREMENT MODEL

The data come from the 1996 Role of Government III survey developed within the framework of the International Social Survey Program (ISSP). All samples are nationally representative of the adult population. The response rates are between 60 percent and 70 percent (ISSP 1996). The study description for Australia is missing, but the response rate in other ISSP surveys is usually slightly above 60 percent.

In relation to the class coding procedures, a number of different occupational classifications were used in order to construct a six-class EGP schema.[11] The service class (occupations characterized as professional, higher technical, administrative, or managerial) is grouped into two fractions, service classes I and II (higher and lower grade, respectively). In a similar vein, those working under a labor contract are divided into skilled and unskilled manuals. An intermediate position in the class structure is taken by the occupations that generally involve a mixed form of employment relations: the so-called routine nonmanuals, often found within clerical and sales occupations. The sixth class is the self-employed.

The principal determinant when allocating individuals into classes follows the dominance model (Erikson 1984). The household is the unit of the class structure. As far as couples in dual-earner households are concerned, the class position of the household is determined by the class position of the family member with the most pronounced attachment to the labor market. The main criterion is number of working hours. The reason for using the dominance model is both theoretical (Goldthorpe 1983) and empirical—where evidence suggests that the individual approach to class assignment may downplay the significance of class, particularly in liberal countries (Erikson & Goldthorpe 1992b; Marshall 1997; Wright 1997; Edlund 2003a). For Australia, data on spouse's employment are not available. Class assignment is therefore determined by the class position of the respondent. Consequently, the effect of class in Australia may be somewhat underestimated.

Another problem of standardization is that data on employment for those currently not working (e.g., the unemployed and pensioners) are available only for Sweden, Norway, and the United States. In Canada, Australia, and New Zealand, data on employment refer only to those currently working. It should also be mentioned that a comparison of the class structures in the countries studied does not raise any suspicion about serious shortcomings in the data, except for Canada. In the Canadian sample, the collapsed working class is peculiarly small, while the collapsed service class is very large. The latter is nearly six times larger than the former. In the other countries, the ratio between the same classes varies from 1.1 to 2.8. Cautious interpretation of the results pertaining to Canada is suggested.

Finally, the class identity variable is requested in different formats across countries. The standard variable contains five categories: lower, working, middle, upper middle, and upper. Canada and New Zealand include an intermediate category—upper working class/lower middle class—presumably because of the overall high propensity for middle-class identification in these countries. This middle category is included in Norway also, but the category "lower" is excluded. In order to reach the highest possible standardization of the variable, it is dichotomized into 1 "working class" (lower, working, upper working/lower middle), and 2 "middle class" (middle, upper middle, upper). It is therefore suggested that aggregate differences in class identity between countries need to be interpreted cautiously.

Following is a description of the dependent variables and coding information:

[A] It is the responsibility of the government to reduce the differences in income between people with high incomes and those with low incomes.
1 = Agree strongly/Agree; 2 = Neither agree nor disagree/Disagree/Disagree strongly.

Listed below are various areas of government spending. Please show whether you would like to see more or less government spending in each area. Remember that if you say "much more," it might require a tax increase to pay for it.
[B] Health.
[C] Education.
[D] Old age pensions.
[E] Unemployment benefits.
1 = Spend much more/Spend more; 2 = Spend the same as now/Spend less/ Spend much less.

On the whole, do you think it should be or should not be the government's responsibility to:
[F] Provide a job for everyone who wants one.
[G] Provide health care for the sick.
[H] Provide a decent standard of living for the old.
[I] Provide a decent standard of living for the unemployed.
[J] Reduce income differences between the rich and poor.
[K] Give financial help to university students from low-income families.
[L] Provide decent housing for those who can't afford it.
1 = Definitely should be/Probably should be; 2 = Probably should not be/ Definitely should not be.

Generally, how would you describe taxes in (Country) today?
[M] For those with high incomes, are taxes . . .
1 = Much too low/Too low; 2 = About right/Too high/Much too high.

Table 2.2 shows the response distributions of the welfare state indicators. Three items are principally about state financial redistribution [A, J, M]. Other items address areas of welfare policy linked to health, retirement, unemployment, education, and housing. The hypothetical size of the recipient groups varies across these areas. Whereas some are universal in character (e.g., health and retirement), others (e.g., housing and financial help for students) are policies targeted toward specific groups. In the analysis, three items were excluded. First, the spending item on education [C] behaved

TABLE 2.2

Attitudes toward the welfare state in six Western countries. Cells indicate welfare state–friendly responses (code 1) expressed as deviations from the grand mean in percentage units.

	Grand mean	Sweden	Norway	USA	Canada	Australia	New Zealand
Government should . . .							
A Reduce income differences	43	+16	+13	-10	-3	-5	-12
B Increase spending: health	74	+2	+11	-7	-22	+4	+12
C Increase spending: education	68	-9	-18	+9	-2	+4	+15
D Increase spending: old-age pensions	47	+10	+10	+3	-20	0	-3
E Increase spending: unemployment benefits	20	+23	21	17	25	-11	-13
F Provide jobs	51	+13	+29	-12	-19	-12	0
G Provide health care	94	+2	+5	-10	0	0	+3
H Provide for the old	93	+5	+6	-7	-4	0	0
I Provide for the unemployed	68	+22	+25	-21	-6	-9	-11
J Reduce differences between rich and poor	54	+17	+19	-7	-8	-7	-14
K Provide financial help for education	83	-4	-5	+2	+1	+4	+2
L Provide decent housing	73	+8	0	-7	-4	0	+3
M Increase taxes on high incomes	46	+17	+1	-7	-3	+3	-12
n (mean)		1095	1121	1205	783	1135	767

SOURCE: ISSP (1996).

very differently compared to the other items, in the sense that education is inversely related to the other items. The more one wants to increase spending on education, the less one is likely to increase welfare state effort in other areas. It is likely that education is perceived as a qualifying policy rather than as a compensatory one. Second, the items on government's responsibility for providing health care [G] and providing a decent living for the old [H] show heavily skewed response distributions. Nearly everyone believes that health care and the well-being of senior citizens are essential government responsibilities.

The structure of the variables is explored with latent class analysis (LCA). For analysis with categorical variables, which are common in the social sciences, LCA is superior compared to traditional measures such as correlation and factor analysis (Hagenaars 1998; McCutcheon 1987; Hagenaars & McCutcheon 2002). The assumption of local independence is fundamental in LCA. The total of associations between observed variables (indicators) are entirely explained by an unobserved (latent) variable. Typically, exploratory LCA applies a 1-class model (the independence model) to data, and then expands the number of classes until a satisfactory fit with the data is reached. This strategy is the nominal level cluster variant of LCA. The cluster model aims to identify clusters/classes (groups of individuals/ cases sharing similar characteristics). The software used for estimation of the latent variables is Latent GOLD (Vermunt & Magidson 2000, 2003).

In Table 2.3, four latent class models are tested against the data. In all four models, the country variable is included as a covariate. While the effect of country is allowed to vary across clusters, all effects between country and indicators are restricted and accordingly set to zero. This means (a) that the characteristics of each cluster are identical across countries, and (b) that cluster membership probabilities can vary across countries.

The 1-cluster model clearly does not fit the data, as small L^2, and BIC statistics are associated with representative or "good" models.[12] While we usually do not expect a good fit of such a model, the L^2 value indicates the maximum association that can be explained by any latent class model. Model 1 is thus a baseline model against which the fit of alternative models can be judged. The 4-cluster model is selected as representing the data. The model has an acceptable fit to data and has the lowest BIC.

Let us examine the characteristics of each of the four clusters distilled by Model 4 in Table 2.3. Table 2.4 shows the probability of each cluster

TABLE 2.3
Attitudes toward the welfare state: model fit for four latent class models. n = 4919.

Model		L^2	BIC	df	p	Reduction in L^2 (a)
1.	1-Cluster	14846.2	−37247.1	6128	.00	0%
2.	2-Cluster	7697.2	−44294.1	6116	.00	48%
3.	3-Cluster	6781.5	−45107.8	6104	.00	54%
4.	4-Cluster	5927.7	−45859.5	6092	.93	60%

NOTES: (a) In relation to model 1.

to respond "welfare state–friendly" (e.g., the probability for indicator response = 1) on each of the 10 indicators. For example, the probability of agreeing that it is the government's responsibility to reduce differences in incomes between high- and low-income earners [A] is 0.84 for respondents classified in cluster 1; 0.02 for cluster 2; 0.07 for cluster 3; and 0.88 for those classified in cluster 4. Thus, respondents in clusters 1 and 4 are strongly in favor of income redistribution, while the opposite is true for respondents in clusters 2 and 3. In the last column, the R^2 is a measure of variance. For each indicator, the more the response probabilities differ across the clusters, the larger is the R^2. Accordingly, the larger the R^2, the better is the discriminatory power of the indicator.

A conclusive reason behind the use of LCA is that attitudinal patterns do not necessarily have to be linear. Therefore, nominal categories can be estimated. To treat attitudinal patterns as nominal categories is in many ways similar to the use of ideal types in theory. At best, the extracted clusters mirror the theoretical ideal types empirically (Hagenaars & Halman 1989). What kinds of theoretical ideal types can be expected to be represented in the data? Here the alternatives might range from the simplest form, which would be a basic distinction between those that are in favor of the welfare state and those that are against it, to a more complex structure, which differentiates between factors such as program coverage (universal/selective), program specificity (whether programs are grouped or valued independently), and institutional aspect (spending, redistribution, responsibility). However, given that the item responses are captured in a four-cluster model, we can expect a model of modest complexity.

A close inspection of the coefficients in Table 2.4 reveals that support for the welfare state tends to be grouped along two separate components. The first is the risk-reducing, social security component provided by the wel-

TABLE 2.4

Welfare state indicator responses in the 4-cluster latent class model. Cells indicate the probability of a welfare state–friendly response by cluster membership.

Cluster		1	2	3	4	R^2
			Social			
		Encompassing	security	Minimalist		
	Government should . . .					
A	Reduce income differences	.84	.02	.07	.88	.68
B	Increase spending: health	.94	.77	.49	.66	.14
D	Increase spending: old-age pensions	.80	.44	.22	.33	.20
E	Increase spending: unemployment benefits	.53	.13	.02	.07	.26
F	Provide jobs	.91	.42	.10	.48	.34
I	Provide for the unemployed	.98	.80	.15	.66	.41
J	Reduce differences between rich and poor	.98	.20	.03	.94	.72
K	Provide financial help for education	.93	.85	.63	.85	.08
L	Provide decent housing	.94	.83	.26	.75	.31
M	Increase taxes on high incomes	.71	.32	.23	.58	.16
	Cluster size	.30	.29	.21	.21	

fare state. The second component is the redistribution of financial resources via taxation and transfers. Thus, two clusters of rather strong welfare state support can be identified. Cluster 1 respondents show strong support for both risk-reducing programs and financial redistribution. Cluster 2 respondents support the risk-reducing social security component but tend to reject the idea of the welfare state as an instrument for explicit redistribution of financial resources. In cluster 3, we find the respondents who seem to be the political opponents of the welfare state; they are not supportive of either social security or redistribution. Finally, as indicated by most of the item responses, cluster 4 is a middle category situated between clusters 1 and 3. Cluster 4 respondents are those that we typically find in the middle of index scales.[13]

It is suggested that clusters 1 through 3 represent three ideal types of the welfare state. The respondents in cluster 1 cherish the *encompassing* welfare model ideal type (Korpi & Palme 1998). Cluster 2 has no immediate correspondence to any established welfare state typology, mainly because the size of the welfare state and its redistributive capacity are intimately associated. Nevertheless, the difference observed with respect to clusters 1 and 2 captures the cardinal political conflict related to financial redistribution through taxation and social transfers pointed out earlier in this chapter. To avoid any confusion with the basic security welfare model (Korpi & Palme 1998), cluster 2 is labeled the *social security* welfare model. In cluster 3, we find the respondents who reject the welfare state. This cluster is therefore labeled the *minimalist* welfare model.

Table 2.5 shows how cluster probabilities correlate with country. Overall, the differences in welfare state support observed across countries are substantial, and particularly so for the encompassing and the minimalist welfare models. Citizens in the social democratic countries are much more likely to embrace the encompassing model than are citizens in the liberal countries. In fact, among the liberal countries, in all cases but one, the encompassing model is the least preferred. Support for the minimalist model is considerably stronger in the liberal countries, and particularly weak in Scandinavia.

Although the main demarcation line runs between the liberal and social democratic countries, some notable variation among the family of liberal nations can be discerned. In the United States and Canada, the minimalist model is the most popular. In Australia and New Zealand, the social security model receives the strongest support. The differences in welfare model preferences may reflect the historically different institutional traits of the North American liberal model and the wage earners' welfare state in Australia and New Zealand.

TABLE 2.5
Attitudes toward the welfare state in six Western countries:
cluster membership probabilities by country.

Cluster	1	2	3	4	
	Encompassing	Social security	Minimalist		(n)
Sweden	.51	.23	.10	.16	892
Norway	.51	.27	.06	.16	914
USA	.18	.26	.34	.23	909
Canada	.13	.27	.31	.30	61
Australia	.19	.33	.24	.25	1001
New Zealand	.19	.40	.25	.16	587
eta	.41***	.14***	.31***	.15***	

Levels of significance: *** = $p < .001$, ** = $p < .01$, * = $p < .05$.

CLASS AND ATTITUDES TO WELFARE POLICY
AND REDISTRIBUTION

We have seen that support for the welfare models differs systematically across countries. This is a general finding that has been noted elsewhere (Svallfors 1997, 2003). Our aim in this section is to analyze whether popular support for these welfare models is differentiated according to class position. Table 2.6 shows two general statistics illuminating the relationships between class and welfare state attitudes. The eta statistic indicates the amount of variation in the dependent variable (the cluster) that can be explained by an independent variable (class). The class cleavage statistic, *ccs*, describes the absolute difference in cluster membership probabilities between workers and service class I, and is defined as

$$ccs = \sqrt{((x_1 + x_2)/2 - x_3)^2}$$

in which x_1 is the cluster membership probability for unskilled workers, x_2 is the cluster membership probability for skilled workers, and x_3 is the cluster membership probability for service class I.

The results indicate the following. First, in relation to the death-of-class debate, there seems to be little evidence that the significance of class is unimportant, except in Canada. However, as already pointed out, the observed class structure in Canada feeds suspicion about data quality. Second, the most pronounced class conflict across countries relates to the encompassing welfare model. Third, only in the United States is the class conflict limited to the encompassing-minimalist dimension. In both of the antipodean, as well as in the social democratic countries, all of the

TABLE 2.6
Attitudes toward the welfare state by class in six Western countries.
Cell entries are measures of association: ccs & eta.

	CLUSTER 1 Encompassing		CLUSTER 2 Social security		CLUSTER 3 Minimalist		CLUSTER 4	
	ccs	*eta*	*ccs*	*eta*	*ccs*	*eta*	*ccs*	*eta*
Sweden	.52	.41***	.31	.30***	.18	.26***	.03	.05
Norway	.36	.32***	.28	.26***	.09	.17***	.00	.11*
USA	.17	.23***	.00	.04	.23	.26***	.05	.14**
Canada	.09	.15*	.01	.08	.06	.10	.03	.08
Australia	.17	.17***	.13	.12**	.15	.14**	.11	.12*
New Zealand	.20	.23***	.13	.17**	.12	.15*	.05	.12

Levels of significance: *** = p < .001, ** = p < .01, * = p < .05.

three welfare models are marked by class conflict. Finally, class differences are comparatively small in cluster 4, a finding reflecting the point made earlier: that these respondents are those we typically find in the middle of traditionally constructed index scales.

Before examining the country-specific relationships between class and welfare models, we will examine whether the strength of class conflict observed across countries varies according to any of the rival hypotheses. Table 2.7 shows the results of the formal testing. Note that the unit of analysis is country. The first lesson learned is that the observed strength of class conflict over welfare policy is systematically associated with the size, scope, and redistributive capacity of the welfare state, as predicted by the HSE. The results also support the notion that the processes through which economic classes are transformed into social classes are shaped by institutional translators to a significant extent. In relation to the HEA, the results are entirely disappointing. The countries exhibiting the highest degree of material equality, welfare policy universalism, and employment security are certainly not the ones showing the lowest degree of class conflict. We can thus conclude that class-based differences in material inequality and social insecurity can be substantial without being transformed into sociopolitical class conflict. The second lesson learned is that systematic association re-

TABLE 2.7

Association between size of welfare state class conflict (ccs & eta shown in Table 2.6) and the HEA and HSE factors (shown in Appendix 2.A). Cell entries are Pearson's r × 100.

	CLUSTER 1 Encompassing		CLUSTER 2 Social security		CLUSTER 3 Minimalist	
	ccs	eta	ccs	eta	ccs	eta
HEA						
Material equality	75	67	83*	88*	−45	−1
Welfare policy universalism	92**	88*	89*	94**	−12	32
Employment security	81*	72	75	74	2	33
HSE						
IT: the political branch	94**	86*	94**	93**	3	37
Size and redistributive performance	92**	88*	89*	94**	−12	32
IT: the industrial relations branch	90**	83*	87*	89*	−8	31
(n)	6	6	6	6	6	6

Levels of significance: ** = p < .01, * = p < .05.

lates to the encompassing and the social security models. When it comes to the minimalist model, the association is weak, mostly because pronounced class conflicts can be observed in both Sweden and the United States.

Table 2.8 shows the class-specific welfare model preferences in each country. A surprising finding is the preferences of the higher echelons of employees observed in Sweden. It has been repeatedly stressed by previous research that service class I employees in Sweden are strikingly hostile toward the welfare state and that this particular group is certainly not "part of any social democratic consensus regarding welfare policies" (Svallfors 2004: 125, 1999b, 2003; Edlund 1999, 2003a, 2003b). It is true that only a minority of service class I respondents embraces the idea of financial redistribution. However, a substantial number supports the social security model. While many of them are not against state organized welfare, they are not too happy with the redistributive aspects of welfare policy. Another surprise is the comparatively strong support for the welfare state expressed by the self-employed. One possible explanation behind these findings is that previous research has not separated the issue of redistribution clearly from the issue of social protection. This, in turn, may partly be explained by the limited ability of conventional statistics, such as correlation and factor analysis, to detect patterns that are not linearly distributed on a singular dimension. As far as the Swedish working class is concerned, there is strong support for the encompassing model. In fact, workers show weak support even for the social security model. Thus, the observed class patterns, in terms of ranks, related to the social security and the minimalist models are similar. The Norwegian patterns resemble those observed in Sweden. A notable difference, though, is that the Norwegian service class I is more welfare state–friendly than are their Swedish counterparts.

In the liberal countries, the welfare model preferences among service class I respondents are somewhat different. Only a small minority supports the encompassing model. In the antipodean countries, preferences are biased toward the social security model, but a substantial number favors the minimalist model. While the opposite is true in North America, the strong support for the minimalist welfare model observed in the United States seems unique. When it comes to workers in the liberal countries, the support is more evenly distributed across different welfare models, both compared to their fellow citizens in the service classes and compared to their working-class counterparts in Scandinavia.

TABLE 2.8
Attitudes toward the welfare state in six Western countries.
Cell entries are cluster membership probabilities by class.

Cluster		1 Encompassing	2 Social security	3 Minimalist	(n)
Sweden	Service class I	.18	.43	.21	158
	Service class II	.46	.25	.11	201
	Routine nonmanuals	.56	.21	.08	134
	Skilled workers	.72	.11	.03	135
	Unskilled workers	.69	.14	.03	178
	Self-employed	.45	.27	.14	86
Norway	Service class I	.33	.42	.11	196
	Service class II	.47	.29	.06	261
	Routine nonmanuals	.57	.23	.04	156
	Skilled workers	.66	.14	.03	100
	Unskilled workers	.71	.14	.02	136
	Self-employed	.41	.29	.05	65
USA	Service class I	.08	.26	.48	240
	Service class II	.14	.26	.40	185
	Routine nonmanuals	.22	.25	.22	172
	Skilled workers	.22	.29	.29	89
	Unskilled workers	.29	.23	.21	153
	Self-employed	.17	.26	.37	70
Canada	Service class I	.10	.25	.34	210
	Service class II	.12	.28	.32	245
	Routine nonmanuals	.21	.30	.22	76
	Skilled workers	.18	.28	.24	36
	Unskilled workers	.19	.24	.31	36
	Self-employed	.07	.10	.36	13
Australia	Service class I	.10	.40	.31	172
	Service class II	.20	.33	.23	327
	Routine nonmanuals	.20	.36	.21	219
	Skilled workers	.29	.30	.16	64
	Unskilled workers	.26	.23	.16	114
	Self-employed	.12	.29	.30	105
New Zealand	Service class I	.06	.45	.35	99
	Service class II	.16	.44	.24	210
	Routine nonmanuals	.28	.35	.20	74
	Skilled workers	.28	.27	.20	71
	Unskilled workers	.25	.37	.26	115
	Self-employed	.14	.61	.11	18

Overall, the class-welfare model preference patterns observed in the six countries indicate some basic similarities across welfare regimes. In both the Scandinavian and the antipodean countries, the class conflict is principally structured along the line of redistribution; preferences for the encompassing model are mirrored in both the social security and the minimalist models, although this tendency is more pronounced in Scandinavia. In contrast, the class conflict in the United States is more about being for or against the welfare state in general, as the conflict is principally structured along the encompassing-minimalist dimension.

In order to test further the argument on the role of institutional translators in political struggles over welfare policy, class identity is brought into the analysis. Class identity is measured with a subjective question on whether the respondent belongs to a class, and if so, which one. The variable distinguishes between middle-class identity and working-class identity. As previously noted, class identity adds a more direct notion of social belonging to the class concept. If the argument about the necessity of positive nutrition for building an identity with solid political orientations is valid, then it is expected that relationships between class and class identity, on the one hand, and between class identity and welfare model preferences, on the other, are considerably stronger in the social democratic countries than in the liberal countries in general, and the United States and Canada in particular.

The linkage between class and class identity is analyzed in Table 2.9. The strength of the relationships is remarkably similar across countries and sufficiently strong to cast doubt on any claim about the declining links between class and class identity (Clark & Lipset 1996; Grusky & Sørensen 1998).

While the ranking of classes in terms of class identity is similar across countries, it is apparent that the most clear-cut pattern is found in Sweden. The deviating pattern is mostly a consequence of the strong middle-class identification among those belonging to service class I in combination with the relatively strong working class identification among the workers. In the other countries, the relative distance between service class I and the working classes is rather similar. In countries where middle-class identification is more common, both workers and service class I are comparatively more likely to subscribe to a middle-class identity. This is the case in Canada and New Zealand. In countries where it is more common to identify with

TABLE 2.9

Class identity by class in six Western countries. Cell entries
are probabilities and measures of association: eta & ccs.

		CLASS IDENTITY				
		Working class	Middle class	(n)	eta	ccs
Sweden	Service class I	.09	.91	178	.46	.62***
	Service class II	.30	.70	232		
	Routine nonmanuals	.49	.51	152		
	Skilled workers	.71	.29	172		
	Unskilled workers	.72	.28	226		
	Self-employed	.41	.59	101		
Norway	Service class I	.22	.78	206	.36	.42***
	Service class II	.24	.76	280		
	Routine nonmanuals	.50	.50	195		
	Skilled workers	.64	.36	114		
	Unskilled workers	.65	.35	155		
	Self-employed	.45	.55	73		
USA	Service class I	.30	.70	326	.32	.40***
	Service class II	.40	.60	250		
	Routine nonmanuals	.62	.38	250		
	Skilled workers	.70	.30	129		
	Unskilled workers	.70	.30	237		
	Self-employed	.54	.46	92		
Canada	Service class I	.13	.87	221	.36	.48***
	Service class II	.26	.74	254		

Routine					
nonmanuals	.44	.56	93		
Skilled workers	.74	.26	38		
Unskilled workers	.47	.53	47		
Self-employed	.27	.73	15		
Australia				.40	.53***
Service class I	.16	.84	193		
Service class II	.24	.76	376		
Routine					
nonmanuals	.50	.50	248		
Skilled workers	.61	.39	74		
Unskilled workers	.76	.24	129		
Self-employed	.43	.57	123		
New Zealand				.32	.43***
Service class I	.09	.91	116		
Service class II	.29	.71	246		
Routine					
nonmanuals	.45	.55	94		
Skilled workers	.55	.45	100		
Unskilled workers	.50	.50	137		
Self-employed	.45	.55	22		

Levels of significance: *** = p < .001, ** = p < .01, * = p < .05.

Share of respondents with assigned class position with no class identity (percentages): Sweden (5); Norway (9); USA (1); Canada (17); Australia (2); New Zealand (10).

the working class, the proportion of workers with a working-class identity resembles or even exceeds the figures observed in Sweden. The most prominent cases are the United States and Australia.

The main impression, however, is that the observed relationship between class and class identity is not distinctly different across welfare regimes. Now, whether class identity carries a political meaning is something different. Table 2.10 displays two measures that attempt to estimate the relative significance of class identity on the formation of welfare policy preferences. The maximum class cleavage statistic, *mccs*, measures the difference in cluster membership probabilities between workers with working-class identity (column 1) and service class I respondents identifying themselves as middle class (column 4). The *mccs* is defined as

$$mccs = \sqrt{(x_{11} - x_{22})^2}$$

in which x_{11} is the cluster membership probability for workers with a working-class identity, and x_{22} is the cluster membership probability for those in service class I with a middle-class identity. The intraclass cleavage statistic, *iccs*, attempts to measure the relative importance of class identity net of class. Membership probabilities between different class identities within each class are estimated using the following equation:

$$iccs = \sqrt{((x_{11} - x_{12}) + (x_{21} - x_{22}))^2}$$

in which x_{11} and x_{12} are the cluster membership probability for workers with a working-class identity and a middle-class identity, respectively, and x_{21} and x_{22} are the cluster membership probability for those in service class I with a working-class identity and middle-class identity, respectively.[14]

As shown in Table 2.10, there is clear evidence that class identity has the potential to carry strong political orientations. In Sweden, and, to a lesser extent, Norway, a middle-class identity decreases encompassing welfare state support, while support for the social security welfare state model increases. This holds for both workers and service class I. The United States offers a striking contrast. Particularly among American workers, class identity does not seem to have any significant political meaning referring to welfare policy. Within the service class, class identity makes a difference, especially when it comes to support for the minimalist welfare model. Nevertheless, compared to the patterns registered in Scandinavia, we have to conclude that class identity does not have a strong impact on welfare state preferences in the United States.

TABLE 2.10
Attitudes toward the welfare state in six Western countries. Cell entries
are cluster membership probabilities by class and class identity,
and measures of association: mccs & iccs.

CLASS:	WORKERS		SERVICE CLASS I			
CLASS IDENTITY:	*Working class*	*Middle class*	*Working class*	*Middle class*	*mccs*	*iccs*
CLUSTER 1						
Encompassing						
Sweden	.79	.48	.47	.15	.64	.32***
Norway	.72	.62	.48	.28	.44	.15***
USA	.27	.25	.15	.06	.21	.06
Canada	.19	.09	.22	.08	.11	.12***
Australia	.32	.18	.17	.08	.24	.12***
New Zealand	.34	.21	.13	.05	.29	.11***
CLUSTER 2						
Social security						
Sweden	.06	.29	.19	.47	.41	.26***
Norway	.12	.18	.25	.46	.34	.14***
USA	.25	.25	.24	.27	.02	.02
Canada	.22	.42	.31	.24	.02	.07
Australia	.23	.30	.24	.43	.20	.13***
New Zealand	.32	.34	.55	.42	.10	.06
CLUSTER 3						
Minimalist						
Sweden	.01	.06	.08	.21	.20	.09***
Norway	.02	.03	.08	.12	.10	.03
USA	.22	.28	.35	.53	.31	.12***
Canada	.27	.25	.28	.33	.06	.02
Australia	.12	.27	.36	.31	.19	.05***
New Zealand	.17	.27	.12	.38	.21	.18***

Levels of significance: *** = p < .001, ** = p < .01, * = p < .05.

Finally, we test whether the strength of conflict observed in the six countries is linked to the institutional feedback effects specified in the HSE. In Table 2.11, the *mccs* and *iccs* measures are correlated with the HSE factors. The results are very similar to those obtained in Table 2.7. The significant relationships indicate that welfare policy–related class conflicts—irrespective of whether statistics refer to maximum class cleavages or internal class cleavages—are comparatively more distinct in advanced welfare states where class organizations are the principal institutional guardians and challengers.

In summary, the observed links between class and class identity are surprisingly strong and similarly structured across countries. Nevertheless,

TABLE 2.11

Association between size of welfare state class conflict (mccs & iccs shown in Table 2.10) and HSE factors (shown in Appendix 2.A). Cell entries are Pearson's r × 100.

	CLUSTER 1 Encompassing		CLUSTER 2 Social security		CLUSTER 3 Minimalist	
	mccs	iccs	mccs	iccs	mccs	iccs
HSE						
IT: the political branch	94**	94**	97**	98**	−18	−20
Size and redistributive performance	91**	93**	87*	89*	−29	−13
IT: the industrial relations branch	88*	96**	91**	96**	−32	−31
(n)	6	6	6	6	6	6

Levels of significance: ** = p < .01, * = p < .05.

the political meaning of class identity differs across welfare regimes. The finding that class identity, net of class, has a more substantial political implication in the social democratic regime compared to the liberal regime—at least as far as welfare politics are concerned—underlines the importance of institutional translators in the process of attitude formation.

CONCLUSION

The short version of the story told in this chapter is a refutation of the claim that countries facing severe material inequality and social insecurity provide an environment that is likely to propel class-based conflict over state-organized welfare policy. If factual differences in material equality would drive class conflict, it would be puzzling that class conflict on the terrain of the welfare state is more salient in Sweden and Norway—countries in which material inequality and social security, regardless of measurement applied, is far less significant than in countries traveling on the liberal welfare regime path. The answer provided to this puzzle is that organized interests in the role of translators of welfare state institutions have a lot to do with the political cleavages that exist in a society. That does not mean, however, that organized interests can dictate to the public and create cleavages at their own will. The point is that *inertia*, not change, is the most likely outcome as far as the contemporary development of political cleavages is concerned. The mutual interactions between the public and institutional translators impose constraints on the actors—a process that facilitates path dependency.

Let us return to the opening statements by Esping-Andersen. Yes, it might be true that the welfare state shapes patterns of stratification. However, whether emerging patterns of stratification—mirrored in material inequality—translate into political mobilization is less than certain. To study social stratification, therefore, is precisely to identify *potential* conflict structures. The major weakness of the *phase II* argument is that the path dependent force of institutional guardians and challengers in the interest formation processes is neglected.

In order for new welfare-related political cleavages to develop, it is suggested that institutional translators either have to be replaced by new actors or must abandon their commonly used strategies and rhetoric. On the latter, it is suggested that even if a change of course would somehow benefit a particular institutional translator, such a move may impose severe difficulties. On the one hand, other institutional translators may effectively block any attempt to a radical change of discourse; and, of course, the same constraints apply to new actors entering the field. On the other hand, institutional translators' past rhetoric and action form a societal collective memory, which severely restricts the number of available options for changing behavior. The relationship between institutional guardians, institutional challengers, and the public can be conceptualized as a dynamic field, which exercises powerful constraints on the behavior of institutional translators. This is a variant of the *Moral Economy* described in Chapter 1 of this volume. In a similar vein, this dynamic field of force obstructs and complicates political mobilization along new structural cleavage dimensions.

The influences on public interpretations and interests exercised by institutions and institutional translators are not fully recognized within the theoretical framework of the regime theory, *phase II*. Rather than promoting alternate conflict sources and deemphasizing the salience of class, the social democratic welfare state configuration serves to maintain conflict patterns structured around the class axis. Moreover, it encourages concerns about social protection and life chances to be addressed to the welfare state. In the archetypal liberal regime, distinctively different behaviors and preferences are promoted. Interests and mobilization formed around class are not encouraged within the realm of politics. Institutions and institutional translators certainly do not underpin public interpretations of the welfare state as an apparatus designed for extensive social protection and redistribution of market-generated inequality.

Another topic addressed in this chapter concerned the role of class in contemporary Western societies. With reference to the claim by anticlass proponents, the results clearly show that class matters. Class has both economic and social meanings. The findings suggest that in countries where classes are heavily differentiated along the economic dimension, corresponding divisions in the social dimension—understood here as attitudes toward the welfare state—do not measure up. In a similar vein, we have seen that in countries where classes in an economic sense are the least distinct, we can observe the greatest differences in the social dimension. Although the relative importance of the social and the economic aspects of class delineated in this chapter resemble the form of a zero-sum game, it has to be underlined that the empirical evidence refers to a specific period in a limited set of countries. Nevertheless, I believe that the results in this chapter highlight the advantages of treating economic and social components of class as distinct entities whose relationships should be judged empirically.

APPENDIX TABLE 2.A1
Macro-level indicators of material and institutional characteristics.

	A	Rank	B	Rank	C	Rank	D	Rank	E	Rank
Sweden	75.0	(1)	951	(1)	52.57	(1)	30.98	(1)	50	(1)
Norway	74.2	(2)	762	(2)	41.77	(2)	26.97	(2)	37	(2)
United States	59.2	(6)	575	(5)	29.13	(6)	14.59	(6)	26	(5)
Canada	68.5	(3)	679	(4)	36.04	(3)	18.03	(4)	32	(3)
Australia	64.8	(5)	697	(3)	31.00	(5)	17.81	(5)	29	(4)
New Zealand	65.0	(4)	528	(6)	34.92	(4)	20.97	(3)		

	F	Rank	G	Rank	H	Rank	I	Rank	J	Rank
Sweden	312	(1)	662.81	(1)	84.15	(1)	4.69	(1)	3.45	(2)
Norway	267	(2)	396.17	(2)	54.70	(2)	4.63	(2)	3.61	(1)
United States	0	(5)	185.35	(6)	13.45	(6)	1.94	(5)	1.12	(5)
Canada	0	(5)	278.12	(4)	34.20	(3)	1.72	(6)	1.18	(4)
Australia	138	(4)	325.13	(3)	31.90	(4)	2.84	(3)	2.73	(3)
New Zealand	139	(3)	200.28	(5)	23.75	(5)	2.31	(4)		

NOTE: see Table 2.1 for descriptions of the macro-level indicators.

APPENDIX TABLE 2.A2

Correlation matrix. Macro-level indicators of material and institutional characteristics. Pearson's r × 100.

	A	B	C	D	E	F	G	H	I	J
A	100	83	90	92	86	80	83	92	83	77
B		100	87	81	98	73	98	96	81	78
C			100	96	99	81	92	97	81	69
D				100	95	93	87	94	91	85
E					100	83	98	99	80	69
F						100	81	85	96	97
G							100	98	84	77
H								100	87	79
I									100	96
J										100

NOTE: see Table 2.1 for descriptions of the macro-level indicators.

NOTES

1. It should be mentioned that whenever the term "universalism" refers to social insurance, it carries the meaning commonly associated with the Nordic welfare model: encompassing social insurance schemes linked to previous earnings. It does not refer to welfare models providing benefits at a relatively low level as citizens' rights, where better-off citizens are supposed to protect themselves via private insurance.

2. Apparently, Stinchcombe made this statement in a class that Erik Olin Wright attended at Berkeley in 1973. See Clark and Lipset (2001: 33).

3. The class schema is known by different names (Goldthorpe classes, the Erikson/Goldthorpe classification of occupations, EGP or CASMIN classes).

4. While there is no consensus among the critics in deciding which strong elements should be included in the concept of class, they all appear to share the conviction that the EGP is too weak an idiom to qualify as a concept of class. See various contributions in Lee and Turner (1996). A strong version of the class concept, disaggregated to the unit-occupational level, is developed by Grusky and associates in a series of works: Grusky and Sørensen (1998); Grusky and Weeden (2001, 2002); Grusky, Weeden, and Sørensen (2001). See also Goldthorpe (2002).

5. For a description and critique of the SCA model, see Emmison (1991).

6. The term "institutional translator" is inspired by the writings of Sartori (1990).

7. Note that for Sartori, *class* is equivalent to *social class* as defined in this chapter.

8. Statements such as "Tax is sexy" and "It's cool to pay taxes" delivered by a Social Democratic Cabinet Minister in the mid-1990s, may sound exotic in the perspective of American politics.

9. See various contributions in Kitschelt et al., 1999; Hollingsworth and Boyer, 1997; Pierson, 2001; also Huber and Stephens, 2001, in which attempts are made to integrate research on welfare state regimes and varieties of capitalism (production regimes).

10. Constructs in the HEA: Material equality = A, Welfare state universalism = C+D, Employment security = B. Constructs in the HSE: Welfare state size and redistributive capacity = C+D, Institutional translators political branch = F+G, Institutional translators industrial relations branch = H+I. Similar results are obtained using multiplicative scales.

11. For details on the occupational codes used for translation into EGP, see Svallfors (2003). In contrast to this chapter, Svallfors complemented the Australian file with data on spouse's occupation and previous occupation for those currently not working. For unclear reasons, the data are not available (anymore) from the Australian National Data Archive.

12. BIC = $L^2 - \ln(n) \times df$. See Raftery (1986).

13. Alternatively, the data structure can be described as containing two dimensions. The first dimension covers the encompassing-minimalist dimension via cluster 1 (strong support for both components), cluster 4 (medium support for both components), and cluster 3 (low support for both components). Cluster 2 captures those that are in favor of the social security component but are much less enthusiastic when it comes to matters of explicit redistribution of financial resources. The assumption of a 2-dimensional solution was tested in an LCA-model containing one trichotomous ordinal latent variable and one dichotomous latent variable, i.e., a 2-factor model in which the first factor has 3 levels and the second 2 levels. The results show that the relationships observed between clusters 1, 4, and 3 correspond to factor 1, while cluster 2 corresponds to factor 2. The model fit is slightly better compared to the 4-cluster model: $L^2 = 5874.38$, d.f. = 6103, p = 0.98. Still, the 4-cluster model is chosen as the best model representing the data, mainly because the three analytically most interesting categories (clusters 1, 2, and 3) are empirically separated in a clear manner.

14. The significance test measures whether attitudes to welfare models are significantly affected by class identity within each of the six classes. However, in the table, results are displayed for only the most analytic interesting classes: the working class and service class I.

REFERENCES

Åberg, R. 1989. Distributive Mechanisms of the Welfare State—A Formal Analysis and an Empirical Application. *European Sociological Review* 5: 167–182.

Armingeon, K., P. Leimgruber, M. Beyeler, & S. Menegale. 2004. "Comparative Political Data Set 1960–2002." Institute of Political Science, University of Berne.

Barnes, S. H. 1966. Ideology and the Organization of Conflict: On the Relationship between Political Thought and Behavior. *Journal of Politics* 28: 513–530.

Budge, I., H-D. Klingemann, A. Volkens, E. Tannenbaum, & J. Bara. 2001. *Mapping Policy Preferences: Estimates for Parties, Electors, and Governments 1945–1998*. Oxford: Oxford University Press.

Castles, F., & D. Mitchell. 1993. Worlds of Welfare and Families of Nations. In Castles, F. (ed.), *Families of Nations. Patterns of Public Policy in Western Democracies*. Aldershot: Dartmouth.

Castles, F. 1996. Needs-Based Strategies of Social Protection in Australia and New Zealand. In Esping-Andersen, G. (ed.), *Welfare States in Transition*. London: Sage.

Clark, T., & S. M. Lipset. 1996. Are Social Classes Dying? In Lee, D. J., & B. S. Turner (eds.), *Conflicts about Class: Debating Inequality in Late Industrialism*. London: Longman.

Clark, T. N., & S. M. Lipset (eds.). 2001. *The Breakdown of Class Politics.* Washington, DC: Woodrow Wilson Center Press.

Coughlin, R. 1980. *Ideology, Public Opinion & Welfare Policy.* Berkeley: Institute of International Studies, University of California.

Edlund, J., & R. Åberg. 2002. Social Norms and Tax Compliance. *Swedish Economic Policy Review* 9(1): 201–228.

Edlund, J. 1999. Progressive Taxation Farewell? Attitudes to Income Redistribution and Taxation in Sweden, Great Britain and the United States. In Svallfors S., & P. Taylor-Gooby (eds.), *The End of the Welfare State? Public Responses to State Retrenchment.* London: Routledge.

Edlund, J. 2003a. The Influence of the Class Situations of Husbands and Wives on Class Identity, Party Preference, and Attitudes towards Redistribution: Sweden, Germany, and the United States. *Acta Sociologica* 46(3): 195–214.

Edlund, J. 2003b. Attitudes towards Taxation: Ignorant and Incoherent? *Scandinavian Political Studies* 26(2): 145–167.

Emmison, M. 1991. Conceptualising Class Consciousness. In Baxter, J., M. Emmison, & J. Western (eds.), *Class Analysis and Contemporary Australia.* South Melbourne: Macmillan.

Erikson, R., & J. H. Goldthorpe. 1992a. *The Constant Flux.* Oxford: Clarendon Press.

Erikson, R., & J. H. Goldthorpe. 1992b. Individual or Family? Results from Two Approaches to Class Assignment. *Acta Sociologica* 35: 95–105.

Erikson, R. 1984. Social Class of Men, Women and Families. *Sociology* 18: 500–514.

Ersson, S. 2001. "OECD Governments." Data file. Umeå University, Department of Political Science.

Esping-Andersen, G. 1990. *The Three Worlds of Welfare Capitalism.* Cambridge: Polity Press.

Esping-Andersen, G. 1993. *Changing Classes.* London: Sage.

Evans, G., & C. Mills. 1998a. Identifying Class Structure. A Latent Class Analysis of the Criterion-Related and Construct Validity of the Goldthorpe Class Schema. *European Sociological Review* 14(1): 87–106.

Evans, G., & C. Mills. 1998b. Assessing the Cross-Sex Validity of the Goldthorpe Class Schema Using Log-linear Models with Latent Variables. *Quality & Quantity* 32: 275–296.

Evans, G. 1992. Testing the Validity of the Goldthorpe Class Schema. *European Sociological Review* 8: 211–232.

Evans, G. 1996. Putting Men and Women into Classes: An Assessment of the Cross-Sex Validity of the Goldthorpe Class Schema. *Sociology* 30: 209–234.

Golden, M., & M. Wallerstein. 2004. "Union Centralization among Advanced Industrial Societies: Update to 1995/2000." Los Angeles: University of California-Los Angeles.

Goldthorpe, J. H., & G. Marshall. 1996. The Promising Future of Class Analysis. In Lee, D. J. & B. S. Turner (eds.), *Conflicts about Class: Debating Inequality in Late Industrialism*. London: Longman.

Goldthorpe, J. H., & A. McKnight. 2004. "The Economic Basis of Social Class." CASE Papers 80, Centre for Analysis of Social Exclusion, LSE.

Goldthorpe, J. H. 1983. Women and Class Analysis: In Defence of the Conventional View. *Sociology* 17: 465–488.

Goldthorpe, J. H. 2000. *On Sociology: Numbers, Narratives, and the Integration of Research and Theory*. Oxford: Oxford University Press.

Goldthorpe, J. H. 2002. Occupational Sociology, Yes: Class Analysis, No: Comment on Grusky and Weeden's Research Agenda. *Acta Sociologica* 45: 211–217.

Grusky, D., & J. Sørensen. 1998. Can Class Analysis Be Salvaged? *American Journal of Sociology* 103: 1187–1234.

Grusky, D., & K. Weeden. 2001. Decomposition without Death: A Research Agenda for a New Class Analysis. *Acta Sociologica* 44: 203–218.

Grusky, D., & K. Weeden. 2002. Class Analysis and the Heavy Weight of Convention. *Acta Sociologica* 45: 229–236.

Grusky, D., K. Weeden, & J. Sørensen. 2001. The Case for Realism in Class Analysis. *Political Power and Social Theory* 14: 291–305.

Hacker, J. S. 2002. *The Divided Welfare State: The Battle over Public and Private Social Benefits in the United States*. Cambridge: Cambridge University Press.

Hagenaars, J., & L. Halman. 1989. Searching for Ideal Types: The Potentialities of Latent Class Analysis. *European Sociological Review* 5: 81–96.

Hagenaars, J. A., & A. L. McCutcheon (eds.). 2002. *Applied Latent Class Analysis*. Cambridge, England: Cambridge University Press.

Hagenaars, J. A. 1998. Categorical Causal Modeling: Latent Class Analysis and Directed Log-linear Models with Latent Variables. *Sociological Methods and Research*, 26, 436–486.

Hanson, R. L. 1994. Liberalism and the Course of American Social Welfare Policy. In Dodd L., & C. Jillson (eds.), *The Dynamics of American Politics*. Boulder, CO: Westview Press.

Hollingsworth, J. R., & R. Boyer. 1997. *Contemporary Capitalism. The Embeddedness of Institutions*. Cambridge: Cambridge University Press.

Holton, R. 1996. Has Class Analysis a Future? In Lee, D. J., & B. S. Turner (eds.), *Conflicts about Class: Debating Inequality in Late Industrialism*. London: Longman.

Huber, E., & J. D. Stephens. 2001. *Development and Crisis of the Welfare State*. Chicago: University of Chicago Press.

ILO. 2004. *Economic Security for a Better World*. Geneva: ILO.

ISSP. 1996. *Role of Government III*. Codebook and datafile compiled at the ZA. Köln: University of Köln.

Jacobs, J. A. 1993. Careers in the US Service Economy. In Esping-Andersen, G. (ed.), *Changing Classes*. London: Sage.

Kangas, O. 1991. *The Politics of Social Rights. Studies on the Dimensions of Sickness Insurance in OECD Countries*. Stockholm: Almqvist & Wiksell.

Karlsson, L. 2005. *Klasstillhörighetens subjektiva dimension: klassidentitet, sociala attityder och fritidsvanor.* [The Subjective Dimension of Class: Class Identity, Social Attitudes and Leisure Habits] Series: Doctoral Theses at the Department of Sociology, Umeå University. Umeå, Department of Sociology.

Kitschelt, H., P. Lange, G. Marks, & J. D. Stephens (eds.). 1999. *Continuity and Change in Contemporary Capitalism*. Cambridge: Cambridge University Press.

Korpi, W., & J. Palme. 1998. The Paradox of Redistribution and Strategies of Equality: Welfare State Institutions, Inequality, and Poverty in the Western Countries. *American Sociological Review* 63: 661–687.

Korpi, W., & Palme, J. 2003. New Politics and Class Politics in the Context of Austerity and Globalization: Welfare State Regress in 18 Countries 1975–1995. *American Political Science Review* 97: 426–446.

Korpi, W. 1980. Social Policy and Distributional Conflict in the Capitalist Democracies. A Preliminary Comparative Framework. *West European Politics* 3: 296–316.

Lee, D. J., & B. S. Turner (eds.). 1996. *Conflicts about Class: Debating Inequality in Late Industrialism*. London: Longman.

Lipset, S. M. 1996. *American Exceptionalism: A Double-edged Sword*. New York: W. W. Norton.

Marshall, G. 1997. *Repositioning Class. Social Inequality in Industrial Societies*. London: Sage.

Matheson, G. 1993. *The Decommodified in a Commodified World*. Unpublished PhD Thesis, University of New England, Armidale.

McCutcheon, A. L. 1987. *Latent Class Analysis*. Newbury Park, CA: Sage.

McDonald, M., & Mendes, S. 2002. "Governments, 1950-1995. Codebook." Department of Political Science, Binghamton University, Binghamton, NY.

McFate, K., R. Lawson, & W. J. Wilson (eds.). 1995a. *Poverty, Inequality and the Future of Social Policy. Western States in the New World Order*. New York: Russell Sage Foundation.

McFate, K., T. Smeeding, & L. Rainwater. 1995b. Markets and States: Poverty Trends and Transfer System Effectiveness in the 1980s. In McFate, K., R. Lawson, & W. J. Wilson (eds.), *Poverty, Inequality and the Future of Social Policy. Western States in the New World Order*. New York: Russell Sage Foundation.

Mettler, S., & J. Soss. 2004. The Consequences of Public Policy for Democratic Citizenship: Bridging Policy Studies and Mass Politics. *Perspectives on Politics*, 2: 55–73.

OECD. 1990. *The Personal Income Tax Base*. Paris: OECD.

Pahl, R. 1996. Is the Emperor Naked? In Lee, D. J., & B. S. Turner (eds.), *Conflicts about Class: Debating Inequality in Late Industrialism*. London: Longman.

Pakulski, J., & M. Waters. 1996. *The Death of Class*. London: Sage.

Palme, J. 1990. *Pension Rights in Welfare Capitalism*. Stockholm: Almqvist & Wiksell.

Peters, G. 1991. *The Politics of Taxation*. Oxford: Blackwell.

Pierson, P. 2001. *The New Politics of the Welfare State*. Oxford: Oxford University Press.

Pontusson, J. 2005. *Inequality and Prosperity. Social Europe vs. Liberal America*. Ithaca, NY: Cornell University Press.

Raftery, A. E. 1986. Choosing Models for Cross-classifications. *American Sociological Review* 51: 145–146.

Rose, R. 1991. Is American Public Policy Exceptional? In Shafer, B. E. (ed.), *Is America Different? A New Look at American Exceptionalism*. Oxford: Clarendon Press.

Rothstein, B. 2000. Trust, Social Dilemmas and Collective Memory. *Journal of Theoretical Politics*, 12: 477–501.

Sartori, G. 1990. The Sociology of Parties: A Critical Review. In Mair, P. (ed.), *The West European Party System*. Oxford: Oxford University Press.

Scott, J. 2002. Social Class and Stratification in Late Modernity. *Acta Sociologica* 45: 23–35.

Siaroff, A. 1994. Work, Welfare and Gender Equality: A New Typology. In Sainsbury, D. (ed.), *Gendering Welfare States*. London: Sage.

Siaroff, A. 1999. Corporatism in 24 Industrial Democracies: Meaning and Measurement. *European Journal of Political Research* 36: 175–205.

Steinmo, S. 1993. *Taxation and Democracy*. New Haven, CT: Yale University Press.

Svallfors, S. 1997. Worlds of Welfare and Attitudes to Redistribution: A Comparison of Eight Western Nations. *European Sociological Review* 13: 283–304.

Svallfors, S. 1999a. The Class Politics of Swedish Welfare Policies. In Evans, G. (ed.), *The End of Class Politics? Class Voting in Comparative Context*. Oxford: Oxford University Press.

Svallfors, S. 1999b. The Middle Class and Welfare State Retrenchment: Attitudes to Swedish Welfare Policies. In Svallfors, S., & P. Taylor-Gooby (eds.), *The End of the Welfare State? Public Responses to State Retrenchment*. London: Routledge.

Svallfors, S. 2003. Welfare Regimes and Welfare Opinions: A Comparison of Eight Western Countries. *Social Indicators Research*, 64(3): 495–520.

Svallfors, S. 2004. Class, Attitudes and the Welfare State: Sweden in Comparative Perspective. *Social Policy and Administration* 38: 119–138.

Tåhlin, M. 1993. Class Inequality and Post-industrial Employment in Sweden. In Esping-Andersen, G. (ed.), *Changing Classes*. London: Sage.

Vermunt, J. K., & J. Magidson. 2000. *Latent GOLD 2.0 User's Guide.* Belmont, MA: Statistical Innovations.

Vermunt, J. K., & J. Magidson. 2003. *Addendum to Latent GOLD User's Guide: Upgrade for Version 3.0.* Boston: Statistical Innovations.

Wright, E. O. 1997. *Class Counts.* Cambridge: Cambridge University Press.

CHAPTER THREE

Overloaded or Undermined?

European Welfare States in the Face
of Performance Dissatisfaction

Staffan Kumlin

There is some consensus that the challenges and pressures faced by mature welfare states are becoming more severe. However, as discussed in Chapter 1, the political responses will hardly involve an apocalyptic neoliberal retrenchment race to the bottom. While during the 1980s it was common to predict the sudden death of the welfare state, recent studies conclude that radical retrenchment has occurred in only a limited number of policy areas and countries (see Ferrera and Rhodes 2000; Lindbom 2001; Pierson 2001; Swank 2002; Scharpf 2002).

Such countries are marked by uncommon institutional and political traits. They typically combine Westminster-style polities and few veto points with liberal welfare and production regimes, providing fewer institutional and attitudinal barriers to retrenchment. Elsewhere, widespread popular support (Borre and Scarbrough 1995; Svallfors and Taylor-Gooby 1999), combined with institutionalized needs for compromises between parties, decision-making levels, and interest groups, have meant that radical retrenchment policies are rarely advocated. And if they are, they usually fail to attract sufficient political support.

But just as rumors of its death are exaggerated, the welfare state has seen the end of its glory days. It is increasingly pressured both by external factors such as international and European integration and by arguably more important internal ones related to aging populations and decreasing fertility rates. On top of this there is the slow-growth and structural unemployment that seems to characterize post-industrial service societies. Taken together, these factors increasingly contribute to an environment of "permanent austerity" (Pierson 2001) in which it is becoming difficult

80

to finance previous commitments to welfare state services and insurance systems. And while the responses are unlikely to involve radical welfare backlash, chances are that more moderate adaptation and cost-containment efforts within existing systems will become more common. As prophesied by Pierson (2001: 417), "neither the alternatives of standing pat or dismantling are likely to prove viable in most countries. Instead, as in most aspects of politics, we should expect strong pressures to move towards more centrist—and therefore more incremental—responses. Those seeking to generate significant cost reductions while modernizing particular aspects of social provision will generally hold the balance of political power."

Some cost-reducing policy changes have already been implemented. Korpi and Palme (2003) investigated net replacement rates in the public insurance systems for sickness, work accident, and unemployment for 18 OECD countries.[1] While their analysis confirmed the moderating impact of institutional factors related to veto points and welfare state regimes, the data also suggested that many welfare states changed in the 1980s and 1990s, also outside the liberal Anglo-Saxon countries: "we find that the long gradual increase in average benefit levels characterizing developments up to the mid-1970s has not only stopped but turned into a reverse" (Korpi and Palme 2003: 445; cf. Allen and Scruggs 2004). Similarly, results indicating gradual service deterioration and increasing resource-scarcity—rather than radical system change—have been reported in comparative studies of public services such as education and health care (Clayton and Pontusson 1998).

Even gradual changes in institutions and policies may instigate public dissatisfaction with outputs. Not least, the perception that "the same public systems still exist, but do not deliver what they once did" may spread. There is some anecdotal evidence to suggest that this may be exactly what we have seen in Europe during the latter half of the 1990s and the early 2000s. Consider, for example, the spread of popular dissatisfaction with health services and public education in Sweden and the UK, or the massive popular protests and strikes against pension and labor market reforms in Italy, Germany, and France. Such powerful outbursts of anger about proposed or implemented reforms suggest that it will not take a neoliberal apocalypse for widespread dissatisfaction to arise in increasingly pressured welfare states.

The increasing risk of welfare state dissatisfaction raises interesting questions for this book. First, what are the effects of dissatisfaction with welfare state policy outputs on political orientations and behavior? More specifically, I investigate how dissatisfaction affects three types of dependent variables: (1) general ideological variables related to the left–right conflict, (2) support for the incumbent government as expressed through voting, and (3) general trust in politicians and political institutions.

A second aim is to analyze how such effects vary across institutional contexts. Thus, I allow not only the possibility that evaluations of policy outputs feed back into the political system in the shape of updated political orientations and behavior, but also the possibility that the nature of that feedback may be different, depending on the institutional configuration in particular countries.

The theoretical part of the chapter will now proceed in two steps. First, I outline two theoretical perspectives for thinking about feedback effects of dissatisfaction. Both are concerned with the three main categories of dependent variables, but their predictions about the nature of feedback effects are different: whereas one predicts that widespread dissatisfaction may help to "undermine" welfare states, the other predicts it will "overload" them. The second step is to consider the nature of *political decision-making institutions* as well as *welfare state institutions*, as explanations for why different types of feedback effects may occur in different institutional environments.

UNDERMINED OR OVERLOADED?

One common hypothesis is that reduced capacities and increasingly poor policy outcomes will decrease public support for the welfare state. As citizens discover that social security systems and public services do not deliver what they once did, they gradually abandon the idea of public solutions to social and economic problems, turning instead to the private market, the family, or civil society. Hence, pressured welfare states undermine themselves in a vicious circle where unsatisfactory performance reduces normative support, which may result in less public spending, less generous benefits, but more demands for nonpublic insurances and services. This may further constrain already fiscally pressured public sectors, and in turn produce even more dissatisfaction, and so on.

This *undermined-welfare-state perspective* can be cast in rational choice terms: citizens are assumed to weigh benefits and costs related to welfare state services, and support becomes more likely the more positive net benefits are perceived. The assumption implies that at any given level of costs in terms of tax payments and other personal contributions, dissatisfaction with benefit levels and public service quality produces less support for the idea of the welfare state, "big government," "the strong state," and so on. As argued by Goul Andersen (2001: 5), "The immediate reaction to such problems may be willingness to spend more but in the long run it may result in a decline of confidence and perhaps in a search for private alternatives. Even the most solidaristic person cannot in the long run be assumed to be willing to contribute to a system that is considered inefficient."

Such predictions can be contrasted against the *overloaded-welfare-state perspective*. This line of reasoning goes back to Crozier, Huntington, and Watanuki's (1975) *The Crisis of Democracy*, which debated democratic consequences of the economic malaise of the early 1970s. This period saw the first wave of serious pessimism about both the economic outlook of industrial nations and their political problem-solving capacities. It was frequently feared that the postwar economic boom was over at the same time as the modern state had grown to limits; that it could hardly expand further without jeopardizing incentives for investment, work, and other growth-generating activities.

Crozier, Huntington, and Watanuki stipulated that citizens were not adapting to new realities. People's largely positive experiences of welfare state expansion during the postwar boom had promoted an irreversible belief that any new societal problem was a state responsibility; that it was best dealt with by means of political regulation, intervention, spending, and so on. Therefore, welfare states heard an ever-growing and increasingly complex cacophony of demands at the same time as their problem-solving capacity had come to a halt. In Kaase and Newton's (1995: 71–72) words, it was assumed that "the revolution of rising expectations makes today's luxuries tomorrow's necessities. . . . Politicians promise more and more at election time, but the more demands they recognize . . . the less likely they are to deliver. . . . Government becomes overloaded and society becomes ungovernable."

On top of this, there also seemed to be signs that the irreversible demands were now expressed and communicated more forcefully to political authorities. Citizens had become more individualist, self-confident, and critical of authorities, expecting their demands to have immediate and visible effects on public policy. Politicians seemed to have become more sensitive to public opinion due to increased voter volatility, a less partisan and loyal mass media, and the growing use of opinion polls.

Overload theory gives rise to a somewhat paradoxical hypothesis, one that flies in the face of the undermined-welfare-state perspective. Dissatisfaction with welfare state–related performance is predicted to *increase* support for public solutions and spending. Decades of essentially positive experiences with state intervention and big government have cemented the inclination to remedy political and social problems with increased public spending and state intervention. When performance problems appear in the shape of, say, more pupils per public school teacher, longer waiting time for specialist treatment, or raised medical fees, citizens will do what they always do according to overload theory: they will demand a political solution by means of (even more) expansionist policies.

When it comes to support for political actors and political institutions, *both* the theoretical perspectives predict negative effects. For example, if overload assumptions were true, dissatisfied citizens would lose faith in the incumbent government that is immediately responsible for not taking enough public action to tackle problems. Because people strongly support the normative idea of the welfare state but have come to perceive that it is currently performing more poorly that it should, citizens can be expected to punish those presently responsible. People throw out the rascals who are thought to be making a practical mess of good ideas and principles. An alternative possibility here is that particular governments are able to escape voters' wrath, and that dissatisfaction instead translates into more generalized political cynicism. This may be so especially if dissatisfaction lingers on over several elections and governments or if the political system tends to simultaneously involve several major political forces in policymaking (cf. Powell and Whitten 1993). We shall return to this point.

The undermined-welfare-state perspective, too, implies negative effects on support for political actors and political institutions. However, because the thrust of this theory is that dissatisfaction undermines normative welfare state support, people punish parties and politicians for having taken *too much* public action, for having let government become too big for its own good. Although this is a rather different sort of dissatisfaction from the one identified by overload theory, its effects are similar: It may result in specific animosity toward a particular incumbent government (if there is one party that has been the main actor behind welfare state outputs).

Alternatively, it may produce generalized antipathy toward political parties and institutions (to the extent that outputs are the results of compromises among several actors).

The specific question of how dissatisfaction with welfare state performance affects political orientations has rarely been the subject of comparative research. What we have are mainly single-country studies or comparative findings addressing the two theoretical perspectives without testing their specific implications with regard to dissatisfaction effects.

In the latter category, there are several studies relevant to overload theory, but they send mixed signals about its viability. On the one hand, overload theory has fared miserably as a grand theory of developments in *aggregate* public opinion. Western European surveys do not reveal a spiral of rising demands on governments (Borre and Scarbrough 1995). Rather, the main feature of welfare state attitudes appears to be stability, and the over-time variation that can be detected is cyclical rather than linear. Moreover, in stark contrast to what is predicted by overload theory, demands for state expansion have proven to be higher in countries with less developed welfare states and a higher level of socioeconomic inequality (see also Pettersen 1995; Roller 1995; Huseby 1995). This suggests that "public opinion is not irreversible," but that "demands for government spending on some services seem to level off in wealthier nations compared with poorer ones. In short, the spiral of rising expectations of the public sector has been replaced—to some extent at any rate—by a spiral of falling expectations" (Kaase and Newton 1995: 73).[2] These results, then, suggest that overload theory was a rather time-specific intellectual product of the early 1970s. As such, it does not work as a general developmental theory of public opinion in welfare states. Therefore, it "seems to have gone the way of bell-bottoms, Afghan coats and patchouli oil" (Norris 1999: 5).

GIVING OVERLOAD THEORY A (SECOND) CHANCE

Nevertheless, as much as the macro predictions of overload theory have faltered, some studies imply that it could still be a useful tool for the micro-level question about welfare state dissatisfaction effects on orientations. For instance, Johansson, Nilsson, and Strömberg (2001) report that dissatisfaction with the performance of a particular public service tends to *increase* support for spending on that particular service. Similarly, Edlund (2006) investigated the effects of "institutional trust" in a number of welfare state institutions on spending preferences. He found that a general distrust factor—based mainly on distrust in social insurances and health care—has no bivariate correlation with "general spending preferences." However, he also found that general distrust, as well as trust in labor market–related welfare, increased support for selective spending on "families with children," "social assistance," and "active labor market policies." These findings are consistent with overload predictions in that perceived problems seem to fuel demands for even more public spending and state expansion.

In this chapter, I add to these findings by analyzing dissatisfaction effects on less specific and concrete orientations. Specifically, an important dependent variable in this chapter is the individual's position along a general "state intervention" value dimension. It can be defined in terms of attitudes toward how much public schemes, policies, and regulation should *generally* intervene in the market economy, and toward the *general* size and generosity of the welfare state. This classic ideological dimension is intimately related to the industrial-age, class-based conflict between workers and capitalists, and between the left and the right (see Lipset and Rokkan 1967; Franklin, Mackie, and Valen 1992). It is often measured in surveys through questions on the preferred general size, generosity, or form of welfare state arrangements. Such questions include suggestions about "reducing the size of the public sector," or about the general extent of "privatization," "redistribution," or "equality."

Why do we focus on this dependent variable? Because it is a very general value dimension, one that is typically more important than specific welfare state support in structuring public preferences and party competition in Western Europe (Granberg and Holmberg 1988; Aardal and van Wijnen 2005; Knutsen and Kumlin 2005). Therefore, general values must be taken into account if we are to understand the *political* ramifications of dissatisfaction; it must be analyzed if we are interested in the overloaded- and undermined-welfare-state perspectives as general theories about welfare state *politics*.

Not many studies have gone down this particular path. An exception is my previous analysis of Swedish data, which on the one hand confirmed the idea that dissatisfaction breeds demands for increased spending on the particular policy area in question. On the other hand, such effects were not to be found at the ideological level. In fact, there was even a modest tendency for negative views on welfare procedures and distributive outcomes to be associated with *less* general welfare state support (Kumlin 2004: Chapter 8). Other findings suggested that personal, short-term, economic self-interest affected general orientations. The data showed rather sizeable differences in general welfare state support among people who frequently benefit personally from welfare state institutions, compared to those who do not. All these findings are in line with the rational choice–inspired tenets of the undermined-welfare-state perspective, in that dissatisfaction and failure to satisfy personal interests reduce general support for the welfare state and state intervention.

So taken together, previous research indicates that overloading and undermining processes can occur *simultaneously*, albeit at different levels of attitude abstraction. Whereas dissatisfaction indeed seems to "overload" the welfare state with ever more demands at a concrete attitude level, it may well undermine support at a more general—and politically more important—level. Testing for this latter type of impact in a large number of countries is one of the two primary purposes of this chapter. We now turn to the second purpose.

DOES THE NATURE OF FEEDBACK EFFECTS DEPEND ON THE INSTITUTIONAL CONTEXT?

Our two perspectives are attractive as they provide general and parsimonious accounts of the impact of dissatisfaction. But parsimony and generality are sometimes problematic. Theories can fail as general "laws" and may be better described as more modest context-specific models. Therefore, this section discusses institutional macro-level factors that may regulate the strength and direction of dissatisfaction effects. In other words, they are factors that could alter the explanatory power of the undermined- and overloaded-welfare-state perspectives.

One source of inspiration is the extensive research on "economic voting" (see Kinder and Kiewiet 1981; Lewis-Beck 1988; Norpoth 1996). My purpose here is not to review the many nuances of this gargantuan field. We just take as our point of departure the general finding that voters in Western democracies tend to punish the government in times of unemployment, inflation, and low GDP growth, only to reward them when things get better. However, as pointed out by Lewis-Beck and Paldam (2000), electoral reward and punishment for economic outcomes is also highly unstable. Much of the time, views on economic performance play at least a certain role for voters' party choices and, in turn, election results. But sometimes this role does not seem to be very important. There are in fact many elections at which governments are not held accountable for economic performance, as reflected in very weak correlations between citizens' evaluations of the economy and their propensity to support incumbent parties.

This begs the question: Under what circumstances do dissatisfied citizens hold politicians to account? On the basis of comparative analyses of aggregate data as well as of individual-level survey data, it seems that systemic *clarity of political responsibility* functions as a crucial contextual factor directing which causal path performance dissatisfaction travels by (see Powell and Whitten 1993; Taylor 2000; Bengtsson 2002). The clarity of responsibility is in turn adjusted by many potential factors, but so far studies have mainly examined the role of basic *political* institutions and contexts, such as the presence of a single majority government, the number of parties involved in decision making, the existence of a second-chamber opposition majority, and so on.

This research suggests that performance variables have stronger effects on voter choice when policy-making powers are concentrated in fewer actors. Under such circumstances, there is hardly any correlation between economic variables and more general political trust in politicians and the representative political system. If responsibility is clear and concentrated, it seems, dissatisfied citizens strike at particular actors *inside* the political system. Conversely, in contexts where the locus of responsibility is fuzzy, performance dissatisfaction does not find an outlet in voting. Instead, performance dissatisfaction will undermine general trust in politicians and the representative political system.

I extend this research in two ways. First, I consider dissatisfaction with welfare state–related policy outputs. As pointed out by several authors, we know surprisingly little about when and how strongly such variables affect attitudes and behavior (see Miller and Listhaug 1999; Huseby 2000; Holmberg 1999; Kumlin 2004); this is especially true when it comes to comparative research. Second, the chapter takes into account a broader range of dependent variables than economic voting research, which has usually investigated only support for the incumbent government.

Several hypotheses will be tested. First, consistent with past research on economic voting, we expect dissatisfaction to do less damage to incumbent governments and more damage to general political trust, where policy-making power is dispersed across nongovernmental actors. Second, we investigate how the impact of dissatisfaction on state intervention support varies depending on the clarity of responsibility. Such effects are expected to fade where policy-making power is dispersed, the logic being that it will be harder to draw ideological conclusions from perceived welfare state failures where several ideological forces have constant opportunities to shape policies. Conversely, such conclusions should be drawn more frequently where only one ideological force at the time bears the main responsibility.

The last hypothesis rejects an assumption made by the undermined-welfare-state perspective—one that may not immediately catch the eye. This perspective actually presupposes that the welfare state is always regarded by citizens as a genuinely leftist/social democratic ideological project. And this is why dissatisfaction with welfare state outputs always reduces support for leftist ideology and state intervention. Those dissatisfied lose faith in the ideological camp that is generally perceived to have given birth to a poorly functioning system.

Of course, this way of thinking makes some sense in that the very idea of the welfare state is intimately intertwined with typically leftist strategies such as state intervention, expansion, regulation, and taxation. Still, it is not the whole ideological story of the welfare state. Previous research tells us that different welfare state regimes can embody very different ideological ideals (Rothstein 1998; Mau 2003) and that different types of political actors have been involved in the construction of welfare states (Baldwin 1990; Esping-Andersen 1990). For instance, "conservative" welfare states have been partly created by Christian Democratic parties to partly embody conservative values. A parallel logic applies to liberal welfare states. To the extent that such historical complexity is present, dissatisfied citizens should have more difficulty in drawing clear-cut political conclusions.

These remarks open up the possibility that dissatisfied citizens draw different ideological conclusions in different welfare state regimes. Specifically, we expect citizens in social democratic welfare regimes to most clearly conform to the predictions of the undermined-welfare-state perspective. Since such welfare states most obviously build on leftist and egalitarian principles, and because such welfare states have been most consistently shaped by leftist political forces, it should be clearer than otherwise to those dissatisfied that it is a leftist and social democratic system that has "failed" and needs to be partly replaced by new ideological ideas. In contrast, liberal and conservative welfare states are (even) more ambiguous mixtures of values and political forces; while they rest on inherently leftist strategies such as state intervention and expansion, the causes and nature of these welfare states are to a significant extent nonleftist. Therefore, it may be less clear to those dissatisfied which ideological conclusions one "should" draw. This may result in weaker effects on ideological orientations.

One can also imagine that the effects of dissatisfaction on incumbent support and political trust are different in social democratic regimes. By analogy with the predictions about clarity of responsibility, one hypothesis is that there are stronger effects on incumbent support in social democratic regimes (at least when a social democratic party is in power). Under such circumstances, it may be easier than otherwise for citizens to assign blame to the government, compared to citizens in welfare states where a greater variety of political values and forces share historical responsibility for the welfare state. In such welfare regimes, output dissatisfaction may be more likely to hamper generalized trust in politicians and politics.

In summary, both political institutions as well as welfare state institutions may affect how responsibility for policy outputs is perceived among citizens. That is why such institutions could also structure the impact of dissatisfaction on ideological state intervention support, incumbent government support, and political trust. Specifically, where the institutional environment diffuses responsibility, we should expect dissatisfaction to do less damage to specific political actors and their underlying ideological positions, but more damage to general trust in political actors and politics.

DATA, MEASUREMENT, AND CAUSALITY

As the literature review suggests, there are almost no previous comparative studies of the effects of dissatisfaction with welfare state–related policy outputs (Huseby 2000 is an exception). Thus, we know little about how welfare state dissatisfaction should be measured in a cross-country setting, how multi- or unidimensional it is, or how it affects, and is affected by, political orientations. This lack of knowledge means we are forced to make a number of assumptions regarding measurement and causality, assumptions that we have no good way of testing yet. What we can do is to spell out clearly these yet-untested assumptions so that they can be analyzed further by future studies.

The data come from the 2002 wave of the European Social Survey, focusing on 16 Western European welfare states.[3] For several reasons, this data set fits our purposes better than other reasonably recent comparative surveys. Most crucially, it simultaneously contains measures of all dependent attitude variables (state intervention orientations, voting, political trust) *and* evaluations of welfare state–related outcomes. As for the latter, the survey included two questions on how the respondent evaluated "the state of health services in [COUNTRY]" and the "state of education in [COUNTRY]," respectively, along scales ranging from 0 (extremely bad) to 10 (extremely good). These two variables were combined into an additive welfare state dissatisfaction index. The index varies between 0 and 10 where higher values represent more dissatisfaction.[4]

This way of measuring welfare state dissatisfaction builds on the assumption that citizens to a large extent evaluate the public sector and the welfare state as an overarching phenomenon. That is, they do not tend to form separate evaluations of the outputs of individual institutions and policies. Instead, we assume that new incoming information about the public sector is incorporated into an overall "running tally" (cf. Lodge and Stroh 1993) of how public schemes and programs generally tend to perform. One empirical implication here is that output evaluations of different policies tend to correlate with each other. This is indeed the case for evaluations of education and health care ($r = .51$).

Beyond this simple correlation, however, the assumption has to remain largely untested for now. But there are a couple of preliminary arguments for it. First, studies on normative welfare state attitudes give us reasons to believe that citizens tend to think about the public sector and the welfare state as overarching phenomena. For instance, attitudes toward spending on health care and education tend to blend in a more general spending dimension (see Kaase and Newton 1995). Second, results from the economic voting field—the one area in which there is plenty of research on effects of policy output evaluations—imply that citizens tend to evaluate "the country's economy" as an overarching phenomenon although, in reality, economic development consists of potentially diverse trends in many areas and aspects of society. Given this inclination among citizens to simplify complex situations, an overall welfare state dissatisfaction index seems a sensible way to approach a largely uncharted territory. Future studies, however, may want to relax this assumption and look more closely into the internal structure of welfare state–related policy evaluations.

Another possible problem with a welfare state dissatisfaction index is that the questions do not explicitly refer to public state-run health care and education institutions. It is thus possible that some respondents answer the questions based on assessments of nonpublic services. While we cannot rule out this possibility, a couple of observations speak against it. For instance, comparative research concludes that in most countries large majorities think that health care and education are and should be public responsibilities (Borre and Scarbrough 1995; Svallfors 2003). In other words, even where quite a number of these services are nonpublic, many citizens seem to perceive that the political sphere has a responsibility for the overall functioning of these sectors. Moreover, analyses show that evaluations of health care and education are consistently and rather strongly related to attitudinal approval of the government in one's country. It is hard to see why this would be the case if most respondents were not answering the questions based on services for which they think politicians carry a significant responsibility.

A final assumption that needs to be spelled out has to do with the direction of causal impact: It is obviously conceivable that correlations between dissatisfaction and the dependent variables are partly due to the latter affecting the former. For instance, it is possible that normative support for the welfare state, or trust in politicians, tends to produce satisfaction rather than the other way around. While we cannot analyze this issue empirically—as there are no comparative "panel data" offering the right sorts of measures—a couple of things can be said in defense of the results and interpretations offered here. First, while reversed causation is almost certainly present to some extent, it is not necessarily the dominant process: a previous study (Kumlin 2006) using panel data from Sweden indicated that dissatisfaction with policy outputs has a significant effect on *changes* in state intervention orientations and left–right self-placement. This was true for both long-term (four years) and short-term (one month) changes. The reciprocal possibility also received empirical support but only for short-term changes. Similarly, Evans (1999) used British election study data and found that negative evaluations of the British National Health Service were significantly related to changes in individual voting patterns between 1992 and 1995. Examining whether these conclusions hold in other countries and also for other dependent variables such as political trust will be an interesting task for future research.

Second, much of our interest is directed toward explanations of *effect differences* across countries or across dependent variables, rather than toward estimating the exact magnitude of effects. Therefore, given that the problem of reversed causation is not more pronounced in one country compared to the other, most of our conclusions should still have some validity in spite of some reciprocal causation.

EMPIRICAL RESULTS: IDEOLOGY

Two very different measures of ideological orientations are offered by the European Social Survey. The first one registers respondents' self-placement on a scale between 0 (far to the left) and 10 (far to the right). This is a widely used measure of ideological positions and has proven valid and useful for analyzing political behavior in Western Europe (see Inglehart and Klingemann 1976; van der Eijk, Schmitt, and Binder 2005). Still, it has a couple of drawbacks for our purposes. One is that the left–right semantic tends to accommodate several empirically interrelated but conceptually distinct topics of conflict: while state intervention is certainly one of these in the investigated countries, it is also true that conflicts such as "postmaterialism vs. materialism" and "moral conservatism vs. libertarianism" could color the responses (Fuchs and Klingemann 1989; Knutsen 1995). A second drawback is that answers to questions about left–right self-placement partly reflect respondents' party preferences. This interpretation is typically referred to as the "partisan component" of left–right self-identification (Inglehart and Klingemann 1976; Granberg and Holmberg 1988; Knutsen 1998). According to this interpretation, people who say that they stand "far to the left" have inferred their position from their party preference, or mean that they support a leftist party. However, this does not necessarily reveal all that much about policy-related values or attitudes. For instance, it could be a sign that dissatisfied voters are punishing an incumbent right-leaning government without changing their ideological orientations. Of course, the opposite may also apply here: in countries with leftist governments, welfare state dissatisfaction could make ideologically stable individuals more prone to support rightist parties, as reflected in more rightist placements on the left–right self-placement scale.

So while left–right self-placement is clearly relevant for our purposes, we would ideally want to supplement it with a measure that comes closer to the substantive content of conflicts over state intervention. Unfortunately, the European Social Survey does not abound with such variables. What we have are four indicators, at least two of which are less than ideal. However, I hope to demonstrate that they are all of sufficient interest as less-than-optimal supplements to the left–right self-placement variable.

The four state intervention items form the basis for two alternative additive indices that have served as dependent variables. One is based on two agree–disagree items: "The government should take measures to reduce differences in income levels" and "Employees need strong trade unions to protect their working conditions and wages." The first item is a relatively straightforward measure of state intervention support. The second item is somewhat more indirect but nevertheless brings up several stimuli that tend to be endorsed more strongly by those who support state intervention (strong unions, protection of working conditions and wages).

The second index adds two further items that were not strictly intended by the primary researchers to measure general state intervention support but which nevertheless deal with adjacent topics: "important that government ensures safety against all threats, and that the state is strong so it can defend its citizens," and "important that every person in the world is treated equally, and that everyone should have equal opportunity in life." These items are more ambiguous in several ways. For example, while the first one indeed asks respondents to give their opinion on a strong state and a government that ensures safety for its citizens, it is not quite clear what kind of safety, threats, or defense are at issue. Similarly, the second additional item prompts respondents to think about equality, a stimulus that tends to be more frequently endorsed among leftist citizens. On the negative side, however, our assumed link to state action is not made clear to the respondents; although the combination is uncommon in Western Europe, it is intellectually possible to be strongly in favor of equality while at the same time despising state intervention as a vehicle for its creation. Moreover, the reference to "the world" may make respondents think about global injustices, a topic that could bring to mind a very different type of intervention compared to the previous items.

Because of these ambiguities, all analyses were performed with both the two-item and the four-item index. Fortunately, it turns out that the substantive conclusions are almost always the same, but effects tend to come out more strongly when using the four-item index. This applies for both positive and negative effects of dissatisfaction. The stronger effects should be taken as a sign of greater construct validity and I will therefore generally report results for the four-item index only. Moreover, it will be evident that the analyses of the state intervention orientations yield the same substantive conclusions as those of the left–right self-placement. The fact that different measures with different weaknesses nevertheless lead to the same conclusions suggests that not only the conclusions but also the indicators have some validity.

Table 3.1 provides a pooled analysis of the relationship between the welfare state dissatisfaction index and the ideological variables. Because respondents from all countries are tossed together in one analysis, any country differences in the effects of dissatisfaction are lost. However, pooling the data provides an opportunity to assess the overall explanatory potency of the two theoretical perspectives in Western Europe.

Looking first at the bivariate relationship between dissatisfaction and state intervention support, one sees no significant effect. But this coefficient probably lies about the actual impact. When taking a host of relevant control variables into account, the relationship becomes significantly negative $(-.02)$. So while the bivariate relationship may lead one to believe that welfare state dissatisfaction has no effect at all, the multivariate analysis indicates that the impact is more likely slightly negative: holding constant the control variables, higher levels of dissatisfaction tend to be associated with lower levels of state intervention support.

The explanation for the suppressed bivariate effect is that the welfare state dissatisfaction index correlates with several other variables that have *positive* effects on support for state intervention. In particular, welfare dissatisfaction correlates with negative feelings about the household income ($r = .17$), a variable that strongly pushes intervention support upward. Thus, the actual impact of welfare state dissatisfaction is suppressed and masked unless one specifies a properly controlled multivariate model. In turn, this raises a question mark concerning certain analyses in past research—which have usually been bivariate—showing positive effects of dissatisfaction on concrete spending preferences. The question is whether

TABLE 3.1

Regression models of general state intervention orientations and left–right self-placement (unstandardized OLS coefficients).

	DEPENDENT VARIABLE: State intervention orientations (0–10, higher values = more state intervention support)		DEPENDENT VARIABLE: Left–right self-placement (0–10, higher values = further to the right)	
	Model 1	*Model 2*	*Model 3*	*Model 4*
Welfare state dissatisfaction index (0–10)	−.01	−.02***	−.06***	−.02*
Negative evaluation of country's economy (0–10)	—	.03***	—	.03***
Negative feeling about household's income (1–4)	—	.14***	—	−.03
Woman	—	.21***	—	−.15**
Age	—	−.003	—	.001***
Education (1–7)	—	−.05***	—	−.08***
Life satisfaction	—	.00	—	.08***
Income	—	−.05***	—	.03***
Class (reference category: Unskilled manual labor)				
Skilled manual labor	—	−.04	—	.06
Service class 1	—	−.52***	—	.21***
Service class 2	—	−.23***	—	.13**
Routine nonmanual labor	—	−.22***	—	.16***
Self-employed	—	−.63***	—	.57***
Constant	8.36***	8.34***	5.39***	4.48***
Adjusted R-squared	.09	.15	.03	.06
Number of respondents	14,323	14,323	16,238	16,238

*p < .10 **p < .05 ***p < .01

COMMENT: Data from the 2002 European Social Survey. The models also contain 13 country dummies, the coefficients of which are not displayed. The data have been weighted according to population size.

those results would remain the same in more rigorously controlled statistical models.

Models 3 and 4 employ left–right self-placement as the dependent variable. They continue to underscore the importance of properly specified statistical models. While the bivariate coefficient seems to support the overloaded-welfare-state perspective (greater dissatisfaction correlates with leftist positions), this effect is reduced from −.06 to a hardly significant −.02 in the multivariate Model 4. In sum, therefore, the pooled analysis in Table 3.1 does not yield clear-cut support for any of the two theoretical perspectives. While dissatisfaction has a tendency to undermine support for state intervention, it tends to push citizens to the left in the subjective sense.

TABLE 3.2
Regression models of state intervention
orientations (unstandardized OLS coefficients).

	$b_{welfare\ state}$ dissatisfaction (four items)	$b_{welfare\ state}$ dissatisfaction (four items) $b_{self-employment}$
Austria	.03	
Belgium	.02	
Switzerland	−.06***	90%
Germany	−.04**	63%
Denmark	−.06*	90%
Spain	−.05*	79%
Finland	.01	
UK	.02	
Greece	.01	
Ireland	.01	
Italy	NA	
Luxemburg	NA	
Netherlands	.03 (p = .14)	
Norway	−.05**	79%
Portugal	.06**	90%
Sweden	−.07***	111%

*p < .10 **p < .05 ***p < .01

NA = Dependent variable not available

COMMENT: Data from the 2002 European Social Survey. Country-specific versions of the model in Table 1, column 4. The third column reports the magnitude of country-specific effects of dissatisfaction expressed as percentages of the impact of the self-employment dummy in the pooled sample (see Table 3.1). These country-specific models contain the same controls as the pooled ones in Table 3.1.

Table 3.2 breaks down the analysis of state intervention support by country. This yields three interesting observations. First, in many countries, dissatisfaction does not have a significant impact at all; there, neither the overloading nor the undermining processes seem to be at work. Second, consistent with our hypothesis, undermining effects are to be found in the three Scandinavian welfare states (Denmark, Norway, Sweden), though also in some other countries (Germany, Spain, Switzerland). Third, the overall negative effects in Table 3.1 hide the fact that at least one of the dependent variables indicate that dissatisfaction *increases* support significantly in Portugal and almost significantly in the Netherlands (p = .14). In other words, it seems that whereas undermining mechanisms are more pronounced overall, overloading processes may well be under way in a small subset of countries. This observation reinforces the need to take institutional and contextual factors into account.

How strong are the effects of dissatisfaction in those countries where they can be found? In any absolute sense, the answer must be "not very strong." In Sweden, where one finds the strongest impact, a maximum leap from total satisfaction (0) to total dissatisfaction (10) is still predicted to produce only a .70 change along the 11-point state intervention support scale. So perhaps "erode" would be a more appropriate description than "undermine," in that it better captures the weakness of the effects.

On the other hand, it may be more appropriate to compare dissatisfaction effects with those of other, better-known independent variables. The prime example is perhaps occupational class, which many see as the single most successful perspective for analyzing general state intervention support (cf. Pettersen 1995). The third column thus compares the maximum effect of dissatisfaction on the four-item index with the predicted effect of moving between unskilled manual workers to the self-employed (.63 according to Table 3.1). This comparison is more flattering for the impact of dissatisfaction. Still, of the countries that display significant dissatisfaction effects, Sweden is the only country where differences between the dissatisfied and the satisfied are greater than the differences between unskilled workers and the self-employed (111%).

Table 3.3 looks at dissatisfaction effects on left–right self-placement in the various countries. Again, the main feature of the data is tremendous country variation in the impact of welfare state dissatisfaction. In seven countries, dissatisfaction correlates significantly with leftist positions, with coefficients ranging from −.05 to −.14. The opposite is true for Norway (.10) and Italy (.07; not significant), whereas we find no detectable impact at all in the remaining countries.

Compared with the class effect, the overloading impact of dissatisfaction on left–right positions seems stronger than its undermining impact on state intervention support. However, we must remember that some of the impact on left–right positions is almost certainly related to the partisan component registered by the left–right self-placement measure, rather than to the value component. For example, the many leftist effects among countries with right-leaning governments are probably partly due to a process in which the dissatisfied punish the rightist government directly, rather than necessarily adjusting values. And of course, it is the latter we want to tap here. Similarly, the rightist effect in Norway (which had a center-right government in 2002) is probably partly due to dissatisfied voters choosing

TABLE 3.3
Regression models of economic left–right
self-placement (unstandardized OLS coefficients).

	$b_{welfare\ state\ dissatisfaction}$	$\dfrac{b_{welfare\ state\ dissatisfaction}}{b_{self\text{-}employment}}$	Ideological tendency of national government
Belgium	−.09***	158%	Left
Germany	−.05**	88%	Left
Sweden	.03		Left
UK	.02		Left
Greece	.02		Left
Finland	−.11***	192%	Mixed
Switzerland	−.03		Mixed
Luxemburg	−.14***	246%	Right
Spain	−.11***	192%	Right
Ireland	−.10***	175%	Right
Norway	.10***	175%	Right
Austria	−.08***	140%	Right
Italy	.07		Right
Portugal	−.06		Right
Denmark	−.01		Right
Netherlands	−.01		Right

COMMENT: Data from the 2002 European Social Survey. Country-specific versions of Model 4 in Table 3.1, column 4. The second column reports the magnitude of country-specific effects of dissatisfaction expressed as percentages of the impact of the self-employment dummy in the pooled sample (see Model 4, Table 3.1).

the populist, rightist, and highly welfare state–oriented Progress Party. Still, there is a lot of country variation in the impact of dissatisfaction even among countries with similar government. For instance, dissatisfied Germans stand further to the left on the self-placement scale, despite having a left-leaning government. Conversely, dissatisfied citizens of Portugal, Denmark, and the Netherlands are not further to the left, even though they have right-leaning governments. Such variation cannot be explained merely by the notion of partisan effects. Rather, they are more in line with the idea that that left–right self-placement also captures values and ideology.

INSTITUTIONS AND DISSATISFACTION EFFECTS ON STATE INTERVENTION SUPPORT AND IDEOLOGY

What accounts for the sizable country variation in the strength and direction of dissatisfaction effects on state intervention support and ideological self-placement? One of the hypotheses in this study has to do with the

TABLE 3.4
Powell and Whitten's measure of clarity of power dispersion (clarity of responsibility).

Austria	1.2
Belgium	2.6
Switzerland	5.0
Germany	2.6
Denmark	2.8
Spain	NA
Finland	3.3
UK	0.2
Greece	0.0
Ireland	0.7
Italy	3.2
Luxemburg	NA
Netherlands	3.2
Norway	2.8
Portugal	NA
Sweden	1.4

NA = Not available
COMMENT: From Powell and Whitten (1993:406). See main text for more information. The country mean is 2.1; unweighted n = 13.

extent to which decision-making power tends to be dispersed in the policy-making process. The measure used comes from Powell and Whitten's study of the impact of "clarity of responsibility" (1993: 406) and is displayed in Table 3.4. Specifically, this variable counts a number of central characteristics in the institutional and political context environment, all of which can be expected to affect clarity of responsibility and power dispersion. These are (1) the existence of a bicameral opposition majority, (2) the existence of a minority government, (3) the existence of a coalition government, (4) a lack of party cohesion, (5) the existence of participatory, inclusive, and proportionally composed committees in the legislature, and (6) each additional competing party that is added to a governing coalition. The scores for individual countries are averages over elections held in the period 1969–1988.[5]

There is quite notable variation in power dispersion. Power tends to be concentrated in countries such as the UK, Ireland, and Greece (on average, less than one), but dispersed in Italy, the Netherlands, Finland, and Switzerland (three or more dispersion-inducing characteristics). Other countries fall somewhere between the extremes.

Table 3.5 contains the same type of analyses as Tables 3.1 and 3.2, but with the difference that they are now conducted separately among citizens

TABLE 3.5

How contextual power dispersion and welfare state regime types
interact with the impact of welfare state dissatisfaction on state intervention
orientations and left–right self-placement (unstandardized OLS coefficients).

	DEPENDENT VARIABLE: *State intervention orientations (0–10, higher values = more state intervention support)*	DEPENDENT VARIABLE: *Left–right self-placement (0–10, higher values = further to the right)*
Social Democratic Welfare States		
Welfare state dissatisfaction (0–10)	−.19***	.20*
Welfare state dissatisfaction × Power dispersion	.07***	−.08*
Liberal or Conservative Welfare States		
Welfare state dissatisfaction (0–10)	−.02	.07*
Welfare state dissatisfaction × Power dispersion	.03	−.04***

*p < .10 **p < .05 ***p < .01

COMMENT: Data from the 2002 European Social Survey, using 14 countries (EU15 + Norway and Switzerland − Italy and Luxemburg). The data have been weighted according to population size. The significance tests are based on cluster-corrected robust standard errors. In addition to the welfare state dissatisfaction variables, the models include the same control variables as Table 3.1, as well as the main effect of power dispersion.

of social democratic welfare states, and liberal/conservative welfare states. A further novelty is that the models include a contextual interaction term based on the power dispersion measure.

The first column reports the results for state intervention support. They show support for the prediction that dissatisfied Scandinavians are more prone than other dissatisfied Europeans to abandon ideological support for leftist state intervention, as evidenced by a rather strong main effect (−.19). It is crucial to note, however, that this is the predicted impact in a social democratic welfare state lacking all of the power-dispersing features tapped by the Powell and Whitten index. But of course, there is no such country in the world. Rather, as soon as a couple of power-dispersing institutional features are introduced, the impact of dissatisfaction is predicted to shrink to the more modest levels that we actually observed for Scandinavia in the country-specific analysis.

As for liberal and conservative welfare states, there is no significant impact in any direction on state intervention support. This seems to be largely true regardless of how power-dispersing the political-institutional environment is. These observations fit our predictions, the explanation being that liberal and conservative welfare states are (even) more of ideological compromises than social democratic regimes. Therefore, dissatisfied citizens might become more bewildered and heterogeneous in their attempts to draw ideological conclusions.

The results for left–right self-placement are also in line with our theoretical predictions. In Scandinavia, there is again a rather sizable "undermining" main effect, where the dissatisfied are more inclined to stand further to the right (.20). But much of this effect washes away as soon as a couple of power-dispersing institutional traits are introduced (−.08). In other types of welfare states, there is a very weak—but still significant—undermining tendency (.07). This provides more support for the notion that it is less likely that welfare state dissatisfaction moves ideological positions outside the social democratic world of welfare. Finally, our expectations are borne out also in the sense that the predicted weak undermining main effect is virtually obliterated as soon as the political institutional environment begins to disperse power (−.04).

Taken together, these findings explain why such inconclusive patterns were found both in the pooled as well as in the country-by-country analyses. For example, very weak overall effects on state intervention support were found in the pooled analysis: neither the overload nor the undermining perspective received overall support. It now becomes clear that the pooled coefficient masks tremendous country variation, and that this variation can be partly explained by the nature of political institutions and of the welfare state itself.

Moreover, while the country-by-country analysis seemed to suggest that dissatisfied Scandinavians are indeed more prone than others to abandon leftist values as measured by the state intervention indicators, no such pattern could be spotted for left–right self-placement. But now we know that not only welfare regimes but also political-institutional power dispersion matters. What is more, most Scandinavians must deal with higher-than-average power dispersion. This in turn means that the social democratic regime effect was attenuated in the previous analyses as they did not take power dispersion into account. In contrast, Table 3.5 does exactly that, with results suggesting that among people who live under *equally* power-dispersing institutional arrangements, dissatisfaction indeed translates more readily into decreased support for leftist values in social democratic welfare regimes.

INCUMBENT GOVERNMENT VOTING

Let us now look at Table 3.6, which shows dissatisfaction effects on the probability of government support (as measured by having voted for a government party in the last election). The analyses are conducted among respondents who have stated that they voted for a specific party in the last election. The statistical method is binary logistic regression, with the dependent variable coded 1 if the respondent voted for a government party, and 0 if another party was chosen.

This dependent variable brings with it a couple of methodological issues. First, countries differ in how much time has passed since the last election. Respondents who voted recently should give more accurate recollections than when several years have passed. Moreover, such measurement error could be partly unsystematic (where some people randomly forget which party they voted for). Additionally, measurement error may be partly systematic—for instance, if people in fact report their *current* party preferences rather than actual past votes, or tend to think that they voted for a party they currently like, even if they did not. We will keep an eye on this problem by eventually performing separate analyses among countries that did and did not have recent elections.

A second problem is that some countries experienced a government shift after the last election. Where this is the case, it is difficult to construct a meaningful dependent variable as there is more than one appropriate electoral target for dissatisfied citizens. Some may punish the current government as implied by our coding of the dependent variable (especially where much time has passed). On the other hand, some may in fact have voted for a party currently in government exactly because they wanted to punish the old government for previous welfare state failures. In all likelihood, both these phenomena are occurring to some extent. This is obviously problematic as our dependent variable will not be able to properly capture the dissatisfaction effects. This ambiguity means we will exclude from the analysis those countries where government shifts occurred after the last election.

Significant negative dissatisfaction effects in the predicted direction

TABLE 3.6

Regression models of having voted for the current government in the last election (logit estimates).

	GERMANY Social Democrats, Greens	SWEDEN Social Democrats	UK Labour	AUSTRIA Christian Democrats, Freedom Party	SWITZERLAND SPS, SVP, FDP, CVP	SPAIN Partido Popular	IRELAND Fianna Fáil, Progressive Democrats	FINLAND Social Democrats, National Coalition, Swedish People's Party, Green, League Left Alliance	GREECE PASOK
Welfare state dissatisfaction	.01	−.08**	−.04	−.15***	.07	−.01	−.12***	.24***	−.15***
Left–right distance to government	−.44***	−.73***	−.29	−.66***	−.09	−1.00***	−.20***	−.25***	−1.43***
Negative evaluation of country's	−.15***	−.06*	−.17	−.04	−.03	−.35***	−.11***	−.02	−.16***
Woman	.21*	−.04	.27*	−.03	−.44**	−.05	.46***	.11	.21
Age	−.02***	.00	−.01*	.01*	.01	.01	.01	.00	.01
Education (1–7)	.04	−.21***	−.12**	−.04	−.25***	−.03	.10*	.11*	−.04
Class (reference category: Unskilled manual labor)									
Skilled manual labor	.06	.50**	−.14	.30	−.11	.26	.49**	.54**	
Service class 1	−.10	.00	−.73***	.70**	.45	.65	.16	.70***	−1.29***
Service class 2	.16	−.12	−.74***	.41**	−.05	.17	.05	.32	−.58
Routine nonmanual labor	.02	.10	−.85***	.52**	−.14	−.54	−.22	.50**	−.76**
Self-employed		−.54*	−.93***	1.13***	.14	.46	.29	−1.07***	−.47
Constant	.94**	.88**	.35	−1.01*	2.20***	−.53	−1.08***	1.55***	1.03
Pseudo R-squared	.08	.20	.07	.03	.03	.32	.06	.08	.50
Number of respondents	1,779	1,378	1,153	1,137	817	685	1,102	1163	1,036
Maximum effect of welfare dissatisfaction on prob (govvote), at country means of other variables	.02	−.17	−.10	−.34	.11	−.01	−.29	.37	−.36

*p < .10 **p < .05 ***p < .01

COMMENT: Data from the 2002 European Social Survey. The dependent variable is coded 1 as if the respondent voted for one of the government parties in the top row, and 0 if another party was chosen. The ideological distance variable was created by calculating the absolute distance between the respondent's own position along an 11-point scale, and the position of the government. The latter was obtained by calculating the average position of the various voter groups for government parties, as weighted according to the relative share of votes in the last election.

can be discerned in four of the nine countries: Sweden, Ireland, Austria, and Greece. Additionally, in the UK there is a nonsignificant effect in the right direction. In these countries, citizens dissatisfied with welfare state performance are significantly more likely than others to vote against the incumbent government. Elsewhere, government voting does not correlate with welfare state dissatisfaction.

There are two exceptions, however: the effect is reversed in Finland and Switzerland (not quite significant, p = .189). Dissatisfied Finnish and Swiss citizens are *more* prone than others to vote for a government party. This observation in fact yields some preliminary support for the hypothesis that dispersion of power and responsibility will generally thwart attempts among dissatisfied citizens to punish incumbent governments. Finland and Switzerland had at the time of data collection coalitions that were arguably the most complex and ideologically wide that Europe had to offer. And in the Finnish case, retrospective punishment was further complicated by the uncertainty of future government alternatives. In the face of such complexity many voters may give up retrospective voting altogether for the benefit of more forward-looking concerns. For example, a speculation would be that retrospectively dissatisfied voters in Finland and Switzerland were nevertheless drawn to the government parties by promises of future improvements, increased spending, or other types of policy changes.

The next step in the analysis is found in Table 3.7, in which we have pooled the data in order to more formally account for country variation by introducing two familiar contextual interaction terms. One tests whether welfare state dissatisfaction does less damage to governments the more power is dispersed; the other tests whether more damage is done to governments in Scandinavian welfare state regimes.[6]

The results are in line with the predictions. Model 1 is estimated among all relevant countries. Consistent with previous comparative European research (van der Eijk, Franklin, and Oppenhuis 1996), the most influential variable is left–right ideological distance (−.43). The runner up in this respect is evaluation of the national economy (−.13). Controlling for these variables, welfare dissatisfaction also plays a role where the dissatisfied are less prone than other citizens to vote for the incumbent government parties (−.05).

It is important to note, however, that −.05 is the predicted impact when our two institutional interaction variables are zero: that is, among non-

TABLE 3.7
*How contextual power dispersion and welfare state regime types
interact with the impact of welfare state dissatisfaction on voting
for the current government in the last election (logit estimates).*

	Countries with no government shift after last election (Austria, Finland, Germany, Greece, Ireland, Sweden, Switzerland, UK)	Countries with no government shift after last election, and where last election was held in 2002 or later (Austria, Germany, Ireland, Sweden)
Welfare state dissatisfaction	−.05***	−.14***
Left–right distance to government (0–10)	−.43***	−.50***
Negative evaluation of country's economy (0–10)	−.13***	−.10***
Power dispersion	.33***	.46***
Social democratic welfare state (Sweden)	−.35***	−.10
Welfare state dissatisfaction × Power dispersion	.02***	.06***
Welfare state dissatisfaction × Social democratic welfare state (Sweden)	−.02***	.004
Constant	−.50***	−.67***
Pseudo R-squared	.07	.08
Number of respondents	10,052	5,660

*p < .10 **p < .05 ***p < .01

COMMENT: Data from the 2002 European Social Survey. The data have been weighted according to population size. The significance tests are based on cluster-corrected robust standard errors. Spain did not experience a government shift after the 2000 election, but is not part of these analyses due to missing data on power dispersion.

Scandinavian respondents who live in political systems with the smallest possible power dispersion. Interestingly, the impact of welfare state dissatisfaction withers away rapidly with each introduced power-dispersing institutional feature. Once we reach the European average number of power-dispersing features, our data suggest that it has become nonexistent (.008 = −.05 + .02 ×2.1).

Also consistent with our hypotheses, there is evidence that dissatisfaction has stronger effects on incumbent support in social democratic welfare regimes. For several reasons, however, this result is less conclusive than in the case of the power dispersion interaction. First, there is only one social democratic welfare regime (Sweden) that did not experience a government shift in the last election, which weakens our basis for conclusions. Second, while the interaction is significant, it is somewhat weaker than that for power dispersion; of course, "social democratic welfare regime" is a dummy that only varies between 0 and 1; the power dispersion measure varies between 0 and 5. Third, the second model does not lend support to the hypothesis. In other words, the prediction is not supported where the methodological problems associated with the dependent variable are the smallest—that is, among the four countries with both recent elections and stable governments. Dissatisfied Swedes are not significantly more prone to punish the incumbent governments when compared with dissatisfied Austrian, German, or Irish citizens.[7]

Finally, the fact that we have access only to Sweden means we cannot tell from this analysis whether the stronger effect in social democratic regimes is in turn dependent on the fact that Sweden had a social democratic, single-party government in 2002. Our hypothesis is that because of the smaller degree of historical responsibility-sharing in a social democratic welfare state, it is particularly easy for dissatisfied citizens in social democratic regimes to blame a social democratic government for poor policy outputs. Of course, this implies that the stronger effects that we have estimated for Sweden would shrink once a non–social democratic government comes to power. Interestingly, while the current analysis cannot help us further, I have previously found some support for the prediction in a longitudinal analysis within Sweden (Kumlin 2003). Specifically, Sweden had a nonsocialist government between 1991 and 1994 and, consistent with our prediction, this period was the only time between 1989 and 2002 that welfare state dissatisfaction did not reduce the probability of incumbent support. In contrast, such effects were found for both previous and subsequent Social Democratic governments.

POLITICAL TRUST

Before drawing conclusions, we have one last political orientation to analyze: general political trust. It is measured by an index adding responses to two items on "trust in politicians" and "trust in country's parliament," respectively. The index was scaled between 0 and 10 with higher values denoting more trust. Table 3.8 displays country-specific regression analyses using political trust as the dependent variable. For purposes of presentation, only the coefficients for welfare state dissatisfaction are shown, although all equations include a series of control variables.

There are two key observations here. First, welfare state dissatisfaction

TABLE 3.8
*Country-specific regression models of political
trust (unstandardized OLS coefficients).*

	$b_{welfare\ state}$ dissatisfaction
Denmark	−.24***
Greece	−.24***
Norway	−.24***
Italy	−.22***
Luxemburg	−.22***
Netherlands	−.20***
Finland	−.19***
Belgium	−.16***
Sweden	−.16***
Germany	−.15***
UK	−.13***
Austria	−.12***
Spain	−.12***
Switzerland	−.11***
Ireland	−.10***
Portugal	−.08**

*p < .10 **p < .05 ***p < .01
COMMENT: Data from the 2002 European Social Survey.
Country-specific versions of Model 1 in Table 3.9.

tends to correlate with general political distrust in all the 14 investigated countries. Second, there is considerable country variation around this large average effect. Denmark, Greece, and Norway top the effect league: in these countries, a leap from maximum welfare state satisfaction to maximum dissatisfaction is predicted by our model to bring about 2.4 units less political trust. This must be seen as quite a loss, considering the fact that the dependent variable ranges between 0 and 10. At the bottom of the table we find Portugal where the coefficient is −.08. However, the Portuguese effect is still clearly significant, both in a statistical as well as in a substantive sense.

The latter becomes clearer if we move on to Table 3.9, which offers two pooled versions of essentially the same analysis. The small difference is that Model 1 includes 13 country dummies, whereas Model 2 lets the impact of welfare state dissatisfaction vary across institutional settings. Model 1 reveals that even the dissatisfaction coefficient in Portugal is roughly at par with that of other explanatory variables—for instance, education (.14). More generally, we see that welfare state dissatisfaction has a rather strong overall negative impact on political trust (−.17). Thus, a maximum leap

TABLE 3.9
Regression model of political trust (unstandardized OLS coefficients).

	Model 1	Model 2
Welfare state dissatisfaction index (0–10)	−.17***	−.17***
Satisfaction with national government (0–10)	.37***	.37***
Negative evaluation of country's economy (0–10)	−.11***	−.09***
Life satisfaction (0–10)	.02***	.02
Negative feeling about household's income (1–4)	−.11***	−.10***
Woman	−.07***	−.07
Age	.00	.00
Education (1–7)	.14***	.15***
Income	.04***	.03
Class (reference category: Unskilled manual labor)		
Skilled manual labor	−.04	−.02
Service class 1	.22***	.23***
Service class 2	.32***	.35***
Routine nonmanual labor	.25***	.26***
Self-employed	.24***	.33***
Power dispersion	—	.17**
Social democratic welfare state	—	.40**
Welfare state dissatisfaction × Power dispersion	—	−.01
Welfare state dissatisfaction × Social democratic welfare state	—	.00
Constant	1.18***	.57**
Adjusted R-squared	.38	.38
Number of respondents	18,772	18,772

*p < .10 **p < .05 ***p < .01

COMMENT: Data from the 2002 European Social Survey. The analysis includes the 14 countries that have nonmissing values in Table 2. The dependent variable is an additive index adding responses to two items on "trust in politicians" and "trust in country's parliament," scaled between 0 and 10 with higher values denoting more trust. Model 1 also contains 13 country dummies (the coefficients of which are not displayed), whereas significance tests in Model 2 are based on cluster-corrected robust standard errors. The data are weighted according to population size.

from total satisfaction (0) to total dissatisfaction (10) is generally predicted to produce a 1.70 change along the political trust index among Western Europeans. This makes welfare state dissatisfaction the second most influential variable in the pooled model, second only to satisfaction with the national incumbent government (.36). Of course, it must once again be acknowledged that some unknown part of the covariation could well be due to a reciprocal causal process, in which already trusting citizens develop negative policy output evaluations. Unfortunately, there is currently no comparative data set with which one could analyze this particular issue. But when there is, it will tell us more about the extent to which the causal hypotheses are in fact correct.

Concentrating now on Model 2, the country variations in Table 3.8 cannot be explained by our two institutional interaction terms, the coefficients of which are basically zero. In other words, welfare state dissatisfaction tends to be equally detrimental to general political trust, regardless of how much policy-making power is dispersed, and regardless of welfare state regime. Thus, while dissatisfaction effects on state intervention support and voting are weak and highly sensitive to the institutional context, dissatisfaction seems to have a both stronger and more universal negative impact on political trust.

CONCLUSIONS

Because of the scarcity of comparative studies of welfare state dissatisfaction, this chapter has been obliged to make a number of yet-untested assumptions regarding measurement and causality. Therefore, it is important to remember that the following conclusions have a somewhat preliminary status until those assumptions are themselves tested by future empirical efforts.

We started the chapter by pitting against each other two lines of thought on how output dissatisfaction in the welfare state feeds back into the input side of the democratic process. One line predicts that widespread dissatisfaction undermines welfare states by reducing general ideological state intervention support. The other line predicts that dissatisfaction will overload the welfare state, fueling demands for even more public spending and problem solving. The models are united, however, in their prediction that dissatisfaction will undermine support for political actors and institutions.

While none of the two models comes out as a clear "winner," I would—if forced to choose—say that there is more support for the undermined-welfare-state perspective: our data predict that in social democratic welfare states with little political power dispersion, dissatisfied citizens become less supportive of state intervention but more inclined to report rightist ideological left–right self-placements. And although such institutional conditions are not simultaneously present in Europe, the results do suggest that the undermined-welfare-state perspective has an explanatory *potential*. In the absence of power-dispersing institutions, it seems, welfare state dissatisfaction *would* undermine the ideological support that European welfare states currently rest on.

In the real world, however, the explanatory potential of the under-mined-welfare state is heavily suppressed by existing institutional configurations. Because most existing European political environments tend to be rather power-dispersing, and because most European welfare states can be seen as ideological compromises rather than pure implementations of a single ideology, most Europeans do not dramatically change their ideological orientations, even when they are seriously dismayed with core welfare state outputs.

Still, the results are interesting as they tell a different story from past studies reporting *positive* effects of dissatisfaction on more specific policy and spending preferences (Edlund 2006; Johansson, Nilsson, and Strömberg 2001). If we add our findings to this research, it seems that overloading and undermining processes occur *simultaneously*, albeit at different levels of attitude abstraction. Whereas dissatisfaction overloads the welfare state with ever more demands at a concrete attitude level, this chapter suggests that it has at least a potential for undermining support at a more general level.

So we must distinguish between these levels in order to understand the political ramifications of dissatisfaction. When political discourse is focused on concrete policies and institutions, output dissatisfaction feeds back into the input process by creating more demands for specific spending. Political parties may sometimes feel a need to respond to these demands in widely salient welfare state areas that have a potential to dominate the agendas of election campaigns, and where single-issue voting may matter (examples include health care and pensions). More frequently, however, voting behavior and party competition in Western Europe are guided by more general ideological concerns. When this is the case, the results indicate that the feedback effect will be negligible in most existing countries, not really altering the parameters of electoral politics. In the few countries with very little power dispersion, we may even expect dissatisfaction to make political actors move to the right in an ideological sense.

Similar conclusions emerge from our analyses of government voting: dissatisfaction has a *potential* to hamper the electoral fortunes of incumbent governments, as evidenced by significant negative effects in four out of nine countries. However, analogous with the pattern for ideological orientations, this feedback effect is frequently suppressed by institutional configurations. Effects are weakened in liberal and conservative welfare states, as well as by power-dispersing institutional features. And, of course, such institutional environments are commonplace in Western Europe.

Finally, both the undermined-welfare-state perspective and the overloaded-welfare-state perspective predict that dissatisfaction damages general political trust. Empirically, we have seen strong evidence that this is the case in all countries. Moreover, while there is country variation in the strength of this impact, it seems rather unsystematic, at least in the sense that it cannot be explained by our institutional variables. Also, the impact is actually rather strong even at its weakest.

In conclusion, then, whereas feedback effects on ideological state intervention support and incumbent government support are both weak overall, as well as highly sensitive to the institutional context, there is a strong and universal negative impact on political trust. In other words, the dominant feedback effect of welfare state dissatisfaction is that it undermines general support for political institutions, parties, and politicians. It is the legitimacy of the democracies of Western Europe—rather than its welfare states or its incumbent governments—that will really suffer from increasing welfare state dissatisfaction.

NOTES

*I would like to thank the following individuals and groups for useful comments: Johannes Lindvall, Martin Rhodes, Edeltraud Roller, Michael Shalev, Erik Olin Wright, the other contributors to this book, and the participants in the seminar "Elections, Public Opinion, and Democracy" (VOD) at the Department of Political Science, Göteborg University.

1. Thus, they were able to draw on a theoretically more satisfying operationalization of the dependent variable, compared to the many quantitative studies that have been obliged to rely on social expenditure data. At the same time, they could include a larger number of countries than focused small-N retrenchment studies (cf. Pierson 1994; Lindbom 2001).

2. In Sweden, Johansson, Nilsson, and Strömberg (2001: Ch. 6) found that demands for increased public efforts in different public service areas have typically *decreased* over time as actual services have expanded. In seeming support of overload predictions, however, Birgersson (1975) reported the existence of a "service paradox" in Sweden. That is, evaluations of public services were more negative, and demands for more public efforts higher, in Swedish municipalities whose services were already more developed. However, in a later analysis that was also extended to the individual level, Sannerstedt (1981: 132–53) could not

find support for the service paradox. Similarly, in a Danish study, Lolle (1999) found virtually no effects at all of the level of public spending on different service areas and citizens' satisfaction with those areas (see also Johansson, Nilsson, & Strömberg 2001: 177–8)

3. France was excluded due to problematic deviations in the wording of the questions measuring welfare state dissatisfaction.

4. All the empirical analyses presented here assume that the relationship between dissatisfaction and political orientations is linear. However, empirical tests have been carried out where the impact was allowed to vary depending on the level of dissatisfaction. Such analyses revealed that very little explanatory power was gained by, for instance, splitting the dissatisfaction scale into a number of dummy variables.

5. There are two arguments for why this period should serve our purposes reasonably well. First, the index taps relatively stable political-contextual circumstances: it is unlikely that the rank-order between countries would have looked much different with more recent data. Second, because welfare state institutions tend to develop slowly over time, it can actually be seen as an advantage that the power-dispersion index covers a longer period.

6. The pooled analysis omits many of the controls previously included as these do not change any of the interpretations or conclusions.

7. I have also examined models that included the controls used previously. However, they did not have any impact on the results and conclusions of interest here.

REFERENCES

Aardal, Bernt, and Pieter van Wijnen. 2005. "Issue Voting." Pp. 192–212 in *The European Voter: A Comparative Study of Modern Democracies*, edited by Jacques Thomassen. Oxford: Oxford University Press.

Allan, James P., and Lyle Scruggs. 2004. "Political Partisanship and Welfare State Reform in Advanced Industrial Societies." *American Journal of Political Science* 48:496–512.

Baldwin, Peter. 1990. *The Politics of Social Solidarity. Class Bases of the European Welfare State 1875–1975*. Cambridge: Cambridge University Press.

Bengtsson, Åsa. 2002. *Ekonomisk röstning och politisk kontext. En studie av 266 val i parlamentariska demokratier*. Åbo: Åbo Akademis förlag.

Birgersson, Bengt Owe. 1975. *Kommunen som serviceproducent: kommunal service och serviceattityder i 36 svenska kommuner*. Stockholm: Stockholms Universitet.

Borre, Ole, and Elinor Scarbrough (eds.). 1995. *The Scope of Government*. Oxford: Oxford University Press.

Clayton, Richard, and Jonas Pontusson. 1998. "Welfare State Retrenchment

Revisited: Entitlement Cuts, Public Sector Restructuring, and Inegalitarian Trends in Advanced Capitalist Societies." *World Politics* 51:67–98.

Crozier, Michel, Samuel P. Huntington, and Joji Watanuki. 1975. *The Crisis of Democracy*. New York: New York University Press.

Edlund, Jonas. 2006. "Trust in the Capability of the Welfare State and General Welfare State Support: Sweden 1997–2002." *Acta Sociologica* 49:395–417.

Esping-Andersen, Gøsta. 1990. *The Three Worlds of Welfare Capitalism*. Cambridge: Polity Press.

Evans, Geoffrey. 1999. "Economics and Politics Revisited. Exploring the Decline in Conservative Support 1992–1995." *Political Studies* 47:139–151.

Ferrara, Maurizio, and Martin Rhodes. 2000. "Recasting European Welfare States: An Introduction." *West European Politics* 23:1–10.

Franklin, Mark N., Tom Mackie, and Henry Valen (eds.). 1992. *Electoral Change. Responses to Evolving Social and Attitudinal Structures in Western Countries*. Cambridge: Cambridge University Press.

Fuchs, Dieter, and Hans-Dieter Klingemann. 1989. "The Left-Right Schema." Pp. 203–234 in *Continuities in Political Action. A Longitudinal Study of Political Orientations in Three Western Democracies*, edited by M. Kent Jennings and Jan W. van Deth. Berlin: Walter de Gruyter.

Goul Andersen, Jørgen. 2001. "Ambivalent Values: The Value Foundations of the Universal Welfare State, Citizens' Attitudes and Potential for Change." Paper presented at the Fifth Conference of the European Sociological Association, Helsinki, August 2001.

Granberg, Donald, and Sören Holmberg. 1988. *The Political System Matters. Social Psychology and Voting Behavior in Sweden and the United States*. Cambridge: Cambridge University Press.

Holmberg, Sören. 1999. "Down and Down We Go: Political Trust in Sweden." Pp. 103–122 in *Critical Citizens. Global Support for Democratic Governance*, edited by Pippa Norris. Oxford: Oxford University Press.

Huseby, Beate M. 1995. "Attitudes towards the Size of Government." Pp. 87–120 in *The Scope of Government*, edited by Ole Borre and Elinor Scarbrough. Oxford: Oxford University Press.

Huseby, Beate M. 2000. *Government Performance and Political Support. A Study of How Evaluations of Economic Performance, Social Policy and Environmental Protection Influence the Popular Assessments of the Political System*. Trondheim: Department of Sociology and Political Science, Norwegian University of Technology (NTNU).

Inglehart, Ronald, and Hans-Dieter Klingemann. 1976. "Party Identification, Ideological Preference, and the Left-Right Dimension among Western Mass Publics." Pp. 243–273 in *Party Identification and Beyond*, edited by Ian Budge, Ivor Crewe, and Dennis Farlie. London: John Wiley.

Johansson, Folke, Lennart Nilsson, and Lars Strömberg. 2001. *Kommunal demokrati under fyra decennier*. Malmö: Liber.

Kaase, Max, and Kenneth Newton. 1995. *Beliefs in Government*. Oxford: Oxford University Press.

Kinder, Donald R., and D. Roderick Kiewiet. 1981. "Sociotropic Politics: The American Case." *British Journal of Political Science* 11:129–161.

Korpi, Walter, and Joakim Palme. 2003. "New Politics and Class Politics in the Context of Austerity and Globalization: Welfare State Regress in 18 Countries, 1975–95." *American Political Science Review* 97:425–446.

Knutsen, Oddbjørn. 1995. "Value Orientations, Political Conflicts and Left-Right Identification: A Comparative Study." *European Journal of Political Research* 28:63–93.

Knutsen, Oddbjørn. 1998. "The Strength of the Partisan Component of Left-Right Identity. A Comparative Longitudinal Study of Left-Right Party Polarisation in Eight West European Countries." *Party Politics* 4:5–31.

Knutsen, Oddbjørn, and Staffan Kumlin. (2005). "Value Orientations and Party Choice." Pp. 125–166 in *The European Voter*, edited by Jacques Thomassen. Oxford: Oxford University Press.

Kumlin, Staffan. 2003. "Politiskt ansvarsutkrävande i Sverige 1986–2002." Pp. 261–70 in *Fåfängans marknad*, edited by Sören Holmberg and Lennart Weibull. Göteborg: SOM Institute.

Kumlin, Staffan. 2004. *The Personal and the Political: How Personal Welfare State Experiences Affect Political Trust and Ideology*. New York: Palgrave-Macmillan.

Kumlin, Staffan. 2006. "Learning from Politics: The Causal Interplay between Government Performance and Political Ideology." *Journal of Public Policy* 26:89–114.

Lewis-Beck, Michael S. 1988. *Economics & Elections. The Major Western Democracies*. Ann Arbor: University of Michigan Press.

Lewis-Beck, Michael S., and Martin Paldam. 2000. "Economic Voting: An Introduction." *Electoral Studies* 19:113–121.

Lindbom, Anders. 2001. "Dismantling the Social Democratic Welfare Model: Has the Swedish Welfare State Lost Its Defining Characteristics?" *Scandinavian Political Studies* 24:171–193.

Lipset, Seymour Martin, and Stein Rokkan (eds.). 1967. *Party Systems and Voter Alignments*. New York: Free Press.

Lodge, Milton, and Patrick Stroh. 1993. "Inside the Mental Voting Booth: An Impression-Driven Process Model of Candidate Evaluation." Pp. 225–263 in *Explorations in Political Psychology*, edited by Shanto Iyengar and William J. McGuire. Durham, NC: Duke University Press.

Lolle, Henrik. 1999. *Serviceudgifter og brugertilfredshed i danske kommuner*. Aalborg: Aalborg Universitetsforlag.

Mau, Steffen. 2003. *The Moral Economy of Welfare States: Britain and Germany Compared*. London: Routledge.

Miller, Arthur, and Ola Listhaug. 1999. "Political Performance and Institutional

Trust." Pp. 204–216 in *Critical Citizens. Global Support for Democratic Governance*, edited by Pippa Norris. Oxford: Oxford University Press.

Norpoth, Helmuth. 1996. "The Economy." Pp. 299–318 in *Comparing Democracies. Elections and Voting in Comparative Perspective*, edited by Lawrence LeDuc, Richard G. Niemi, and Pippa Norris. Thousand Oaks, CA: Sage.

Norris, Pippa (ed.). 1999. *Critical Citizens. Global Support for Democratic Governance.* Oxford: Oxford University Press.

Pettersen, Per Arnt. 1995. "The Welfare State: The Security Dimension." Pp. 198–233 in *The Scope of Government*, edited by Ole Borre and Elinor Scarbrough. Oxford: Oxford University Press.

Pierson, Paul. 1994. *Dismantling the Welfare State?* Cambridge: Cambridge University Press.

Pierson, Paul (ed.). 2001. *The New Politics of the Welfare State.* Oxford: Oxford University Press.

Powell, G. Bingham, and Guy D. Whitten. 1993. "A Cross-national Analysis of Economic Voting: Taking Account of the Political Context." *American Journal of Political Science* 37:391–414.

Roller, Edeltraud. 1995. "The Welfare State: The Equality Dimension." Pp. 165–198 in *The Scope of Government*, edited by Ole Borre and Elinor Scarbrough. Oxford: Oxford.

Rothstein, Bo. 1998. *Just Institutions Matter. The Moral and Political Logic of the Universal Welfare State.* Cambridge: Cambridge University Press.

Sannerstedt, Anders. 1981. *Attityder till kommunal service.* Stockholm: Ds Kn 1981:22, Rapport 9 från kommunaldemokratiska forskningsgruppem.

Scharpf, Fritz. 2002. "The European Social Model: Coping with the Challanges of Diversity." *Journal of Common Market Studies* 40:645–667

Svallfors, Stefan. 2003. "Welfare Regimes and Welfare Opinions: A Comparison of Eight Western Countries." *Social Indicators Research.* 64: 495–520.

Svallfors, Stefan, and Peter Taylor-Gooby (eds.). 1999. *The End of the Welfare State?* London: Routledge.

Swank, Duane. 2002. *Global Capital, Political Institutions, and Policy Change in Developed Welfare States.* Cambridge: Cambridge University Press.

Taylor, Michaell A. 2000. "Channeling Frustrations: Institutions, Economic Fluctuations, and Political Behavior." *European Journal of Political Research* 38:95–134.

van der Eijk, Cees, Mark N. Franklin, and Erik Oppenhuis. 1996. "The Strategic Context: Party Choice." Pp. 332–365 in *Choosing Europe? The European Electorate and National Politics in the Face of Union*, edited by Cees van der Eijk and Mark N. Franklin. Ann Arbor: University of Michigan Press.

van der Eijk, Cees, Hermann Schmitt, and Tanja Binder. 2005. "Left-Right Orientations and Party Choice." Pp. 167–191 in *The European Voter: A Comparative Study of Modern Democracies*, edited by Jacques Thomassen. Oxford: Oxford University Press.

CHAPTER FOUR

Social Risk, Policy Dissatisfaction, and Political Alienation

A Comparison of Six European Countries

Maria Oskarson

Some people don't care about politics. In most cases, people who don't care about politics also don't engage in political action (Verba, Schlozman, and Brady 1995: 2). From a democratic perspective this is not necessarily a problem, as long as there are equal opportunities to actually engage in politics. However, if political involvement follows structural cleavages, and those who care and who don't care represent different groups in society, there is a risk that some groups are systematically underrepresented. This could be seen as a democratic problem. As stated in the final report of the APSA Task Force on Inequality and American Democracy, "American Democracy in an Age of Rising Inequality," produced by some of the most prominent American political scientists: "Citizens with lower or moderate incomes speak with a whisper that is lost on the ears of inattentive government officials, while the advantaged roar with a clarity and consistency that policy-makers readily hear and routinely follow" (APSA 2004: 2).

The political involvement of citizens is not independent of politics. As stated in Chapter 1, there are several indications that the economic development of the advanced democracies during recent decades has led to increased differences between various social groups, not only in material living conditions but also in relation to politics. This chapter presents an analysis of the relation between a vulnerable social risk position and political integration in the context of welfare state policies and retrenchments.

The relationship between economic evaluations and political support is well proven (Dalton 2004; Listhaug 1995; Miller and Listhaug 1999), so increasing economic differences between rich and poor might result in increasing social differences also in political support or trust. Lack of political support, however, does not necessarily indicate political passivity. It is sometimes claimed to imply a well-informed and "sound" skepticism toward politics. But since we also know that political interest varies with individual resources such as education and occupational status, the combination of low trust and low interest in politics is most probably overrepresented in weaker social groups. This combination, here labeled *political alienation,* is more problematic from a democratic point of view. Citizens who are politically alienated do not seek information on political matters, and even if political information reaches them anyhow, they are not receptive to the information since they do not trust the political actors. This combination of lack of interest and lack of trust is probably fertile ground for populist or extremist movements (Rydgren 2003). The concept of political alienation is presented in this chapter as a qualitative concept indicating citizens "out of reach" of the political system.

The focus of the chapter is to investigate the relationship between social risk position and political alienation in six European countries, with the hypothesis that the relationship is stronger in countries that have experienced more substantial retrenchment in their social insurance systems than other countries. How the welfare state is organized under different regimes is often claimed to matter for the political integration of weaker social groups. Here the underlying question is whether we can detect a "feedback effect" from retrenchments and increased recommodification in welfare systems, alienating the most risk-exposed groups from politics (Mettler and Soss 2004). The analysis is based on the European Social Survey 2002 (ESS 2002) presented in Chapter 1, and includes Belgium, Germany, Great Britain, the Netherlands, Norway, and Sweden.

The chapter proceeds with a presentation of the marginalization hypothesis and a discussion of retrenchments in the social insurance systems of the six countries. It then presents the definition and measurement of the dependent variable *political alienation*, followed by a discussion of the independent variables—*social risk groups*. In line with previous research, political dissatisfaction is introduced as a possible intermediate variable between social risk position and political alienation.

THE MARGINALIZATION HYPOTHESIS

In recent years much attention has been directed to decreased political trust in Western democracies (Dalton 2004; Norris 1999a). One hypothesis presented is that "increasing inequality in economic conditions may lead to growing cynicism among those at the lower end of the status ladder"(Dalton 2004: 84). The argument is that globalization processes lead to increasing social differences when citizens with lower education, "unqualified" jobs, or weak relation to the labor market bear greater costs and receive fewer benefits from changing economic conditions (Bobbio 1987), and that this social and economic marginalization would lead to political alienation in the sense of decrease in political trust (Dalton 2004; Goul Andersen and Hoff 2001). However, the consequences of post-industrialist economic development on inequality depend, of course, on how the political sphere of society and the welfare state are handling the situation.

It seems most probable that the link between increasing economic and social inequalities and political alienation (however defined) is politics in general, and welfare policies in particular. To act as a mediating link between the direct consequences of competitive market forces and the social and economic well-being of individuals is more or less the "raison d'être" for the welfare state (Esping-Andersen 1990). One related perspective on the welfare state is to regard welfare states or welfare systems in terms of "risk management" where the welfare state or system shares the responsibilities for management of risks such as poverty, ill-health, or unemployment with the individual in a fair and just way. In this perspective, the balance between individual and collective responsibility differs among various welfare states and also among different systems within a state. The structure of this sharing of responsibilities for risk management has to be seen as legitimate and reliable in delivery in order to be sustainable since the collective responsibility is generally collectively paid for through the tax system.

The social risks we have mentioned are not equally distributed; hence the dependence on "risk sharing" is unequal. Some citizens are more prepared than others to take more individual responsibility by means of their better financial as well as cognitive resources. Consequently, there is also reason to believe that the degree to which changes in the welfare systems are seen as legitimate differ among groups because of differences in ideology as well as differences in self-interest and need. When welfare systems change or "recommodify," the differences can accordingly lead to deepening cleavages between those who are "able to play by the new rules" and those who are not.

Another aspect of the welfare state is that welfare states embody and create norms about what is fair and just, and form citizens' expectations and demands (Mau 2003, 2004; Rothstein 1998; Svallfors 2003). In Chapter 1, it was stated that the norm-building capacity of the welfare state through the interaction of institutions, orientations, and cleavages formed a "moral economy," where "social transactions are grounded upon a socially constituted, and subjectively validated, set of shared moral assumptions. These background assumptions regulate which demands, needs, and entitlements are regarded as justified" (Mau 2003: 2). Support for the welfare state and specific welfare policies cannot be understood solely from a self-interest or rational perspective, nor can evaluations of actual welfare policies. It is also necessary to consider the norms about justice, entitlement, and reciprocity embedded in the design of welfare systems and welfare plans. This is the main argument in the moral economy of welfare state institutions: "The moral economy of welfare state institutions can be defined as the ongoing logic of social support for, and acceptance of, the redistributive nature of welfare provision whereby a commitment to the fate of the less well-off, the disadvantaged and people at risk is recognized" (Mau 2004: 59). But the institutional structure of the welfare states also tells us what is legitimate to expect and demand (Aarts, Macdonald, and Rabinowitz 1996; March and Olsen 1989; Mau 2004; Rothstein 1998; Soss 1999). The way in which welfare institutions are designed gives rise to different norms about what is fair and just, or unfair and unjust. In this perspective, the welfare state institutions tend to create or destroy their own moral support (Rothstein 1998). A correspondence between values (or norms), institutions, and policies is the foundation of virtually every typology of welfare states (Cox 2004), and in times of "stable policies" this learning process helps to keep up the legitimacy of the welfare systems by setting the norms.

In times of "unstable policies" on the other hand—that is, when the welfare systems are put under pressure and reformed—the very same logic might reverse the process, and the legitimacy could accordingly be open to challenge. When the dividing line between individual and collective responsibility changes, there is a risk that the legitimacy is threatened, that the system is seen as unfair. If, as previously hypothesized, the expectations and demands are stable and deep-rooted, changes might create a gap between what citizens consider "fair and legitimate" and what the welfare state actually delivers (Cox 2004; Taylor-Gooby 2004), thus leading to dissatisfaction with the actual policies presented and implemented. Policies redefining the balance can then be expected to become critical issues, when the actual policies deviate from the norms and expectations of citizens (Borre 2000; Miller 1974; Miller and Listhaug 1999).

It is furthermore plausible that the consequences of increased social and economic inequality have stronger political implications among more risk-exposed groups with low or few political resources, leading to political dissatisfaction and alienation. One outcome might be that political alienation is overrepresented in identifiable groups in society, with consequences for the representation of interests of these groups and thus for political decisions made and policies implemented. To take the argument one step further, if we can find that the probability for political alienation is linked to certain policy arrangements, the lack of political articulation of this group might lead to policies that do not take the group into consideration, and thus might bring about political alienation and even the growth of this group. This perspective applies what Suzanne Mettler and Joe Soss call "the political tradition of scholarship on mass politics," that is, to "explain mass opinion and behavior as outcomes constructed through a political process" (Mettler and Soss 2004: 3).

From the marginalization perspective, one general hypothesis for this chapter is as follows: The degree to which the consequences of increased economic competition (globalization) on economic and social inequalities lead to increased differences in political integration among groups depends on how the welfare state is organized and how welfare policies are formulated. This means that we expect a stronger correlation between social position and political integration in countries where substantial retrenchments have occurred in the welfare systems than in countries where there have been fewer changes. From the moral economy perspective, a complementary hypothesis is this: In more generous welfare states where expectations of the welfare state are high, retrenchment challenges the legitimacy of the welfare systems to a higher degree than elsewhere, leading to larger social differences in political integration.

Since the effects of supposed dissatisfaction with welfare policies might work differently or be of different magnitude under different welfare regimes, it is necessary to analyze the relationship between social position and political alienation in different welfare states. In general, when welfare regimes are discussed, the categorization encompasses a wide range of welfare programs and services as well as the main political actors (Esping-Andersen 1990). One explanation for the lack of correspondence between institutional design and normative attitudes that is sometimes found could be that actual institutional welfare design is not homogenous across different programs and services. For that reason, the analysis here follows the more specific typology of social insurance institutions presented by Korpi and Palme (Korpi and Palme 1998). The typology is based on three dimensions: basis of entitlement, benefit level principle, and whether there is employer-employee cooperation in program governance. These are highly relevant dimensions of the welfare state in relation to social risk groups and the marginalization hypothesis presented here.

Whether welfare states have actually experienced retrenchment or not is the subject for an academic debate, as is the relevance of partisan politics for retrenchment. Many studies have shown that welfare state spending has in most countries *not* decreased in recent years, thus generating conclusions about welfare state resilience as well as about the decreasing relevance of partisan politics for welfare policies (Pierson 2001). However, others claim that there are several reasons why measures based on expenditures give the wrong picture. Expenditure data do not capture structural changes such as decreased GDP growth, increased unemployment, or political changes such as reforms of the tax system (Allan and Scruggs 2004; Korpi and Palme 2003). Rather, both Allan and Scruggs, as well as Korpi and Palme, argue that the relevant data for questions of retrenchment should be based on individual entitlements and net replacement for type households or individuals (Allan and Scruggs 2004; Korpi and Palme 2003).[1] Both analyses of developments of net individual income replacement show the same pattern, as is shown in Table 4.1.

The results presented in both of the cited studies show a striking similarity. The correlation between the figures presented in the two studies is

TABLE 4.1

Comparisons of retrenchment trends in unemployment benefits and sickness insurance program (sick pay) reported by Allan & Scruggs (2004) and Korpi & Palme (2004).

Country	UNEMPLOYMENT BENEFITS		SICKNESS INSURANCE	
	Allan & Scruggs	Korpi & Palme	Allan & Scruggs	Korpi & Palme
Basic security systems				
Canada	−3.5	−13.1	−3.5	−15.4
Denmark	−20.5	−24.5	−21	−21.4
Ireland	−29.5	−34.9	−29.5	−33.5
Netherlands	−14	−13.2	−14	−14.7
New Zealand	−14	−25.0	−16.5	−34.7
Switzerland	−2.5	0	−3.5	0
Great Britain	−30.5	−39.9	−31	−43.1
USA	−10	−12.8		
Corporatist systems				
Austria	−2	−10.1	0	−4.6
Belgium	−12	−28.1	−6.5	−9.3
France	−5	−7.2	−4.5	−6.8
Germany	−3.5	−6.4	−6.5	0
Italy	0	−23.8	−6.5	0
Japan	0	−1.0	0	0
Encompassing systems				
Finland	−6	−5.0	−18	−10.3
Norway	−1	−10.0	0	0
Sweden	−14	−7.3	−11.5	−13.8
Targeted systems				
Australia	−6	−10.1	−6	−10.1
Mean	−9.67	−15.13	−10.5	−12.81
Standard deviation	9.40	11.52	9.78	13.37

COMMENT: Entries are maximum percentage differences between peak and target year, Allen & Scruggs (1999); Korpi & Palme (1995). Classification of type of social insurance institutions is from Korpi & Palme (Korpi and Palme 2003; Korpi and Palme 1998).

$r = 0.78$ for unemployment insurance, and $r = 0.87$ for sickness insurance. Both studies show a clear pattern of retrenchment for most of the selected countries.[2] Even though Table 4.1 shows considerable variation within the typologies, some patterns are discernible. The most pronounced retrenchment is found in "basic security systems" and the smallest retrenchment is found in some countries within the "state corporatist systems." Finland and Sweden, as examples of "encompassing systems," show retrenchment in parity with many other European countries. Retrenchment in Norway, the third country representing "encompassing systems," is lower than in Finland and Sweden.

	Limited retrenchment	Substantial retrenchment
Basic security systems	Netherlands	Great Britain
Corporatist systems	Germany	Belgium
Encompassing systems	Norway	Sweden

Figure 4.1. Countries selected for analysis.

From these two analyses of retrenchment over the last decade, it is possible to separate countries with substantial retrenchments in social insurance systems from those with little retrenchment. The following analysis includes six countries, two from each category of social insurance system—one that has experienced substantial retrenchment, and one that has not. Apart from these differences, the countries were chosen to be as similar as possible, which is why only Western European countries are included. The selected countries are presented in Figure 4.1.

Of countries classified as "Basic security" by Korpi and Palme, the Netherlands is chosen to represent "limited retrenchment" although this country has experienced some retrenchment according to Table 4.1. Of European countries with basic security institutions, the cutbacks are smallest in the Netherlands. That Great Britain has experienced the largest retrenchment is beyond doubt. Among state corporatist countries, Germany has experienced the smallest retrenchment of the European countries included, and Belgium the largest when both programs are considered. Among the countries with encompassing social insurance systems, Norway has experienced limited retrenchment, whereas retrenchment has been more substantial in Sweden.

In the following discussion, the relationship between political alienation and social risk position will be analyzed for these six countries, with the hypothesis that the relationship will be stronger in countries that have experienced substantial retrenchment in social insurance policies. The organization of the welfare systems as well as actual retrenchment in social insurance systems will be treated as contextual factors; we will not, of course, be able to state any firm causal relationship between actual retrenchment and individuals' relations to politics. However, irrespective of whether retrenchments have affected the actual situation of the individual respondent, we expect the public debate and the political agenda to pay more attention to social insurance systems, the position of social risk groups, and the like in countries where retrenchment policies actually have been implemented, than in countries where this has not been the case. This increased attention is expected to make more people aware of what is going on and thus react to the developments. But before starting the analysis, let us introduce and define the concept of political alienation.

POLITICAL ALIENATION

In general, the concept of political equality is restricted to the formal rights and opportunities of citizens to participate in politics. Whether citizens actually choose to participate is usually seen as an individual decision, depending on the individual's interest and resources. Studies of political participation have taught us a lot about what lies behind actual political participation and how political equality in modern democratic states is reflected in such participation (Verba, Schlozman, and Brady 1995). Most of these studies state that a central prerequisite for actual participation is some degree of political involvement or engagement. As Verba and his co-authors write, "It is hard to imagine that at least some psychological engagement with politics is not required for almost all forms of political participation" (Verba, Schlozman, and Brady 1995: 343). Political involvement could accordingly be seen as a prerequisite for democracy and for fulfillment of political citizenship.

Political involvement or engagement is generally seen as an umbrella concept, indicating the psychological and emotional "link" between the individual and politics. It could be said to point to the psychological aspects of the political citizenship and relate to the psychological feeling of being incorporated or even participating in the political sphere. Usually, political involvement is linked to interest or motivation for actual participation or the like. By political interest is usually meant "the degree to which politics arouses a citizen's curiosity" (van Deth 1989: 278). Self-reported political interest, participation in discussions of politics, media usage, and, possibly, political information are considered to be main components of the internal aspect of political involvement (Goul Andersen and Hoff 2001; van Deth and Elff 2004; Verba, Schlozman, and Brady 1995).

Variations in political interest among different social groups, as well as any increase over time within one country, is commonly explained by "push theories," that is, psychological and sociopsychological theories, stating that variations are due to different individual resources and skills. That political interest co-varies with social characteristics such as education, age, and gender is well proven (van Deth and Elff 2004; van Deth 1989; Verba and Nie 1972; Verba, Schlozman, and Brady 1995).

Variations in the level of political interest among countries, on the other hand, are often attributed to "pull theories," that is, the level of political interest in a country depends on the relevance of political and social arrangements (van Deth and Elff 2004). This means that the more interventionist politics are in daily life, the more visible and salient politics become, and political interest is thus aroused. This is supposed to explain the high degree of political interest in the Scandinavian welfare states, compared to welfare systems in other Western countries. Not the least is this the case for "weaker groups" in society, since the organization of the Scandinavian welfare state is supposed to compensate for social inequalities present elsewhere. (Goul Andersen and Hoff 2001; Rothstein 1998). Here the perspective generally used to explain differences in political involvement among countries will also be applied at the individual level—that politics also matter for explaining differences in political interest and involvement among different individuals or groups. We would claim, however, that involvement in the political sphere of society has one more dimension, namely, trust and support. One requirement for citizens to feel like participants and supporters of the system is for them to believe the political system or sphere can be trusted to treat them as participants—that is, with respect (Rothstein 1998).

In general, political trust is included in the wider concept of political support, which is theoretically closely linked to David Easton's classic work. Easton distinguished between support at three levels of political objects: the political community, the regime, and the authorities (Easton 1965); and the regime level can be further divided into principles, norms and procedures, and institutions (Dalton 2004; Easton 1975; Norris 1999b). The support (or lack of support) for these different political objects is usually seen as based either on actual performance at the level in question (evaluative or specific support) or on more generalized or affective orientations (affective or diffuse support). Specific support is naturally closely linked to actual performance and thus to whoever is incumbent. Affective support is more vague and generally seen as rooted in political socialization and values (Dalton 2004; Klingemann and Fuchs 1995; Norris 1999a).

Political trust is more closely linked to politics at the individual level than is political interest, and it is closely related to ideology or political preferences—voters tend to have more trust in the political party or the politician they have voted for than in the opposition party or candidate. This, however, could hardly explain variations in trust over time. A general conclusion from earlier research was that evaluation of policy and/or government performance was one of the strongest explanations for political support, that is, trust in politicians and in political institutions (Miller and Listhaug 1999). When there is a continuing discrepancy between the citizens' expectations and the actual policies implemented by the government, this situation might lead to growing distrust (Borre 2000; Miller 1974).

In recent studies on political trust, the opposite of political trust is usually labeled *political alienation*. The debate has been whether one should incorporate trust in government, or restrict it to trust in democracy (Borre 2000; Lockerbie 1993; Miller 1974). When political alienation is linked to the social and economic marginalization hypothesis in Dalton's book *Democratic Challenges, Democratic Choices*, it is defined in the same way as in most recent studies—as the opposite to political trust (Dalton 2004). Dalton concludes, also in line with other findings, that there is no strong relation between "lower status" (operationalized as "low education") and low trust. Rather, it is among the well-educated younger generations that he finds the decrease in trust. This finding is in line with the argument presented by Inglehart that post-materialists are demanding and distrustful citizens (Dalton 2004; Inglehart 1997).

The argument in this analysis is that political alienation includes more than lack of political trust, and that this is why the marginalization hypothesis has not found support. The concept of alienation originates from the concept of *entfremdung* used by Marx and by Weber. In political sociology, political alienation has come to refer to the opposite of "political engagement" of any kind and to include various aspects of inefficacy, apathy, cynicism, and displeasure (Citrin et al. 1975; Mason, House and Martin 1985). A general definition presented by Lane in 1962 is that "political alienation refers to a person's sense of estrangement from the politics and government of his society. . . in this sense a disidentification. It implies more than disinterest; it implies a rejection" (Lane 1962: 161). In a classic article from 1960, political alienation is discussed as a consequence of inefficacy and "involves not only apathy or indifferences but also diffuse displeasure at being powerless and mistrust of those who do wield power" (Thompson and

Horton 1960: 190). In empirical analyses, mainly from the 1970s, political alienation has come to include all sorts of aspects of the relation between citizens and politics such as low efficacy, low trust, and political apathy. All these different aspects tap into concepts that could be understood as aspects of alienation from politics, but these different aspects are multidimensional (Mason, House, and Martin 1985).

To treat political alienation as the opposite of trust does not include the involvement or participatory aspect at all, which might be misleading since lack of trust does not necessarily lead to apathy or rejection. The argument here is that the consequences of social and economic inequalities on the relationship to politics should not be restricted to incorporating only political trust. Citizens could report low political trust but still be interested in politics and be ready to participate, yet at the same time report a low level of political trust as a result of feelings of marginalization. To regard political alienation as solely a lack of engagement, apathy, or passivity is also too narrow, since apathy could be a result of trust in others to handle politics in which one still feels included. The multidimensional aspect of political alienation is vital.

In line with this argument, political alienation is explicitly treated in this study as multidimensional by combining the dimensions of trust and interest. Political alienation is used as a label for the combination of low political interest and low political trust. This two-dimensional concept of political alienation enables us to make a distinction between the "cynical" with low political trust but high political interest, and the "alienated" who report neither political trust nor interest. The post-materialistic "low trusters" found by Dalton and others tend to be highly educated and to have fairly high efficacy, even if they tend to sometimes choose unconventional political channels for participation (Dalton 2004; Inglehart 1999). The alienated, on the other hand, are much less likely to engage in any form of political participation.

Alienated, Cynical, Loyal, or Integrated

Political alienation is here seen as a two-dimensional concept for the relation between the citizen and the political sphere, including political trust alongside political interest.[3] Political interest is consequently seen as a necessary, but not sufficient, condition for involvement. The argument is that

	High political interest	Low political interest
High political trust	Integrated	Loyal
Low political trust	Cynic	Alienated

Figure 4.2.   Four types of relations to politics.

the combination of both dimensions better describes different qualities in political involvement, and that full citizen engagement builds on both interest and trust. The combination of the two dimensions forms four categories of relations between the individual citizen and the political sphere, as shown in Figure 4.2. To make a distinction from the conventional use of the term "political engagement" as political interest in a wide sense, the opposite to alienation will here be labeled "political integration," describing citizens who, by a combination of high interest and high trust, could be said to be well integrated into the political sphere of society.

The first category, the *integrated*, includes politically interested citizens who also trust politicians and political institutions. The second category, the *loyal* citizens, comprises citizens who report political trust but take a low interest in politics. The third, *cynical* citizens, are highly interested in politics, but report low trust. Finally, the politically *alienated* citizens are citizens with low interest in politics and low political trust. The combination of low or no interest in politics with low trust of political institutions and actors, here labeled political alienation, constitutes what could be termed a risk group for democracy. Citizens with low interest in politics do not seek information, and if information on political matters reaches them anyway, their low trust would lead them to disregard it. The next section addresses issues involved in measuring of political alienation, and is followed by a description of the model.

Measurement of Political Alienation

The most central variable for this analysis is, of course, the variable for political alienation. As stated previously, this variable incorporates two dimensions—interest and trust—which is why we must start with the matter of measurement. The European Social Survey 2002, on which this analysis is based, included several questions addressing political interest as well as political trust, enabling us to construct two additional indices.

Political interest is measured with an index including items on "watching news or other programs about politics on TV," "reading about politics in newspapers," "discuss politics," "how important politics is in respondent's life," and the traditional question on "subjective political interest." All items are standardized to range from 0 (low interest) to 10 (high interest), then added together and divided by five. The index thus ranges from 0, indicating no interest to 10, indicating extremely high political interest.[4] For the continuing analysis the extreme categories 0 and 1 are collapsed.

Political trust is also measured with an index. The items included here are two questions about the relations between the public and the politicians—"Do you think that politicians in general care what people like you think?" and "Would you say that politicians are just interested in getting people's votes rather than people's opinions?"—and three items on explicit trust (in the country's parliament, politicians, and the European Parliament). The European Parliament is included since in the countries under study here the EU is definitely a relevant part of the political system. The item values are added together and divided by five, giving an index ranging from 0 = no trust at all to 10 = extremely high political trust. Thus, we have an additive index constructed from five issues.[5] For the continuing analysis the extreme categories 0 and 1 are collapsed.

Political alienation is operationalized as a combination of the indices for political interest and political trust. Several strategies are possible for combining these into one variable—quantitative or qualitative. We have already presented a qualitative strategy, where the two dimensions are combined according to "low" or "high." It is not self-evident, however, how best to delineate the categories—that is, a level is not stated for *how low* political interest and political trust should be for the person reporting to be classified as alienated. A numerical cutoff point such as the numerical mid-value for all countries could, for example, lead to a situation where some citizens reporting higher political trust than most respondents in their particular country could still be classified as "alienated." In the absence of any firm theoretical argument for a certain numerical cutoff point, it would be better to make the cutoff at the *national mean* for each index, in order to control for national variations. This means that "low political interest" would be operationalized as less political interest than the average citizen in that country, and the same with political trust. This mode of categorization means that comparisons of the distributions among the four categories are

TABLE 4.2

Political alienation in four citizen categories. Mean values 1–10 where 1 indicates total integration (high political interest and high political trust) and 10 indicates total alienation (low interest and low trust).

	BASIC SECURITY SYSTEMS		CORPORATIST SYSTEMS		ENCOMPASSING SYSTEMS	
	Limited retrench- ment	*Substantial retrench- ment*	*Limited retrench- ment*	*Substantial retrench- ment*	*Limited retrench- ment*	*Substantial retrench- ment*
	Netherlands	*Great Britain*	*Germany*	*Belgium*	*Norway*	*Sweden*
Alienated	6.99	7.97	7.45	7.68	6.80	7.15
Cynics	5.73	6.57	6.40	6.24	5.62	5.83
Loyals	5.68	6.41	5.91	6.17	5.61	5.79
Integrated	4.30	4.75	4.59	4.64	4.20	4.20
Total	5.51	6.32	5.97	6.01	5.48	5.59
Difference alienated − integrated	2.69	3.22	2.86	3.04	2.6	2.95
N	1680	1392	2181	968	1606	1512

not relevant. A third option—the one to be followed here—is to construct an index of political interest and political trust. The position that these are two separate dimensions is supported by modest bivariate correlations. The two dimensions are combined in a multiplicative index for political alienation ranging from 1, the most involved, to 10, the most alienated.[6] This strategy means that only the end points of the index have a firm meaning (total involvement versus total alienation) and at the same time the ordinary least square regression is applicable. By combining the two strategies in this way, it is possible to make some comparisons of the mean values on the index across the four categories as well as among the six countries. Table 4.2 presents the mean values of the alienation index for the four qualitative categories presented—*alienated, cynics, loyals,* and *integrated*.[7] The cutoff point for the categorization is the national mean on each index.

From Table 4.2 it is clear that the four qualitative categories actually form a more or less uniform distribution since the "cynics" in all countries have a higher value on the alienation index (are more alienated) than the "loyals." It is also clear that there is some variation both among the countries and among the four categories in the mean values on the alienation index. The difference in the mean values between "alienated" and "integrated" ranges from 2.6 in Norway to 3.22 in Great Britain. There is hardly any systematic difference in the pattern among the countries classified under three different welfare systems, though there is a pattern indicating that the difference between alienated and integrated is largest in countries that have experienced substantial retrenchments (Great Britain, Belgium, and Sweden).

That the definition of political alienation used here measures something substantial in the psychological relationship between individuals and the political sphere can be validated by treating political alienation as an independent variable in relation to more firmly established measures of relation to politics. People who are here classified as politically alienated have a much lower degree of party identification than those classified as integrated, and also lower than that of the cynics and the loyals. The difference in proportions of respondents feeling closer to a certain party varies from 27 percentage points in Sweden to 36 percentage points in Germany. Political alienation is also clearly related to manifest political participation. When the participation rates in all forms of political participation (conventional as well as unconventional) are compared for the four categories, the alienated score lowest on all forms, and the integrated highest with no exceptions. For example, the differences between the two "extreme" groups in turnout at national elections varies from 6.3 percentage points in Belgium (in spite of the fact that voting is compulsory there) to 20.5 percentage points in Great Britain. The differences regarding work in organizations or associations other than political parties vary from 9 to 30 percentage points, and so on.

The first and basic question for the empirical analysis to follow is how political alienation is related to social characteristics indicating various aspects of social risks. Given that there actually is a relationship, the next question is whether this relationship can be linked to social differences in policy dissatisfaction. From the discussion about marginalization and normative expectations earlier, we expect the relation between social and economic risk and political alienation to be stronger than elsewhere in countries that have experienced substantial retrenchments in the social security programs; but we would also anticipate that encompassing welfare systems, where expectations of social security systems would likely be high, would be more vulnerable to the alienating effects of retrenchments. A final hypothesis in this area is that the impact of policy satisfaction on political alienation is of a greater magnitude in countries that have experienced retrenchment of the welfare system (that is, where the norms about the responsibility of the welfare state have been changed or debated) than in countries where the welfare systems are left more intact.

As mentioned earlier, the empirical analysis is based on the European Social Survey 2002 presented in Chapter 1 of this volume. This means that the analysis is cross-sectional, which impedes firm empirical conclusions about causality. The causal relation between social and economic characteristics and political alienation is self-evident, while the causal relation between policy dissatisfaction and political alienation is most probably recursive. However, the theoretical assumption for the present analysis is in line with previous research that policy evaluation precedes political trust (Dalton 2004; Listhaug 1995; Miller and Listhaug 1999), even though we cannot determine empirically whether this is the actual causal order. In a cross-sectional analysis we can only state if there is a relationship. But before describing the empirical testing of the full model, we shall first discuss what is meant by *social risk position*.

SOCIAL AND ECONOMIC RISK GROUPS

The retrenchments of social insurance systems discussed earlier in this chapter could be seen as a process of "rolling back" the decommodification of the welfare systems, thus increasing the market dependence of individuals. This development, sometimes labeled "recommodification," should, however, not be exaggerated. The decommodification aspect of the welfare state has not come to an end. The levels are changing rather than being abolished, as is clear from Table 4.1.

But individuals and groups still have different vulnerability to changes in income redistribution. Some groups face a greater risk of poverty or economic hardship than others, while groups with low-risk potential might have much to gain on recommodification—for example, in terms of lower taxes. The hypothesis here is that such differences are reflected in the relation to politics.

So, which groups are most exposed to risk of poverty?[8] Generally, two factors could be said to decide risk exposure in this respect: "no or very low incomes" and "no alternative way to be supported." All people who are not in full-time employment or self-employment could be seen as dependent on someone else for economic support (Baldwin 1990; Svallfors 1996). As stated previously, the unemployed and those with bad health are two obvious groups. Groups with very low market income or with low education are also exposed to economic risks (Kitschelt and Rehm 2004). Two groups generally lack market income but are still not regarded as risk groups: these are children and married women working in the home. These groups are generally seen as mainly dependent on the family rather than on the welfare state. Single parents and their children are, however, generally considered a very risk-exposed group. A common trait for all these groups is that they are more exposed than others to financial problems.

An index of social risk is constructed by adding the factors of unskilled manual labor, low education (lower secondary or lower), unemployed or permanently sick or disabled during the last seven days, employment on limited contract, being a single parent, and main source of household income from unemployment or social benefit. The index can thus range from 0 (no risk) to 6 (all six social risks).[9] The index measures the risk of financial difficulties but states nothing about how respondents actually evaluate their present economic situation. The analysis therefore includes a question on how the respondent "feels about the household income nowadays." The answers "finding it difficult" or "finding it very difficult" are collapsed to form "difficult to cope on present income." Since this is a highly subjective measure, it is related to the individual's expectation of what it means "to cope." People might adjust their expectations of living standard to their actual incomes as well as to their social class, neighborhood, and the like. From the moral economy perspective discussed previously, the expectations and norms about economic standards could also be related to the individual's expectations of the welfare state, especially if the individual is in a "risk position." For these reasons, it is necessary to also control for net household income.[10] This means that we have three different, but clearly related, aspects of social and economic risk included in the social risk position, difficulty in coping on present household income, and actual household income. The correlations between the three major independent variables for this analysis are presented in Table 4.3.

Social risk position is most clearly related to difficulty in coping on present household incomes in Germany and Belgium, the two countries

TABLE 4.3

Correlations between social risk position, difficulty in coping on present household income, and actual household income. Pearson's r.

	BASIC SECURITY SYSTEMS		CORPORATIST SYSTEMS		ENCOMPASSING SYSTEMS	
	Limited retrench- ment	Substantial retrench- ment	Limited retrench- ment	Substantial retrench- ment	Limited retrench- ment	Substantial retrench- ment
	Netherlands	Great Britain	Germany	Belgium	Norway	Sweden
Social risk position* Difficult to cope on present income	0.184**	0.131**	0.253**	0.255**	0.150**	0.155**
Social risk position* Household income	−0.365**	−0.544**	−0.408**	−0.415**	−0.374**	−0.472**
Difficult to cope on present income* Household income	−0.260**	−0.260**	−0.346**	−0.268**	−0.229**	−0.271**

Levels of significance: *** = p < 0.001. ** = p < 0.01. * = p < 0.05.

classified as "corporatist systems," while it is most clearly related to actual household income in Great Britain, where the retrenchments in the social insurance systems have been most substantial, according to the research by Palme and Korpi, and Allan and Scruggs as presented in Table 4.1. That social risk position and income are related is clear, even though the correlations must be regarded as rather low, considering the general expectation of social risk position leading to poverty. One explanation for these modest correlations is probably that the social risk index is based on the respondent's personal situation while the question on difficulties in coping on present income and the question on actual income refer to "household income." The modest correlation could also be taken as an indicator that the welfare states actually are decommodifying citizens—social risk position does not automatically lead to poverty. But still, people in what is here labeled a "social risk position" have lower incomes and greater difficulty in coping on their present household incomes than other groups in society. These groups are the most vulnerable to changes in welfare state policies in general and social insurance systems in particular. They are politically weak groups, and the expectation here is that they are politically alienated to a higher degree than other groups.

SOCIAL AND ECONOMIC RISK GROUPS
AND POLITICAL ALIENATION

We are now ready to test the base model for this chapter—the relationship between social risk position and political alienation. As discussed earlier in the chapter, a weak social position is generally related to low political interest as well as low political trust. The specified model with social risk position, difficulty in coping on present income, and actual income as main independent variables incorporates the most relevant "usual suspects" for both political interest and political trust.

The social risk index includes the respondent's education, previously stated as important for the level of political interest. The variable of coping on present income as the personal economic evaluation was put forward as an important correlate of political trust. Other variables that have been shown to correlate with political interest and/or political trust are gender and age, so these variables will also be controlled for. Since age is expected to have a nonlinear relation to political alienation, two dichotomous variables for age are used: one for "young" (below 30 years of age) and one for "old" (60 years or older). Gender and age do not by definition relate to social risk, but there are reasons to believe that social risk position might be related to the respondents' gender as well as age. Since earlier studies have shown that political trust is related to party sympathy—people tend to have a higher trust in governments and politicians they voted for or sympathize with—a control variable for whether the respondent voted for any of the government parties (or the government party in case of a one-party government) is introduced into the model.

Table 4.4 presents estimates of the relationships between social risk positions and political alienation in the six selected countries. First, the data in Table 4.4 verify that there is a clear and significant relation between social risk position and political alienation.[11] The difference between a person with no social risk and a person experiencing all six risks included in the social risk index ranges from 0.97 (Germany) to 2.25 (Sweden) on the political alienation index ranging from 1 to 10. Difficulties in coping on present household income are significantly related to political alienation only in the Netherlands and Germany. Household income, however, is also under control for social risk position as well as for the subjective evalua-

TABLE 4.4
Social risk groups and political alienation. OLS regression (unstandardized b-values).

	BASIC SECURITY SYSTEMS		CORPORATIST SYSTEMS		ENCOMPASSING SYSTEMS	
	Limited retrench-ment	*Substantial retrench-ment*	*Limited retrench-ment*	*Substantial retrench-ment*	*Limited retrench-ment*	*Substantial retrench-ment*
	Netherlands	*Great Britain*	*Germany*	*Belgium*	*Norway*	*Sweden*
Social risk index	0.232***	0.327***	0.161***	0.234***	0.266***	0.375***
Difficult to cope on present income	0.359**	−0.134	0.328**	0.146	−0.219	0.019
Household income	−0.054**	−0.065**	−0.089***	−0.097*	−0.065***	−0.064**
Gender	0.316***	0.235**	0.207**	0.209	0.012	0.004
Below 30 years of age	−0.106	−0.119	0.045	−0.138	0.161*	−0.210*
Above 60 years of age	−0.044	−0.340**	−0.368***	−0.072	−0.011	−0.478***
Voted for government parties	−0.262***	−0.417***	−0.485***	−0.115	−0.148*	−0.126
R^2	0.10	0.10	0.10	0.07	0.07	0.09
N	1367	1066	1449	543	1384	1274

Levels of significance: *** = $p < 0.001$. ** = $p < 0.01$. * = $p < 0.05$. Alienation index 1= totally integrated. 10 = strong alienation.

tion of economic difficulties significantly related to political alienation in all countries. One possible explanation of the limited additional effect of difficulties in coping on present income could be that the two aspects of risk position measure the same underlying phenomenon. However, from Table 4.3 we know that even though the social risk index and economic difficulties are not unrelated, the correlations are quite modest, which is why the results in Table 4.4 indicate that social risk position and low incomes are two essentially separate indications of a vulnerable social and economic situation. When the model is evaluated without the variables for economic difficulties and income, the b-values for social risk position are slightly higher than when they are included. This validates the conclusion of two essentially separate effects.[12] The control variables gender and age show different relations to political alienation in the six countries. In the Netherlands, Great Britain, and Germany, women are politically alienated to a significantly higher degree than men, whereas there are no gender differences in Belgium, Norway, and Sweden.

As for differences among countries in the relationship between social risk position and political alienation, the general pattern that the relationship is weaker in the encompassing welfare states does not appear in Table 4.4 but is rather the opposite. Instead, there is a clear pattern that the relationship is somewhat stronger in countries with substantial retrenchment than in the countries with the same type of welfare systems but with limited retrenchment, and the highest b-value for the relationship between social risk position and political alienation is actually found in Sweden. In other words, the analysis so far supports the marginalization hypothesis stating that the relation between social risk position and political alienation is higher in countries where there have been substantial retrenchments in the social insurance systems, regardless of how the welfare systems are organized. The results so far also support the hypothesis derived from the moral economy perspective: that encompassing welfare states where the normative expectations of the welfare state's role in risk management are highest are more vulnerable to a widening gap between expectation and actual delivery.

The next step in the analysis is to include policy dissatisfaction into the model to test the assumption that policy dissatisfaction acts as an intermediate factor between social risk position and political alienation. Policy satisfaction is here measured with an index constructed from questions of satisfaction with the present state of the economy and with how the government is doing its job as well as evaluation of the state of education and health services, respectively. This means that it incorporates specific welfare areas as well as more overarching evaluations. Unfortunately, the ESS 2002 does not include any specific questions on evaluation of social insurance systems, which is why it is not possible to isolate dissatisfaction with this policy area from other policy areas. However, it seems less plausible that the evaluations of policies regarding social insurance policies and other evaluations of both general and specific areas should differ significantly.

All four questions on policy evaluation have response scales ranging from 0 = extremely dissatisfied/extremely bad to 10 = extremely satisfied/extremely good. The items were added together, divided by four, and reversed so that the index for policy dissatisfaction ranges from 0 = extremely satisfied to 10 = extremely dissatisfied.[13] The first step in analysis is to explore the relationship between social risk position and policy dissatisfaction per se, as presented in Table 4.5.

Actual social risk position is not what matters most for policy dissatisfaction. In all six countries, it is subjective difficulty in coping on present

TABLE 4.5
Social risk and policy dissatisfaction. OLS regression (unstandardized b-values).

	BASIC SECURITY SYSTEMS		CORPORATIST SYSTEMS		ENCOMPASSING SYSTEMS	
	Limited retrench-ment	*Substantial retrench-ment*	*Limited retrench-ment*	*Substantial retrench-ment*	*Limited retrench-ment*	*Substantial retrench-ment*
	Netherlands	*Great Britain*	*Germany*	*Belgium*	*Norway*	*Sweden*
Social risk index	0.045	0.055	−0.063	0.031	0.094*	0.041
Difficult to cope on present income	0.740***	0.360**	0.634***	0.713***	0.545***	0.580***
Household income	0.009	0.030	0.055**	−0.013	−0.046**	−0.019
Gender	0.327***	0.418***	0.206**	0.177*	0.144*	0.213**
Below 30 years of age	0.264**	−0.072	−0.299**	0.105	−0.312***	−0.184*
Over 60 years of age	0.052	−0.120	−0.045	0.140	−0.050	−0.165
Voted for government party	−0.039	−0.596***	−0.348***	−0.055	−0.398***	−0.481***
R^2	0.04	0.05	0.03	0.04	0.06	0.04
N	1747	1453	1788	933	1666	1477

Levels of significance: *** = $p < 0.001$. ** = $p < 0.01$. * = $p < 0.05$. Political dissatisfaction measured with index of 4 items where 0 = very satisfied and 10 = very dissatisfied.

household income rather than risk position that is significantly related to policy dissatisfaction. Nor is the effect of social risk position channeled through economic difficulties. As discussed previously, the correlations between social risk position and economic difficulties are not strong. Consequently, when the variable for economic difficulties is left out of the model, the b-value for social risk position is still insignificant in five of the six countries. Only in Norway is there a weak but significant positive relation between social risk position and policy dissatisfaction (b = 0.094). Also worth noting are the significant gender differences—women are more dissatisfied than men in all six countries.

The next and final step in the analysis of the relationship between social risk position and political alienation is to analyze the full model, controlling for political dissatisfaction as a possible intermediate variable. From Table 4.5 we know that social risk position is not strongly related to policy dissatisfaction, but that difficulty in coping on present household income is. From Table 4.6, moreover, it is clear that policy dissatisfaction mainly has an additional effect on political alienation, separate from the effect of social risk position. Table 4.6 presents three regression models. Model 1 is

TABLE 4.6

Social risk, political dissatisfaction, and alienation. OLS regression (unstandardized b-values).

BASIC SECURITY SYSTEMS

	LIMITED RETRENCHMENT NETHERLANDS			SUBSTANTIAL RETRENCHMENT GREAT BRITAIN		
	Model 1	Model 2	Model 3	Model 1	Model 2	Model 3
Social risk index	0.232***		0.185***	0.327***		0.293***
Difficult to cope on present income	0.359**		0.134	-0.134		-0.148
Household income	-0.054**		-0.056**	-0.065**		-0.064**
Gender	0.316***	0.263***	0.224***	0.235**	0.132	0.083
Below 30 years of age	-0.106	-0.199*	-0.162	-0.119	0.046	-0.094
Over 60 years of age	-0.044	0.195*	-0.061	-0.340**	0.105	-0.270*
Voted for government party	-0.262***	-0.331***	-0.277***	-0.417***	-0.169*	-0.217*
Policy dissatisfaction index		0.320***	0.304***		0.303***	0.310***
R²	0.10	0.16	0.19	0.10	0.14	0.21
N	1367	1522	1314	1066	1207	1041

CORPORATIST SYSTEMS

	LIMITED RETRENCHMENT GERMANY			SUBSTANTIAL RETRENCHMENT BELGIUM		
	Model 1	Model 2	Model 3	Model 1	Model 2	Model 3
Social risk index	0.161***		0.164***	0.234***		0.190**
Difficult to cope on present income	0.328**		0.164	0.146		-0.019
Household income	-0.089***		-0.111***	-0.097*		-0.104**
Gender	0.207**	0.170**	0.118	0.209	0.096	0.179
Below 30 years of age	0.045	0.171*	0.160	-0.138	-0.026	-0.124
Over 60 years of age	-0.368***	-0.120	-0.357***	-0.072	0.136	-0.137

(continued)

TABLE 4.6
(continued)

CORPORATIST SECURITY SYSTEMS

| | LIMITED RETRENCHMENT | | | SUBSTANTIAL RETRENCHMENT | | |
| | GERMANY | | | BELGIUM | | |
	Model 1	Model 2	Model 3	Model 1	Model 2	Model 3
Voted for government party	−0.485***	−0.399***	−0.363***	−0.115	−0.235*	−0.106
Policy dissatisfaction index	0.161***	0.276***	0.286***	0.234***	0.348***	0.336***
R^2	0.10	0.15	0.21	0.07	0.12	0.17
N	1449	1792	1407	543	703	510

ENCOMPASSING SYSTEMS

| | LIMITED RETRENCHMENT | | | SUBSTANTIAL RETRENCHMENT | | |
| | NORWAY | | | SWEDEN | | |
	Model 1	Model 2	Model 3	Model 1	Model 2	Model 3
Social risk index	0.266***		0.240***	0.375***		0.352***
Difficult to cope on present income	−0.219		−0.336**	0.019		−0.138
Household income	−0.065***	0.025	−0.054***	−0.064**	0.263***	−0.056*
Gender	0.012		−0.015	0.004	−0.199*	−0.073
Below 30 years of age	0.161*	0.305***	0.216**	−0.210**	0.195*	−0.137
Over 60 years of age	−0.011	0.199*	−0.025	−0.478***	−0.331***	−0.475***
Voted for government party	0.012	−0.135*	−0.052	−0.126	0.320***	0.010
Policy dissatisfaction index		0.267***	0.246***			0.310***
R^2	0.07	0.12	0.15	0.09	0.12	0.20
N	1384	1454	1374	1274	1522	1197

Levels of significance: *** = $p < 0.001$. ** = $p < 0.01$. * = $p < 0.05$. Alienation index 1 = totally integrated. 10= strong alienation. Political dissatisfaction measured with index of 4 items where 0 = very satisfied and 10 = very dissatisfied.

the base model from Table 4.4 with social risk position as the independent variable. In Model 2, social risks are excluded, and policy dissatisfaction is treated as the main independent variable. In Model 3, policy dissatisfaction is added to the base model. Relevant control variables are the same in all three models.

The pattern from Table 4.4 persists also under control for policy dissatisfaction, that is, the relation between social risk position and political alienation is significant and of a relevant magnitude in all six countries. Furthermore, the relation is stronger in countries that have experienced substantial retrenchment in their social security systems, the strongest relation being found in Sweden also under control for policy dissatisfaction. The b-values for social risk position decrease somewhat when policy dissatisfaction is added to the model, but the main effect of policy dissatisfaction is, as expected, separate from social risk position. The same is the case for household incomes, which show a significant relationship with political alienation in all countries also under control for policy dissatisfaction. In the base model (Model 1) difficulty in coping on present income is significantly related to alienation only in the Netherlands and in Germany. When policy dissatisfaction is added to the model these relationships decrease and are no longer significant, indicating that the relationship between difficulty in coping economically and political alienation in these countries is at least partially channeled through policy dissatisfaction. In the other four countries, difficulty in coping is not directly related to political alienation.

This analysis has not proved that policy dissatisfaction is the mechanism between social risk position and political alienation. It does not seem to be the case that social risk groups are more dissatisfied with government policies and therefore are alienated to a higher degree than other groups. Rather, it is primarily when they actually find that coping on present income is difficult that policies are blamed, and this indicates an indirect effect between financial difficulty and political alienation.

CONCLUSIONS

This analysis has stated that there is a clear relation between social risk position and political alienation in all six countries included in the study. The marginalization hypothesis discussed and dismissed by Dalton and others does actually obtain support when political alienation is defined as the combination of low trust and low political interest rather than being restricted to low trust only. Furthermore, the relationship is stronger in welfare states that have experienced substantial retrenchment in their social insurance systems than in those with more limited experiences of retrenchment—a finding that further strengthens the marginalization hypothesis. If there is any pattern among the different modes of organization of the welfare systems, it is the opposite of what might be expected from the concept of Scandinavian encompassing welfare systems as being more integrative of weaker social groups. The relationship between social risk position and political alienation is found to be strongest in Sweden. One possible interpretation of this finding is that the expectations and norms regarding the welfare system's responsibility of "risk sharing" are so high that retrenchments give rise to feelings of disillusionment and deceit among the most risk-exposed groups and eventually lead to political alienation.

Where do these results leave us? The actual fulfillment of political citizenship requires not only legal rights but also political engagement. As a general rule in discussions of lack of political engagement, individual characteristics or lack of individual resources are always put forward as explanations. The results here point also to political explanations. What this analysis has shown is that the way the welfare state is organized—and even more important, whether it delivers what is normatively expected—has the capacity to either engage citizens in politics or to disengage them from political involvement. Politics do matter—not just individual factors. Politics has the capacity to alienate citizens.

In times when social insurance systems are under pressure in most European welfare states, this finding presents a severe challenge. The normative perception of the welfare state having the responsibility to act as a "safety net" for citizens is a deeply rooted one. To implement reforms of social insurance systems without breaking the "social contract" and consequently risking increased political alienation is not easy. What the wider consequences of political alienation might be are not for analysis here. One obvious consequence, however, is that the voices of politically alienated citizens are not heard in the established political channels and these groups risk being overlooked in political representation and in decision making. This situation is likely to increase the alienation even more and deepen the cleavage between those who are "inside" and "outside" the political sphere, laying the ground for populist or extremist political movements (Rydgren 2003).

The moral economy of welfare states might have worked as a foundation for welfare politics in times of stable or growing economies, also helping to legitimize it outside the groups most dependent on the safety net of the welfare state. But in times of retrenchment and cutbacks, the same moral economy risks generating further disillusionment with the welfare state and the alienation of citizens from politics altogether. The full consequences of such disillusionment and alienation are yet to be seen.

NOTES

1. The Korpi and Palme study is based on sickness cash insurance, work accident insurance, and unemployment insurance; it calculates net replacement rates for average wage levels for production workers from single households and four-person households with a dependent spouse. The Allen and Scruggs dataset is very similar to that of Korpi and Palme, but it does not include work accident insurance. The accuracy of basing the analysis on only the average wage level for industrial workers could be questioned since middle-class groups also might be affected by retrenchment actions such as a lowering of the maximum income replacement levels. Also, the relevance of "one-breadwinner households" could be questioned since female work participation has increased in most countries.

2. The two studies also show a clear correspondence between partisan politics and retrenchment, but this relationship is outside the focus for this study.

3. Whether political alienation is an adequate label for this combination of traits is debatable. An alternative could be to follow the terminology of Jan van Deth and use the label "disenchanted" (van Deth 1989). Another alternative could be "marginalized," the term used by Jörgen Goul Andersen for people who are not integrated in political life (Goul Andersen and Hoff 2001).

4. Cronbach's alpha = 0.702.

5. Cronbach's alpha = 0.82.

6. Pearson's r varies from 0.313 in Sweden to 0.172 in Norway. A factor analysis (varimax rotated) presents two factors—interest and trust—in the Netherlands and Sweden. In the other countries, media usage forms a third factor, related also to the variable for trust in politicians (0–10 scale). The index is constructed as the square root of (political interest index × political trust index). For this construction, the values 0 and 1 are collapsed on the political interest index and the political trust index. The index is then reversed so that 10 indicates the most alienated.

7. The political alienation index includes only respondents with valid answers on all 10 questions on which the index is constructed, explaining why the number of respondents varies. Especially for Belgium, this excludes a substantial number of respondents. The dubious strategy of replacing missing answers with the mean value is rejected since this might give more misleading results than the chosen strategy to restrict the analysis to valid answers only.

8. I do not include here risks of other kinds, such as environmental. For a wider discussion see Beck 1992.

9. There are significant correlations between "unskilled manual" and "low education" (from r = 0.34 in Belgium to r = 0.25 in Sweden) and on a lower level between "main source of income" and "unemployed or disabled last seven days." The correlations are considered low enough to see the different risks as mainly additive.

10. Income is measured by a question asking respondents to place their household income in one of 12 income categories. The variable thus ranges between 1 = extremely low income and 12 = extremely high income.

11. The analysis is based on respondents with valid answers to all questions involved. For Belgium, this lowers the number of respondents substantially, due to high internal dropout. See also Note 7.

12. The b-values for social risk position is then for the Netherlands 0.309, Great Britain 0.387, Germany 0.253, Belgium 0.296, Norway 0.307, and Sweden 0.401.

13. The mean and Cronbach's alpha for the policy dissatisfaction index are for Belgium 4.01 (0.646), Germany 6.10 (0.704), Great Britain 5.06 (0,738), Netherlands 4.79 (0.688), Norway 4.53 (0.667), and for Sweden 4.81 (0.715).

REFERENCES

Aarts, Kees, Stuart Elaine Macdonald, and George Rabinowitz. 1996. Issue Competition in the Netherlands. Paper read at Joint Sessions of the European Consortium for Political Research, Oslo.

Allan, James P., and Lyle Scruggs. 2004. Political Partisanship and Welfare State Reform in Advanced Industrial Societies. *American Journal of Political Science* 48 (3):496–512.

APSA. 2004. American Democracy in an Age of Rising Inequality. Task Force on Inequality and American Democracy, American Political Science Association.

Baldwin, Peter. 1990. *The Politics of Social Solidarity. Class Bases of the European Welfare State 1875–1975.* Cambridge: Cambridge University Press.

Beck, Ulrich. 1992. *Risk Society: Towards a New Modernity.* London: Sage.

Bobbio, Norberto. 1987. *The Future of Democracy.* Minneapolis: University of Minnesota Press.

Borre, Ole. 2000. Critical Issues and Political Alienation in Denmark. *Scandinavian Political Studies* 23 (4):285–309.

Citrin, Jack, Herbert McClosky, J. Merrill Shanks, and Paul M. Sniderman. 1975. Personal and Political Sources of Political Alienation. *British Journal of Political Science* 5 (1):1–31.

Cox, Robert Henry. 2004. The Reconstruction of the Scandinavian Model: Ideas, Institutions and Welfare Reform. Paper read at Annual Meeting of the American Political Science Association 2–5 September, Chicago.

Dalton, Russell J. 2004. *Democratic Challenges, Democratic Choices. The Erosion of Political Support in Advanced Industrial Democracies.* Oxford: Oxford University Press.

Easton, David. 1965. *A Framework for Political Analysis.* Englewood Cliffs, N.J.: Prentice-Hall.

Easton, David. 1975. A Re-Assessment of the Concept of Political Support. *British Journal of Political Science* 5:435–457.

Esping-Andersen, Gøsta. 1990. *The Three Worlds of Welfare Capitalism.* Cambridge: Polity Press.

Goul Andersen, Jørgen, and Jörgen Hoff. 2001. *Democracy and Citizenship in Scandinavia.* New York: Palgrave.

Inglehart, Ronald. 1997. *Modernization and Postmodernization. Cultural, Economic, and Political Change in 43 Societies.* Princeton, N.J.: Princeton University Press.

Inglehart, Ronald. 1999. Postmodernization Erodes Respect for Authority, but Increases Support for Democracy. In *Critical Citizens. Global Support for Democratic Governance,* edited by P. Norris. Oxford: Oxford University Press.

Kitschelt, Herbert, and Philipp Rehm. 2004. New Social Risk and Political Preferences. Paper read at international conference of Europeanists organized by the Council for European Studies, March 11–13, Chicago.

Klingemann, Hans-Dieter, and Dieter Fuchs, eds. 1995. *Citizens and the State.* Oxford: Oxford University Press.

Korpi, Walter, and Joakim Palme. 2003. New Politics and Class Politics in the Context of Austerity and Globalization: Welfare State Regress in 18 Countries, 1975–95. *American Political Science Review* 97 (3):425–446.

Korpi, Walter, and Joakim Palme. 1998. The Paradox of Redistribution and Strategies of Equality: Welfare State Institutions, Inequality, and Poverty in the Western Countries. *American Sociological Review* 63 (5):661–687.

Lane, Robert E. 1962. *Political Ideology. Why the American Common Man Believes What He Does.* New York: Free Press.

Listhaug, Ola. 1995. The Dynamics of Trust in Politicians. In *Citizens and the State,* edited by D. F. Hans-Dieter Klingemann. Oxford: Oxford University Press.

Lockerbie, Brad. 1993. Economic dissatisfaction and political alienation in Western Europe. *European Journal of Electoral Research* 23 (3):281–293.

March, James G., and Johan P. Olsen. 1989. *Rediscovering Institutions. Organizational Basis of Politics*. New York: Free Press.

Mason, William M., James S. House, and Steven S. Martin. 1985. On the Dimensions of Political Alienation in America. *Sociological Methodology* 15:111–151.

Mau, Steffen. 2003. *The Moral Economy of Welfare States. Britain and Germany Compared*. London: Routledge.

Mau, Steffen. 2004. Welfare Regimes and the Norms of Social Exchange. *Current Sociology* 52 (1):53–74.

Mettler, Suzanne, and Joe Soss. 2004. The Consequences for Public Policy for Democratic Citizenship: Bridging Policy Studies and Mass Politics. *Perspective on Politics* 2:55–73.

Miller, Arthur. 1974. Political Issues and Trust in Government: 1964–1970. *American Political Science Review* 68 (3):951–972.

Miller, Arthur, and Ola Listhaug. 1999. Political Performance and Institutional Trust. In *Critical Citizens. Global Support for Democratic Governance*, edited by P. Norris. Oxford: Oxford University Press.

Norris, Pippa, ed. 1999a. *Critical Citizens. Global Support for Democratic Governance*. Oxford: Oxford University Press.

Norris, Pippa. 1999b. Introduction: The Growth of Critical Citizens? In *Critical Citizens. Global Support for Democratic Governance*, edited by P. Norris. Oxford: Oxford University Press.

Pierson, Paul. 2001. Coping with Permanent Austerity. Welfare State Restructuring in Affluent Democracies. In *The New Politics of the Welfare State*, edited by P. Pierson. Oxford: Oxford University Press.

Rothstein, Bo. 1998. *Just Institutions Matter. The Moral and Political Logic of the Universal Welfare State*. Cambridge: Cambridge University Press.

Rydgren, Jens. 2003. *The Populist Challenge: Political Protest and Ethnonationalist Mobilization in France*. New York: Berghahn Books.

Soss, Joe. 1999. Lessons of Welfare: Policy Design, Political Learning, and Political Action. *American Political Science Review* 93 (2):363–380.

Svallfors, Stefan. 1996. *Välfärdsstatens moraliska ekonomi. Välfärdsopinionen i 90-talets Sverige*. Umerå: Boréa.

Svallfors, Stefan. 2003. Welfare Regimes and Welfare Opinions: A Comparison of Eight Western Countries. *Social Indicators Research* 64:495–520.

Taylor-Gooby, Peter. 2004. Open Markets and Welfare Values. Welfare Values, Inequality and Social Change in the Silver Age of the Welfare State. *European Societies* 6 (1):29–48.

Thompson, Wayne E., and John E. Horton. 1960. Political Alienation as a Force in Political Action. *Social Forces* 38 (3):190–195.

van Deth, Jan. W. 1989. Interest in Politics. In *Continuities in Political Action*, edited by K. M. Jennings and J. W. van Deth. Berlin: Walter de Gruyter.

van Deth, Jan W., and Martin Elff. 2004. Politicisation, Economic Development and Political Interest in Europe. *European Journal of Electoral Research* 43:477–508.

Verba, Sidney, and Norman H. Nie. 1972. *Particiaption in America: Political Democracy and Social Equality*. New York: Harper & Row.

Verba, Sidney, Kay Lehman Schlozman, and Henry E. Brady. 1995. *Voice and Equality : Civic Voluntarism in American Politics*. Cambridge, Mass.: Harvard University Press.

CHAPTER FIVE

The Relationship between Public Service Dissatisfaction and Political Action
Does Institutional Design Matter?

Maria Pettersson

A number of social scientists acknowledge today that the design of an institution has important consequences, both on the functioning of the institution itself as well as on citizens' preferences and actions (see for example Schneider & Ingram 1993: 79; Schneider & Ingram 1997; Rothstein 1996; Mau 2003).* But the actual democratic effects that different institutional arrangements really have is still an underdeveloped area of research (Mettler & Soss 2004). In short, we possess knowledge about the way institutions matter for various kinds of policy output, and we also know a great deal about people's opinions about the welfare state and welfare state output. But the connection between the two—that is, the interplay between institutional theory and public opinion studies—demands more attention.

As discussed in the first chapter of this volume, the changing nature of welfare states can be traced to changes in decision-making structures and stratification patterns. The changes in decision-making structures are characterized by simultaneous downward and upward shifts in political power, where both the subnational levels and the European Union have gained power and responsibilities. Together, these changes have altered the conditions for citizens' political involvement and participation (see also Norris 2002: 193–195). Today we are witnessing the way transparency declines in political decision making and how what is usually labeled "traditional political involvement," such as being a party member, declines while informal and issue-specific ways to influence politics are on the increase. These informal and issue-specific actions also highlight yet another development: the growing importance of government output or outcome as a basis for citizens' political actions (Goul Andersen & Hoff 2001; Togeby et al. 2003).

Together, then, these developments make it highly important to explore more closely the relationship between citizens' evaluations of welfare state policies, or public service output, and political action and how this relationship differs among various institutional arrangements. The core argument, as the introductory chapter stated, is that just as some institutional settings tend to make certain preferences more likely, some institutional settings may make political action a more or less probable outcome of dissatisfaction. But which are these institutional settings and how can their effect be analyzed systematically?

The welfare regime typology developed by Esping-Andersen (1990) is the usual way to compare countries when measures of welfare state output are the heart of analysis. This chapter, however, also presents an alternative method, comparing not only welfare states but also welfare state institutions. A wide range of criticism has been directed against the regime typology concerning matters such as whether decommodification should be the major criterion, whether the typology neglects change, or whether the regime types should be considered ideal types or "real types." Other authors have tried to develop the regime concept by adding new categories (Mau 2003).[1] The shortcomings of the regime typology are also evident when studying individual political behavior—it has been difficult to empirically establish attitude patterns according to regime clusters (Svallfors 2003). A more fruitful way to analyze the impact of welfare state institutions on citizens' political life is to shift, or at least supplement, the level of analysis from regimes to institutions *within* a welfare state, since the institutional design of welfare state institutions and programs also differs (Schneider & Ingram 1993; Schneider & Ingram 1997; Soss 1999; 2002; Mettler 2002b; Mau 2003). Steffen Mau expresses this view very clearly: "It is also sometimes misleading to treat the welfare state as one single object and not to differentiate between distinct policy sectors. Looking at particular policy areas and their variations seems to be more promising for the understanding of the policies and politics of welfare" (Mau 2003: 59). Therefore, it is important to include both institutional levels in order to investigate both between-country differences and within-country differences regarding institutional design.

The aim of this chapter is to explore the relationship between public service evaluations and citizens' political action. To be more specific, we first explore whether welfare state dissatisfaction is related to political action by comparing a number of countries to determine whether regimes differ. Second, we investigate whether service evaluations of Swedish public schools and Swedish health care have different effects on political actions aimed at these two institutions, and to what extent these effects can be ascribed to differences in institutional design between the two public service areas. By comparing two welfare state institutions within Sweden, we can examine more closely the institutional mechanisms at play in the relationship between policy evaluations and political action.

To answer these two research questions, two different datasets are used. To compare countries, we use data from the 2002 European Social Survey (ESS). To perform the comparison between Swedish public schools and health care, a regional survey from western Sweden is used.

The dependent variable in this study is political action. By political action we mean actions taken by citizens to influence political outcomes (Brady 1999; Teorell 2003). In other words, action is taken to express demands, the target being any political outcome (Teorell 2003). In this definition, everything from voting to petition signing and political consumerism can be included. The definition gives us flexibility when we move between the empirical levels—that is, from the country comparisons to the comparison of public service areas—since our dependent variable changes from general political action to welfare state–targeted political action. However, we use this definition in a more narrow sense than in its original since we exclude activities such as voting, boycotts, and illegal protests. We are interested in how welfare state dissatisfaction might be related to other forms of political action than voting, which takes place only within certain intervals, but we exclude political consumerism and illegal activities. Also, following our definition of political action, the actions must be taken outside the welfare state institution and also be real actions to be counted, thereby excluding activities such as contacting staff and having political discussions.

The analytic tool to be used when comparing institutions is called *institutionalized citizen empowerment* (Hoff 1993; Kumlin 2004). Empowerment can be measured in various ways, typically means-tested versus non-means-tested, degree of discretionary power, and exit options (Soss 1999; Mettler 2002a; Campbell 2003; Kumlin 2004). The advantage of using institutionalized citizen empowerment as a tool when examining the impact of institutional design is that it can be transferred easily between contexts. The same dimensions of institutional design are likely to be found in more than one welfare state, which makes comparisons both within and among welfare states possible. Besides these more explicit forms of design, an underlying dimension also structuring the effects of institutions is their societal interest base. Just as policies and institutions tend to reproduce themselves and create interests on the elite level (Pierson 1993), they also create interests on the mass level, and this affects citizens' political preferences and political actions.

Several empirical studies that have included aspects of institutional design to explain citizens' political behavior show support for the idea that differences in institutional design—that is, degree of institutionalized citizen empowerment—are an important explanation of citizens' (users' and clients') political trust, sense of political efficacy, and level of political participation (Petersson, Westholm, & Blomberg 1989; Petersson et al. 1998; Soss 1999; Goul Andersen & Hoff 2001; Campbell 2003; Kumlin 2004). A common feature among these studies, except for Goul Andersen and Hoff, is that they are single-country studies, several having been conducted within the American context only. In this chapter, comparisons will be made on two levels: comparisons of the impact of welfare state dissatisfaction among countries and among public service areas within one country.

The next section of this chapter provides a brief overview of research on effects of policy dissatisfaction on political behavior and research on political action. This is followed by the first empirical section, where we discuss and empirically test the regime hypothesis concerning the relationship between welfare state dissatisfaction and political action. The second empirical section discusses and tests the importance of empowerment in Swedish public schools and health care regarding the effect of public service dissatisfaction on welfare state–related political action. The chapter ends with conclusions about the empirical work and a discussion of the progress made in understanding how institutional design matters for individuals' political behavior.

DISSATISFACTION AND POLITICAL ACTION

Citizens' evaluations of government output affect their political opinions. Studies of economic voting, focusing on citizens' evaluations of the economy in general as well of their personal economy and its impact on voting, have been conducted for some decades (two well-known studies are Kinder & Kiewiet 1981; Lewis-Beck 1988). Also, several studies have investigated the relationship between economic evaluations and political trust or confidence in political institutions (Listhaug 1995; Holmberg 1999; McAllister 1999; Huseby 2000). A general finding is that negative evaluations of government economic performance have negative effects on citizens' political trust.

During the late 1990s, scholars began to expand the number of policy areas taken into account and to investigate the effects of other areas of government output on voting and political support. An important conclusion from these studies is that not only does the economy matter for individuals' political preferences, but so do evaluations of areas such as public service. Negative evaluations of social policy output lead people to develop feelings of political distrust and render them less inclined to support the governing party (Huseby 2000; Kumlin 2004). The politics of the welfare state cannot be neglected when one is trying to understand citizens' political preferences—an argument, as we will show, that is equally valid when talking about how and when citizens take political action.

However, it is old news that there is a connection of some kind between policy evaluations and political participation. Although the assumptions about the order of causality can be criticized, many studies have taken a similar perspective to the one used in this chapter, that is, that policy dissatisfaction spurs political action (Farah, Barnes, & Heunks 1979; Lyons & Lowery 1989; Petersson et al. 1998; Goul Andersen & Hoff 2001; Dalton 2002). Starting with the political action study, Farah, Barnes, and Heunks (1979) found supporting evidence of policy dissatisfaction having a strong positive effect on protest participation,[2] but a limited effect on traditional or conventional political participation. Strong effect means that the relationship between dissatisfaction and protest potential was found in all the five countries analyzed—the Netherlands, Great Britain, the United States, Germany, and Austria—while a positive relationship between dissatisfaction and conventional participation was found in the Netherlands and the United States only (Farah, Barnes, & Heunks 1979).[3] Comparing the United States, Great Britain, Germany, and France, Russel Dalton (2002) found that citizens dissatisfied with government performance, measured as their satisfaction with the way democracy works, were only slightly more inclined to protest than satisfied citizens. Interestingly, political dissatisfaction proved to have greater effect on protest participation than on conventional participation in all four countries (Dalton 2002).

Moving to a more local context, the Lyons and Lowery (1989) study of two American municipalities also found some support for the hypothesis that dissatisfaction with local public service, measured as a combination of retrospective and present evaluations, had a positive effect on local political action such as contacting officials, signing petitions, and attending meetings (Lyons & Lowery 1989).

The relationship between dissatisfaction and political participation has also been investigated in the two Swedish Citizen Studies (Petersson et al., 1989; Petersson et al. 1998). The aim was to investigate attempts made by citizens to influence their everyday situation, and several citizen roles were included: as a homeowner/renter, as a patient or next of kin, as a parent of small children, as a parent of schoolchildren, as a student, as employed, and finally as unemployed. According to the authors, being able to exert influence is a way for the citizen to exercise power, to become empowered. However, if a citizen dissatisfied with service provision does not take any action to exert influence, the citizen feels powerless. Although this study measures dissatisfaction with "circumstances in your child's school" or "circumstances in the care of you/your next of kin" and thereby emphasizes personal experiences and not policy in general, important lessons can be learned. First, not all citizens take action as a consequence of dissatisfaction. Parents of small children and schoolchildren are more inclined to take action to bring about improvements than are patients and the unemployed. Regarding patients and the unemployed, the authors find patterns of powerlessness, that is, that perceived dissatisfaction with one's situation in these two citizen roles is translated into inaction rather than into any attempt to improve circumstances (Petersson et al. 1998, chapter 2).

The Swedish Citizen Study has also been compared with the Norwegian and Danish counterparts (Goul Andersen Hoff 2001). The comparative study of the Scandinavian Citizen Studies also extends the analysis regarding user participation by taking institutional design into account. Thus, this study can be seen as an attempt to bridge traditional mass opinion studies with an institutional perspective, something this chapter will develop even further. Goul Andersen and Hoff characterize different public service institutions according to their degree of voice opportunities (i.e., formal mechanisms of user influence). Comparable data among the three Scandinavian countries can be found regarding health care, schools, and child care. All three institutions are labeled high voice opportunities and fairly good exit opportunities. The two institutions identified as having bad exit opportunities are present only in the Danish case data (employment office and tax authorities). Dissatisfaction with health care, schools, and child care does affect political action, but the authors also find that satisfied citizens try to influence matters. One interpretation of the effects of institutional design is that formal mechanisms of user influence should lead to a stronger relationship between dissatisfaction and attempts to influence. In general, Denmark takes a leading position regarding institutionalized voice opportunities in all three public service areas; Sweden is second and Norway last. Goul Andersen and Hoff also found empirical evidence supporting this, that is, Danish parents try to exert influence to a higher extent than do Swedish and Norwegian parents (Goul Andersen & Hoff 2001).

In sum, previous research establishes that there is indeed a relationship between welfare state–related output evaluations and citizens' political participation. This research also helps to point out important predictors of political participation. But the question, "Under what institutional circumstances does this relationship appear?" has not been investigated to the same extent.

A REGIME PATTERN?

The first empirical question to be answered is whether there is any relationship at all between welfare state dissatisfaction and political action, and if so, can we trace any regime patterns? There are numerous ways to classify welfare regimes, all originating from Esping-Andersen's three welfare regimes based on the level of decommodification in welfare states. Esping-Andersen defines decommodification as "the degree to which individuals, or families, can uphold a socially acceptable standard of living independently of market participation" (Esping-Andersen 1990: 37).

One can question the relationship between level of decommodification and actual service delivery, and in the long run why the type of regime should have anything to do with what citizens think about welfare state output. But taking into consideration that decommodification both embraces the scale of provision and the delivery of provision, the case becomes clearer; this means that welfare states also encapsulate different norms about welfare provision that are likely to influence attitudes about welfare and welfare states in general (see Mau 2003 for a similar argument). Despite its shortcomings, the regime typology is the most developed tool we have to compare welfare states on a country-by-country basis. It provides us with a somewhat blunt but still usable tool for measuring institutional variation.

As mentioned earlier, much criticism has been directed against the division of welfare states into social democratic, conservative, and liberal clusters; there have also been numerous developments of this categorization (again Mau 2003: 58–60 provides a good overview). Each development becomes the target of additional criticism. However, there seems to be some consensus that European welfare regimes should be classified into four different categories: social democratic, conservative, liberal, and Mediterranean regimes (Leibfried 1992: 37; Bonoli 1997).[4]

The countries chosen for this analysis are all ESS-participating EU countries, except France (due to data problems) and Luxembourg (as it is an outlier and is hard to classify as belonging to a welfare regime). This means that we are left with 13 countries. To this group, Norway has been added. In sum, then, the analysis is performed for 14 different countries:[5] Denmark, Finland, Norway, and Sweden belong to the social democratic regime cluster. Austria, Belgium, Germany, and the Netherlands are conservative regimes. Great Britain and Ireland are liberal welfare states; and Greece, Italy, Portugal, and Spain form the Mediterranean cluster (Leibfried 1992; Bonoli 1997).

The dependent variable in the following analysis consists of a political action index based on a question on political participation in the ESS 2002 survey: "There are different ways of trying to improve things in [Country] or help prevent things from going wrong. During the last 12 months, have you done any of the following?" Ten different participation forms are mentioned and out of those, four were chosen for this study: contacted a politician, government, or local government official; worked in a political party or action group; signed a petition; and took part in lawful demonstration. Since the other forms of participation (worked in other organization; wore campaign badge; boycotted products; bought products for political, ethical, or environmental reasons; donated money; and engaged in illegal protest activities) tap voting-related behavior, political consumerism, and illegal activities, they were defined as less interesting for the purposes of this study.[6] A political action index was developed using the four remaining action forms.

According to research on political participation, one should distinguish between different modes of participation, since the basis or costs and benefits of, for example, party work and demonstrating differ (Verba & Nie 1972). This means that the explanations for why people join political parties or take part in demonstrations are different. In the present study, we mix citizen-initiated contacts with cooperative activity, or in other words, we mix party activity, contacting officials, and protest activity (see further Verba & Nie 1972: chapter 2; Teorell 2003). The main reason for this choice is that we do not have any hypotheses on how dissatisfaction could affect modes of political action differently. Also, to create these modes or dimensions of participation, we need more than one indicator for each mode. ESS 2002 provides, for example, only one item on contacting officials and on party activity, which makes it hard to create an index separating different modes of action.

Although the perspective of political action used here corresponds well with previous research, there is still one problem that needs attention: Citizens take political action for many reasons, and issues dealing with the welfare state comprise just one probable area. Even though welfare protests have been seen in many European countries, action can be taken in other political areas such as environment, war, refugees, world trade, and so on. Of course, this problem always arises in measuring political behavior. If political trust were the dependent variable, a similar argument could have been made. But we have more knowledge of the relationship between policy evaluations and, say, political trust (see the section "Dissatisfaction and Political Action"). Previous research linking welfare dissatisfaction and political actions has often used a more precise dependent variable, taking the target of citizens' political actions into account (Petersson et al. 1998; Petersson et al. 2002; Hoff 1993; Goul Andersen & Hoff 2001). That the measure of political action used in this empirical part does not distinguish between what citizens act against should be kept in mind.[7]

The independent variable used in this first empirical part of the study is welfare state dissatisfaction. This variable consists of an index measuring citizens' evaluations of education and health policy. The questions asked are: "Please say what you think about the state of education in [Country] nowadays" and "Please say what you think about the state of health services in [Country] nowadays." Both response scales run from 0 (extremely bad) to 10 (extremely good). In constructing the welfare state dissatisfaction index, the order of answering categories was first reversed: 0 indicates satisfaction and 10 dissatisfaction. The index was also divided by 2 to keep the 0 to 10 range.[8]

Besides the main actors—welfare state dissatisfaction and political action—a number of control variables need to be included. From previous research we know that level of education is one of the most important explanations of political action (Verba, Schlozman, & Brady 1995; Goul Andersen & Hoff 2001; Norris 2002). Moreover, we know that citizens do not participate at the same rate during different life stages. This means that age is an important control variable. But since the relationship between age and action is curvilinear, age dummies representing different age groups are included instead of the continuous age variables (Norris 2002; Pettersson & Ribbhagen 2003). Ideology is a third important control variable to include. Ideology may have an impact both on evaluations and on levels of political action. For example, citizens to the left are more welfare-friendly (Holmberg & Oscarsson 2004) and take protest action more than citizens with liberal or conservative ideology (Dalton 2002: 67, 73). Class is included as a resource variable taking into account level of welfare dependence. Working-class people show higher support for the welfare state in general and are also more dependent on welfare arrangements (Svallfors 2004). To be able to determine the effect of each class group, dummy variables are used. Finally, gender is used to control for the known relationship of somewhat lower political action among women than men (Norris 2002; Verba & Nie 1972; Verba, Schlozman, & Brady 1995).

On the basis of previous research, a possible outcome could be that the effect of welfare state dissatisfaction on political action would be larger in social democratic welfare regimes than in others. Citizens in social democratic welfare states support their welfare state to a higher extent because universal programs create large interest groups and hence produce self-interest to support the programs they are dependent on. Also, the design of a social democratic welfare state is more empowering compared to other welfare regimes (Goul Andersen & Hoff 2001; Svallfors 2002) due to the high degree of universal solutions. Svallfors (2002: 199) argues that high degree of *universalism* minimizes the degree of bureaucratic discretion, which in turn creates higher support for welfare services.

But given previous research, it is also plausible to expect greater differences within than between clusters of regimes (Svallfors 2003). Also, as discussed above, the problem of measuring political action should not be neglected. Since our aim is more explorative, we will not present any formal hypothesis test. Instead, the objective with this first analysis is primarily to explore whether there is any effect of welfare state dissatisfaction on political action in the 14 countries, and whether any regime differences can be detected at all. If patterns can be detected, despite the problems raised, interesting conclusions on the institutional design at the regime levels can be drawn.

Table 5.1 reveals that evaluations of government performance on education and health services have a weak, but significant, bivariate effect on political action among citizens in Austria, Belgium, Finland, Germany, Great Britain, Ireland, Spain, and Sweden—in 8 of the 14 countries. In general, although these particular effects are significant, they are quite modest, ranging between .02 (Germany) and .07 (Spain). When education, age, left–right ideology, class, and gender are included in the analysis, the initial weak relationship between welfare state dissatisfaction and political action holds in 6 of the 8 countries: Belgium, Finland, Great Britain, Ireland, Spain, and Sweden. In Italy and Norway, the effect of welfare state dissatisfaction on political action becomes significant at the 90 percent level in the multivariate model. In the full model, the effect of welfare state dissatisfaction varies between .02 (Sweden) and .05 (Spain). The total effect on political action if a citizen moves from Very Satisfied to Very Dissatisfied is between .20 and .50. Thus, the difference in political action between a satisfied and a dissatisfied citizen is small in all countries, and the predicted level of political action for a very dissatisfied citizen does not exceed the threshold 1, indicating that one type of action has been taken.[9]

Of the included control variables, education proves to be an important explanatory factor in all 14 countries. Left–right placement has a significant effect in all countries but Portugal. The more to the right, the lower is the level of political action.[10]

Turning to the question on regime differences, no real tendency can be discovered. The relationship between welfare state dissatisfaction and political action exists in all four regime clusters but may be slightly higher in liberal regimes and slightly less in conservative regimes. A significant and controlled relationship between welfare state dissatisfaction and political action exists in two out of two liberal regimes, in one out of four

TABLE 5.1
Effects of welfare state dissatisfaction on political action in 14 countries (OLS regression).

| | Bivariate model, dependent variable: Political Action Index (0–4) | | | | Multivariate model, dependent variable: Political Action Index (0–4) | | | |
| | *b Welfare State Dissatisfaction* | | | | *b Welfare State Dissatisfaction* | | | |
	constant	*Index (0–10)*	R^2	*N*	*constant*	*Index (0–10)*	R^2	*N*
Conservative regimes								
Austria	.60***	.03**	.01	1631	.81***	.02	.08	1631
Belgium	.58***	.04**	.004	1258	.47***	.04**	.06	1249
Germany	.50***	.02**	.002	2331	.82***	.01	.08	2331
Netherlands	.46***	−.00	.00	2019	.27**	.00	.07	2019
Liberal regimes								
Great Britain	.52***	.04***	.01	1758	.07	.03***	.08	1758
Ireland	.53***	.04***	.01	1465	.78***	.03**	.05	1465
Mediterranean regimes								
Greece	.33***	.01	.00	1487	.38**	.01	.03	1487
Italy	.35***	.03	.004	747	−.18	.04*	.13	747
Portugal	.26**	.01	.00	1030	.77***	.00	.07	1030
Spain	.32**	.07***	.02	1061	.71**	.05***	.12	1061
Social democratic regimes								
Denmark	.57***	.02	.001	1280	.80***	.01	.06	1280
Finland	.49***	.03**	.002	1787	.54***	.03**	.07	1787
Norway	.74***	.01	.00	1842	.64**	.03*	.08	1842
Sweden	.61***	.03**	.003	1730	.90***	.02**	.06	1730

COMMENT: ***p≤.01 **p≤.05 *p≤.10. The OLS regressions were performed in each country separately. A design weight was used to account for different probabilities of selection. The regression was performed with robust standard errors. The dependent variable *Political action index* consists of four different actions: contacted politician or government official, work in political party or action group, sign petition, and demonstration. The independent variable, *Welfare state dissatisfaction index*, measures respondents' evaluations of "state of education" and "state of health services" and ranges from 0 (extremely good) to 10 (extremely bad). The control variables in the multivariate model are education, age, left–right ideology, class, and gender. The coefficients have been excluded from the table presentation in order to save space. Complete tables can be found in the Appendix, Table 5.A1.
SOURCE: European Social Survey (ESS) 2002.

conservative regimes, in three of four social democratic regimes, and in two of four Mediterranean countries. Thus, the relationship between dissatisfaction and political action is both present and absent in all regime types.

However, if we take a step back and think about the features in each of these regime types, a different pattern would have been more plausible. To be more precise, a result indicating that the relationship is more common in social democratic regimes would have been more probable; it is generally assumed that citizens in social democratic regimes are empowered to a larger extent, and there are notions that welfare states with more universal solutions generate larger support for the welfare state than other regimes. Since the relationship between dissatisfaction and political action is insignificant in 6 of the 14 countries, and weak in 8 of the chosen countries, no coherent conclusions can be drawn on the usability of the regime typology in understanding cross-national differences in welfare state–related attitudes and behaviors.

These results can have two explanations. The first one is that even though welfare regimes structure some political behavior, they evidently do not structure citizens' political actions. The second explanation of these poor results lies in the measures we have used. In ESS, political action is measured in a too general and unspecific way. We cannot come any closer than this using comparative data. The conclusion, however, only fuels my principal argument: that we need to take the institutional design of different welfare state services into account. The next section takes this chapter one level further by developing the concept of institutionalized citizen empowerment and also by more explicitly testing the impact of institutional design on the relationship between dissatisfaction and political action in Sweden. By comparing the same public service areas as in ESS (school and health care), but keeping the country context constant and using a better designed survey, we can perform a better test of the effect of institutional design on citizens' political actions.

INSTITUTIONALIZED CITIZEN EMPOWERMENT

The main theoretical and analytical tool used in this section of the study is what we refer to as *institutionalized citizen empowerment* (Hoff 1993; Schneider & Ingram 1997; Soss 1999; Goul Andersen, Torpe, & Andersen 2000; Kumlin & Rothstein 2004). As already mentioned, the principal argument presented here is that different institutional arrangements have different effects on the relationship between public service dissatisfaction and political action. When encountering a welfare state institution, the citizen can become more or less empowered, and this affects the relationship between dissatisfaction and political action. In other words, "People can come away from encounters with government feeling informed and empowered or helpless, ignorant and impotent" (Schneider & Ingram 1997: 79). This indicates that feedback mechanisms are at work. The citizen meets public policy in terms of decisions and procedures at a certain welfare state institution, that is, policies go hand-in-hand with institutional design. As policies can create incentives for citizens to act one way or another, which affects their socioeconomic circumstances (Pierson 1993), they could also affect how citizens think and act toward the political system. Suzanne Mettler and Joe Soss express this elegantly: "Policy designs shape citizens' personal experiences with government and hence influence processes of political learning and patterns of political belief" (Mettler & Soss 2004: 62). In other words, to understand why citizens react or not to policy outputs, we need to investigate the relevant dimensions of the institutional design of public service institutions (see also Mettler & Soss 2004 for a similar argument). In this chapter we will try to map exactly these relevant dimensions of design in Swedish public schools and health care, which we refer to as "empowerment."

We should understand institutionalized citizen empowerment as a power balance between the individual and the welfare state institution. The greater a citizen's influence, the greater will be the person's empowerment. Conversely, a lower degree of influence, indicating that the institution has great deal of control over the individual, equals a lower degree of empowerment (Hoff 1993: 78–79; Kumlin 2004: 55–58).

Previous research that has tried to pin down the norms or mechanisms of welfare state institutions and to test them empirically has relied mostly on the distinction between universal and means-tested institutional arrangements (Soss 1999; Mettler 2002a; Campbell 2003). Comparing two means-tested American welfare programs, Soss (1999, 2002) found that the design of welfare programs affected how individuals receiving welfare thought and acted, not only within the program but also in politics generally. *Degree of universality, control,* and *discretionary power* all influenced the individual's perceptions; low levels of empowerment negatively affected recipients' beliefs in the effectiveness of participation and their views on government. Conversely, a high degree of empowerment had positive effects on political action, trust, and sense of political efficacy. Campbell's comparison of Social Security, the most universal U.S. welfare program, and other non-means-tested and means-tested American welfare programs, confirmed this. Interestingly, she also found that controlling for age, income, and other resources, recipients of non-means-tested programs had higher participation levels than recipients of means-tested programs; she considered this to be because of the institutional design of the welfare programs (Campbell 2003). Campbell's conclusion indicates that matters of importance for political action included not just individual background features but also the actual design of welfare state institutions themselves.

By comparison, Verba, Schlozman, and Brady (1995) investigated the participation level among recipients of non-means-tested welfare programs (Social Security, veterans' benefits, Medicare, and student loans), finding that they participated to the same extent as other American citizens; the authors also investigated recipients of means-tested welfare programs (AFDC, Medicaid, Food Stamps), finding that they had considerably lower levels of political participation. The authors' explanation of this pattern does not include welfare program design, or program participation as Soss (2002: 161) labels it. Instead, they find the explanation in the individual characteristics of the recipients. Campbell's work (2003) indicates that individual level explanations are not enough; there also are institutional explanations.

Another dimension common to previous research is the degree of *discretionary powers of caseworkers*—to what extent caseworkers have the power to interpret loosely formulated laws regulating that particular public service area (Soss 1999; Kumlin 2004). The more discretionary power a caseworker has, the lower will be the degree of empowerment for the individual recipient. A third dimension of previous research is the presence or degree of *exit options* (Hirschman 1970; Goul Andersen & Hoff 2001; Kumlin 2004). The presence of exit options provide citizens with an alternative when they feel dissatisfied with current service conditions; the threat of alternatives could also influence the institution toward taking better care of its users.

By combining degree of discretionary power and degree of exit options, Kumlin (2004) classified Swedish public service institutions into three categories: customer institutions (high degree of empowerment), user institutions (medium degree of empowerment), and client institutions (low degree of empowerment). It is noteworthy that public schools and health care in Sweden are both classified as user institutions, with a medium degree of empowerment. Kumlin's main finding was that experiences with customer institutions had positive effects on political trust whereas experiences with client institutions had exactly the opposite effect (Kumlin 2004).

A fourth dimension tested in previous research comprises the formal mechanisms of user influence, or *voice opportunities* (Goul Andersen &

Hoff 2001). As mentioned in the section "Dissatisfaction and Political Action," Goul Andersen and Hoff compared data from Denmark, Sweden, and Norway on, among other things, the relationship between dissatisfaction and political action. In their classification, both health care and public school in Sweden were labeled high voice opportunities. In the comparison, the relationship between public school dissatisfaction and political action was strongest in Denmark, which the authors conclude had to do with the well established user–board channels of influence in Denmark.

In sum, the broad implications of the research referred to here are the same: institutions that are more empowering have positive effects on citizens' participation and political trust. This research also provides four types of variable institutional dimension. Besides these four dimensions, we believe it is important to develop the concept of empowerment and add further dimensions.

The additional dimensions we use are *individual rights* and *accountability*, both dimensions found in a work comparing Swedish and British health care (Karlsson 2003). According to Karlsson, the presence of individual rights in laws regulating public service areas strengthens the power of the individual vis-à-vis the public service area. If the law states rights, the individual can claim these rights when encountering an institution.

Even though the concept of accountability embraces the whole political system—not just the service institution in itself but also the political relationship that surrounds the institution—it is fruitful to discuss accountability, or clarity of responsibility, in terms of institutional design. Today, most countries are complex multilevel democracies, and which level has the responsibility for a certain policy area is not always clear-cut. If the lines of responsibility are blurred, the individual has greater difficulty knowing where to turn or whom to hold accountable when dissatisfied. Clearer lines of responsibility make it easier for citizens to channel their grievances (Karlsson 2003; Taylor 2000).

DIMENSIONS OF EMPOWERMENT IN SWEDISH PUBLIC SCHOOLS AND HEALTH CARE

To be able to determine the degree of empowerment in Swedish public schools and health care, we now turn to a discussion of the actual design features of the two public service institutions, using the six dimensions presented in the previous section: universalism, discretionary power, exit options, voice opportunities, individual rights, and accountability.

Universalism

There is no doubt that both public schools and health care are universal institutions. No means-testing takes place, and both institutions are financed mostly by taxes. This means that everybody has access to both public schools and health care. Public schools are completely free of charge: no tuition fees, no book fees, and free school lunches. When visiting a health care center or a hospital, a patient must pay a patient fee. In general, this fee is considered to be low. If a citizen has frequent encounters, health care becomes free of charge after a certain amount of paid patient fees. However, there are problems of both perceived and actual availability of health care, such as long waiting time at emergency rooms and sometimes months or years of waiting for special medical care, usually surgeries (National Board on Health and Welfare 2002; Socialstyrelsen 2004). Even though availability is not a problem for public schools, large age groups and cutbacks are noticed primarily in larger classes. While these problems do not change the basic principle of universalism, they do affect the quality of public service.

Even though both public schools and health care are universal institutions, I believe there is one important feature that somewhat changes the view of these institutions as equally universal. During life, most people have close, but time-limited contacts with public school. Either you are a pupil yourself or you are a parent of a pupil. Health care, however, is something most people have contact with more or less regularly during all life stages, even though each encounter might be less close than the contact with a public school. We believe this feature makes health care a more clear-cut "public good"[11] than schools, something that actually empowers citizens. This argument could be strengthened using Swedish research on confidence in different institutions. Health care enjoys the highest confidence level of all institutions, higher than any other public, political, or media institution, and this pattern has been persistent for 20 years. Public elementary school also enjoys high confidence and ranks as number 4 out of 20 institutions, but there is still a considerable gap between schools and health care (Holmberg & Weibull 2005a, 2005b). Thus, by adding the notion of public good to the dimension of universalism, the health care sector comes out as a slightly more universal institution than public schools.

Discretionary Power of Caseworkers

Neither public schools nor the health care system can be said to have case-workers in the strict sense. Of course, teachers have a great deal of power over the pupil, in the same way a doctor has power over a patient. Even though teachers and doctors both deal with matters of extreme importance, they do not have to interpret loosely formulated laws to judge how to teach a pupil or treat a patient. Instead this interpretation of laws is done at a higher organizational level, often in the public administration. However, we would argue that regardless of discretionary power, a doctor has a great deal of power over the individual seeking medical treatment. Also, when we encounter the health care system, the contact occurs usually when we are not feeling our best. Therefore, we believe the individual occupies a more exposed position when encountering health care than in encounters with public schools.

Exit Opportunities

In theory, the *exit options* within the school system and within the health care system are fairly good, and this is also the conclusion from an earlier study (Goul Andersen & Hoff 2001). In both cases, exit opportunities exist within and outside the publicly financed system.

Regarding public schools, the law regulating the school system in Sweden clearly states that the parent/guardian has the right to choose a public school for the child within the municipality/district, and that the municipality should obey this wish as long as it does not interfere with the placement of other children or has negative economic consequences (Skollag (1985:1100): chapter 4, 6 §). However, this opportunity is often restrained by economic circumstances and is far less evident in practice. The exit opportunity outside the public system is to change to a so-called independent school. In these schools the municipality is not the responsible authority, but the financing comes mostly from public funds. In 2000/2001 Sweden had 418 independent schools (nine years of compulsory schooling) and 97 independent high schools. However, roughly 100 out of 290 Swedish municipalities lack independent schools (Skolverket 2001). In western Sweden, the area covered by the survey we will use later, 84 percent of users of public school live in a municipality where independent school is an exit opportunity.[12]

Turning to health care, around one-quarter of the visits to local health care centers in Sweden are to centers where the care provider is private (SKL 2005). Although it is hard to compare figures, a rough estimate is that 10 percent of all doctor appointments in primary and special care are appointments with private doctors. However, if the full range of alternative care providers is included—private doctors, foundations, and cooperatives—7.3 million out of 24.8 million appointments in the health care sector are carried out by health care providers other than the regions or the city councils (SKL 2004, 2005).[13] Concerning exit options within the health care system, in theory a citizen has the right to receive his or her medical treatment from any health care center and hospital within the county council. In reality, choosing where to get treatment is not a reality for everyone. In the annual survey on health care, 52 percent of the respondents reported having the opportunity to choose the hospital within the region where they would be treated (Vårdbarometern 2002).

In sum, exit opportunities exist both within and outside the public school system and the health care sector, but exit is far easier in theory than in practice. At first glance, the exit options seem better in the health care sector, but since these exit options are mostly at a regional level for health care, while on a local level for public schools, we consider the exit opportunities to be fairly equal. However, exit is evidently more usual from the health care sector.

Voice Opportunities

Voice opportunities indicate the degree to which citizens or users of public service can be a part of decision making and exert influence over the service institution. There are numerous ways citizens can use their voices, but the most regulated form is the so-called user-board. Sweden has a number of different forms of user-boards. A common feature is that the responsible authority, usually the municipality, delegates power to the users and employees. The most common, but also least powerful, user-board is a form of cooperation between users and employees. The most far-reaching forms of user influence, the so-called self-governance boards, to a varying degree have the power to run an entire institution (Jarl 2001).

User-boards are quite common phenomena within the public school system. Eighty percent of Swedish municipalities report having the least powerful variant of user-boards, and only 42 percent have so-called self-governance boards (Jarl 2001). It is important to point out that the "users" are not primarily the children but their parents. In addition to user-boards, the interaction between parents and teachers is usually extensive, especially through parent-teacher meetings. Also, there are formal complaint boards at the national level through the Swedish National Agency for Education (Skolverket 2005). Hence, the public school system displays several arenas where users and teachers, principals, and other decision makers interact.

Compared to public schools, health care is the public service area where user-boards have had most difficulty in getting established. This difference, of course, mirrors how we encounter the two institutions. As a parent, your child is in the compulsory public school system from age 7 to 16, while the contact of either a parent or a child with a hospital or a health care center may last from only 20 minutes to several months. Since a majority of individuals have fairly short contacts with health care, it is much harder to establish user-boards in this area. Also, people usually need special skills to be able to manage and plan health care, which also works as a barrier to any increase in empowering structures within the health care system. Instead, the efforts made so far by the county councils to strengthen the individual in his or her contact with health care are more in line with the possibility of choosing a health care provider and improving complaint structures (Jarl 2001). Interestingly, the number of complaints received by the Patient Advisory Committees all over Sweden has increased heavily in the last years, attracting considerable media attention (some examples of this media attention are Bahri 2004-04-08; Östersunds-Posten 2004–06–17; Lindskog 2004–07–26; Gustavsson 2005–02–02; Andree 2005–02–03).

Comparing voice opportunities in public school and health care, it is evident that users of the public school system have not only more "voice arenas" but also much greater real opportunities to exert influence and participate in decision making than do users of the health care system. Although it is possible that both institutions could be characterized as having high levels of voice opportunities as described by Goul Andersen and Hoff (2001), our conclusion is that voice opportunities are clearly lower within the health care system.

Individual Rights

As mentioned earlier, the existence of a rights-dimension in laws regulating health care is believed to strengthen the individual when dealing with an institution. A comparison of individual rights in public school and health care shows clearly that the rights-dimension is more strongly stated in the law regulating schools than in the law regulating health care. The obligation to attend school is balanced with a right for the citizen to get an education: every child between 7 and 16 years of age has both an obligation and a right to attend school (Skollag (1985:1100)). Also, the municipalities are obligated to provide schooling.

In Swedish law regulating health care, we can only find obligations for the various regions to provide health care, and these obligations are formulated as aims to be reached. No explicit statement on individual rights can be identified (Karlsson 2003). This indicates that the degree of empowerment through individual rights is higher and more strongly formulated within the public school system than in health care.

Accountability

The last dimension of empowerment that will be introduced here is accountability. In terms of accountability or responsibility, the major difference between public schools and health care in Sweden is the responsible political authority. The municipalities are, in general, the responsible political units for public schooling, while regions or county councils are the responsible health care providers. In both cases, legislation and major policies are the preserve of the government and the responsible ministries at the national level (the Ministry of Education, Research, and Culture and the Ministry of Health and Social Affairs). Consequently, it should be equally easy (or hard) to identify the responsible person or authority. Even though Swedish ministers are not personally responsible for the outcomes of a public service area—as in Great Britain, for example—they usually receive the blame for public policy and legislation (Karlsson 2003). In actual practice, the municipalities/county councils should take responsibility but, just as in other systems, blame avoidance is used. When a municipality cannot fulfill its goals for the public schools, it tries to avoid blame by saying it was simply limited by financial restraints from the government. In other words, level of responsibility is what differs most: public schooling is run on the local level, health care on the regional level. However, since both activities also are governed from the national level, the lines of responsibility seem equally unclear.

*How Does Empowerment Affect Dissatisfaction
and Political Action?*

To sum up, when comparing the Swedish public school and health care systems we find many similarities. Both systems can be characterized as universal user institutions in which bureaucratic discretion, in terms of interpreting laws, is low. Also, the lines of political responsibility are equally unclear. However, we conclude that health care is more of a public good, enjoying a more thorough public support; hence, the dimension of universalism is more strongly emphasized in the health care sector. Exit options are present in both public schools and health care, although the real exit options are generally fewer than in theory. However, exit from the publicly financed health care system is more common than exit from public schools. The greatest differences appear in the empowerment dimension of voice opportunities. While complaint structures can be found in both areas, the individual's influence is much higher within public schools through the channel of user-boards—there are stronger established feedback mechanisms between users and local authority within the public school system. In addition, we find that the emphasis on individual rights is also higher in the school system.

Thus, the overall judgment must be that citizens in their encounters with public schools are empowered to a higher degree than are citizens in their encounters with health care. However, it is important to mention that the empowerment structures we have discussed do not have to form a single dimension. It is possible that some structures are more important than others and that certain features outweigh others. We do not know, for example, whether universalism is more important than voice opportunities.

The question then is, What political consequences do these aspects of institutional design have on citizens' political behavior and preferences? Even though the two institutions share many similarities, the differences that have been pointed out probably produce different feedback mechanisms. This means that citizens learn different things depending on which institution they encounter.

Following previous research, we should expect to find a stronger relationship between public school dissatisfaction and political action since public school offers a more empowering structure. This expectation follows the argument from participatory democratic theory (Pateman 1970; Goul Andersen & Hoff 2001). Participation at the local level, such as through user-boards, fuels further participation at other political levels. This conclusion can be contested; empirical research to more closely investigate the participatory process has found that this learning process is much more complicated. Participation in user-boards does seem to give rise to a learning process for most parents, but usually it is their democratic awareness as parents, that is, their increased interest and participation in school matters, and not their democratic awareness in general that is promoted (Jarl 2005). Therefore, we find it equally possible that because of the well-established forum of user-boards, parent-teacher meetings, and other means, citizens do not have to use the political system and political action to air their grievances. In other words, there are channels within the public school system that can handle dissatisfaction. In this way, the feedback mechanism stays within the public school area.

Turning to health care dissatisfaction and political action, there are also two possible outcomes. Even though health care in general can be regarded as less empowering, this does not mean that citizens lack power. What seems to be an important aspect of institutional design in health care is the availability of exit opportunities from public to private primary care. Since exit in this form is relatively common, a possible outcome is that there is no relationship between dissatisfaction and political action in the case of health care. On the other hand, since most citizens are dependent on public health care, it becomes a very important public service. It is also possible that threats of cutbacks mobilize people to take political action in order to tell politicians that public health care is "untouchable." This hypothesis can be supported by research on the high confidence the public medical service enjoys as an institution (Holmberg & Weibull 2005a).

THE IMPACT OF INSTITUTIONAL DESIGN ON WELFARE STATE TARGETED POLITICAL ACTION

By comparing school and health care services in Sweden, and using welfare state–related political action as a dependent variable, we can more closely isolate the institutional features and add something both theoretically and empirically to the discussion on institutionalized citizen empowerment and feedback mechanisms.

Since user influence seems to be the institutional feature that is most different between the two institutions, this leads us to the conclusion that the degree of institutionalized citizen empowerment is higher within the school area than within health services. Does this have any effect on the extent to which citizens express their dissatisfaction with these two policy areas through different forms of political action? As just discussed, it is not clear that increasing voice opportunities for citizens with a public service institution would fuel further participation. We have also argued that it is equally possible that internal voice mechanisms could handle grievances.

Using ESS, the empirical results show that there is a weak or nonexistent effect of welfare state dissatisfaction on political action in most countries. But if we switch attention to data from the western Sweden survey on society, opinion and mass media from 2000,[14] does a different pattern appear?

First, let us discuss the data and variables. The dependent variable measures political action targeted at different public service institutions. The wording is "Have you, during the last 12 months, expressed your point of view on the activity of any of the following areas by, e.g., writing a letter to the press, signing a petition, demonstrating, or contacting a politician?" The public service areas included in the question are child care, health care, school, employment, and eldercare. For every institution, the response options are Yes, several times; Yes, once/few times; No. In the analysis, the yes-options have been collapsed to a single category, that is, the dependent variable used is dichotomous.

The independent variable measures evaluations of locally produced public service; the question used is, "What is your opinion on the public service of the following areas in the municipality where you live"? For each of the 30 public service areas listed, the response options are Very satisfied, Somewhat satisfied, Neither satisfied nor dissatisfied, Somewhat dissatisfied, Very dissatisfied, and Don't know (excluded in the index). We use a school index measuring evaluations of both public elementary school and high school. In the same way, we use a health care index that consists of evaluations of local health centers and hospital care. To measure public service contact, the question is, "Do you or any close relative use any of the forms of services listed below?" Twenty-two different service areas are listed and, as with the measure of public service evaluations, we analyze users (and users who are close relatives) of public elementary school and high school together, and users of local health care centers and hospital care together. As control variables, we use equivalent measures as in the analysis based on ESS data: level of education, age, left–right placement, class, and gender.[15]

Table 5.2 displays the logistic regression results for evaluation of school and political action aimed at the school area. To ease interpretation, predicted probabilities of political action have been calculated for the evaluation variable and the interaction variable.

Evaluations of public schools at the local level have a positive effect on political action aimed at the public schools area (Model 1). The predicted probability of action among satisfied citizens is 15 percent, compared to 32 percent among dissatisfied citizens. However, this pattern does not hold when the full model is run (Model 4), that is, the effect of dissatisfaction becomes weak and insignificant. The direct effect on political action of being a user of public schools is positive, but it does not hold when other variables besides evaluation are included. In Model 3, the interaction term of service evaluation and user is introduced and displays a significant effect. This indicates that there is an extra effect on political action among dissatisfied users of public schools. The predicted level of political action is 15 percent among satisfied nonusers and 38 percent among dissatisfied users—more than twice as high. However, this interaction effect is no longer significant in the full model. Of the included control variables, the following have positive effects on political action: education; age 30–49 and age 50–64, compared to age under 30; and other workers, white-collar middle class, and farmers, compared to industrial workers. Citizens on the ideological right have taken political action aimed at the schools area to a lesser extent than those on the ideological left.[16]

In sum, citizens dissatisfied with public school service at the local level have not taken political action aimed at the public schools area to a higher extent than have satisfied citizens. Instead, education, age, left–right placement, and class are more important predictors of this sort of political action. This result is contrary to what Petersson et al. (1998) and Goul Andersen and Hoff (2001) found. The conclusion from the comparison of the Scandinavian Citizen Studies is that parents of schoolchildren, more than any other group of users, take initiatives to improve circumstances in the schools. One explanation of this difference is that the target of action differs: While our survey asks for explicit targets *outside* the public

TABLE 5.2

*Effects of evaluations of public school on welfare state–related
political action in Sweden (logistic regression).*

	Model 1	Model 2	Model 3	Model 4
		Dependent variable: *Political action targeted at public school*		
		Public school		
Evaluation of Public School Service (1–5)	.23***	.25***	.10	.05
User of Public School (0–1)		.49***	−.18	−.10
Evaluation*User (0–5)			.24*	.23
Education (1–4)				.41***
Age				
Age 30–49				1.15***
Age 50–64				.65**
Age 65–85				−.50
Left-right ideology (1–5)				−.20***
Class				
Other workers				.70**
White collar, lower				.29
White collar, middle				.70**
White collar, professionals				.60
Self-employed				.41
Farmers				1.49***
Gender				
Woman				−.04
Constant	−1.93***	−2.30***	−1.86***	−3.52***
Pseudo R^2	.01	.02	.02	.11
N	1411	1384	1384	1103
P (action) if evaluation = 1 (satisfied)	.15	.15	.18	.17
P (action) if evaluation = 5 (dissatisfied)	.32	.33	.25	.20
P(action) if evaluation*user = 0			.15	.13
P(action) if evaluation*user = 5			.38	.33

COMMENT: ***p≤.01 **p≤.05 *p≤.10. The dependent variable *Political action targeted at public school area* consists of two categories, 0 (no action taken) and 1 (action taken). The independent variable, *Evaluation of public school service*, is an index consisting of evaluations of public school and evaluations of public high school and ranges from 1 (very satisfied) to 5 (very dissatisfied). The variable *User of public school* distinguishes between nonusers (0) and users, including close relative of users (1). Evaluation*User is a interaction variable. The *Education* variable ranges between 1 and 4, where 1 is Low education and 4 is High education. Four *age dummies* were made to measure the impact of age on political action. The category with respondents of age 29 and younger was chosen as the reference category. *Left–right placement* is a question measuring ideology, and the respondent chooses a number between 1 (far to the left) and 10 (far to the right). Class has been recoded using the Swedish election study class scheme based on occupation. Industrial worker has been chosen as reference category.

SOURCE: Society, Opinion and Mass Media (SOM) Survey of Western Sweden 2000.

school—that is, politicians and civil servants, not teachers or principals—the results of the Swedish Citizen study indicate that initiatives are more often *within* the institution in question (see Petersson et al. 1998: chapter 3).

Turning to evaluations of health care, we can trace a different pattern. The results in Table 5.3 indicate, just as in the case of public schools, that citizens dissatisfied with health care are more inclined than satisfied citi-

TABLE 5.3
*Effects of evaluations of health care on welfare
state–related political action in Sweden (logit regression).*

	Dependent variable: Political action targeted at health care			
	Health care			
	Model 1	Model 2	Model 3	Model 4
Evaluation of Health Care Service (1–5)	.21***	.21***	.24**	.27**
User of Health Care (0–1)		.54*	.62	.69
Evaluation*User (0–5)			−.03	−.04
Education (1–4)				.10
Age				
Age 30–49				.70**
Age 50–65				.70**
Age 65–85				.41
Left–right ideology (1–5)				−.22**
Class				
Other workers				−.26
White collar, lower				−.28
White collar, middle				−.05
White collar, professionals				−.21
Self-employed				.03
Farmers				.51
Gender				
Woman				.22*
Constant	−2.11***	−2.65***	−2.72***	−3.17***
Pseudo R^2	.01	.01	.01	.03
N	2678	2577	2577	2160
P (action) if evaluation = 1 (satisfied)	0.13	0.13	0.13	0.12
P (action) if evaluation = 5 (dissatisfied)	0.25	0.26	0.27	0.29
P(action) if evaluation*user = 0			0.17	0.18
P(action) if evaluation*user = 5			0.16	0.15

COMMENT: ***p≤.01 **p≤.05 *p≤.10. The dependent variable *Political action targeted at health care area* consists of two categories, 0 (no action taken) and 1 (action taken). The independent variable, *Evaluation of health care*, is an index consisting of evaluations of local health care and evaluations of hospital care and ranges from 1 (very satisfied) to 5 (very dissatisfied). See Table 5.2 for information on other variables and categories.

SOURCE: Society, Opinion and Mass Media (SOM) Survey of Western Sweden 2000.

zens to take political action targeted at the health care area. But contrary to the public schools area, the relationship between evaluations of health care and political action is stable when other variables are introduced (Model 4). Based on Model 1, the predicted probability of political action is 13 percent among satisfied citizens and 25 percent among citizens dissatisfied with health care services. Neither being a user of health care nor the interaction term of service evaluation and user reach significance (Models 3 and 4). As noted earlier, citizens between 30 and 49 years of age and 50 and 64 years of age have higher levels of political action than citizens under 30 years of age. We also recognize the well-known negative sign of left–right ideology, indicating that citizens to the right take less action than citizens to the left. In general, none of the included class variables have significant effects on political action, compared to the reference category of industrial workers.

To sum up, we find a significant positive effect of evaluations of health care on political action aimed at the health care area. This means that citizens who are dissatisfied with health care delivery take more political action than citizens satisfied with health care delivery—for example, through petition signing and contacting politicians.

Comparing the public schools area and the health care area, the results indicate that citizens dissatisfied with public schools do not voice their grievances through political activities aimed at this area. However, there is a tendency for dissatisfied users of public schools to take political action. Citizens who are dissatisfied with health care delivery do use political action to express their points of view to decision makers on issues of health care, and no difference between users and nonusers can be traced. These results support a conclusion that dimensions of empowerment work in different ways, that is, different mechanisms come into play, depending on the institution in question.

DOES INSTITUTIONAL DESIGN MATTER?

From the empirical material analyzed in this chapter, two separate sets of conclusions can be drawn. The first empirical section investigated whether we could find any regime patterns and whether there was any relationship at all between welfare state dissatisfaction and political action in general. We can state that there is a weak relationship between welfare state dissatisfaction and non-targeted political action in some countries, but we know little about the reasons why. The regime typology did not help us understand and interpret the results; the relationship was found, or not found, in all regime families. The conclusions drawn from this are twofold. First, the problem of finding mass attitudes in coherence with the regime typology is not new. Even though it has been hard in some cases to establish regime attitude patterns, the regime typology is the most well-known tool we have when measuring institutional design of welfare state at the macro level. Nevertheless, it is possible that welfare regimes do not structure citizens' political action. Second, the attempt to find a relationship between welfare state evaluations and non-targeted political action was a challenge from the start, considering the poor measurements available through ESS. Still, the fact that we found relationships, although weak, in half of the countries points in a certain direction. We know that welfare state dissatisfaction affects political trust negatively (see Kumlin, Chapter 3 in this volume), but if this dissatisfaction has any effect on political action, it is evidently positive, leading to more action.

To sum up, the conclusion of the first section of this chapter is precarious. Our results do not support the hypotheses derived from previous research that different regimes produce different feedback mechanisms and that this, in turn, affects citizens' political action. However, considering the imprecise survey questions used, we can neither support nor reject these hypotheses.

To examine more closely the impact of institutional design, a more explicit comparison was made between the public schools and health care systems in Sweden. By comparing public schools and health care using six dimensions of empowerment, we reached the conclusion that the degree of institutionalized citizen empowerment was higher within the public school system than within the health care system. The main difference between Swedish public schools and health care is the dimension of voice opportunities. While institutionalized channels of user influence are relatively well established within public schools, they are almost nonexistent in health care. However, we could also see that the law regulating schools puts more emphasis on individual rights, but that the notion of universality is more strongly emphasized within the health care sector because of its clearer characteristic of being a "public good."

By using political action aimed at different public service institutions as the dependent variable, we were able to better tap welfare state–related political action, compared to the general question on political action in the European Social Survey. The conclusion of the analysis is that dissatisfaction with public schools is not related to political action aimed at public schools, but we did find this relationship regarding the health care area. In other words, what we have found is that citizens dissatisfied with health care take political action to a higher extent than citizens satisfied with health care.

The immediate interpretation of these results is that fewer voice opportunities tend to make citizens more inclined to take political action instead, and the relatively large number of voice opportunities within public schools deals with parents' grievances. However, it is important to nuance this conclusion. Both previous research and the discussion on empowerment in school and health care in this chapter share a common conclusion: Both public schools and health care are institutions with relatively high degrees of empowerment. Following this, it could have been equally valid to expect no differences in the relationship between dissatisfaction and political action for public school and health care, that is, we would have found a positive relationship in both cases. Also, it is possible that citizens think differently about these two institutions. While our contact with public schools is usually limited to our own schooling and that of our children, contact with the health care system continues throughout life. It is plausible that this difference between school and health care makes health care more of a public good—an institution worth fighting for. This feature may produce different feedback mechanisms than those in the public schools area and may explain why we also see a positive effect of health care dissatisfaction on political action and no similar effect regarding public schools.

Since the measure of institutional contact, the user/nonuser distinction, did not have any significant effect, it is hard to draw conclusions on the impact of institutional design. We did find that dissatisfied users of public schools were more inclined to take political action than satisfied nonusers, but this result was not statistically significant. Instead, individual characteristics, such as education, age, and class, proved to be important explanations of political action in both public schools and health care. However, since the interaction variable between evaluation of public school and political action just barely loses its significance, we may have something interesting here. This result points in a direction that actually supports some previous research—that experience of user-influence spills over to other forms of political action. What we see as a tendency is that parents also voice their grievances in school matters by contacting politicians, signing petitions, and contacting media. Thus, what we may have identified is that voice opportunities empower parents and pupils to express their opinions on school issues through political action, while universalism and widespread public support empowers citizens dissatisfied with health care to take political action, regardless of whether they are users by these definitions or not.

The overall conclusion in this chapter gives us something to think about when discussing the impact of institutional design. We can say that institutional design evidently matters, for we have traced the pattern that different dimensions of empowerment work in different directions. A comparison of less similar institutions could provide us with better answers to our questions on how empowerment works. Also, empowerment might affect modes of political action differently. We might find a more nuanced answer if we investigate whether voice opportunities within schools empower parents and make certain modes of action more likely outcomes than others. Hence, future research should compare institutions with more striking design differences and analyze modes of political action separately. In other words, we need to further investigate, with better comparative measures and more elaborate measures of institutional design, the relationship between welfare dissatisfaction and political action if we are to better understand the interplay between institutions and citizens' political attitudes and actions.

TABLE 5.A1

Effects of welfare state dissatisfaction on political action in 14 European countries (OLS regression).

	Dependent variable: Political action index (0–4)			
	Conservative regimes			
	Austria	Belgium	Germany	Netherlands
Welfare state dissatisfaction (0–10)	.02	.04**	.01	.00
Education (1–7)	.13***	.11***	.09***	.10***
Age				
Age 30–49	.12*	−.03	.02	.16***
Age 50–65	.10	.11	.08	.16***
Age over 65	−.01	−.14*	−.14**	.15**
Left–right ideology (0–10)	−.07***	−.02*	−.07***	−.04**
Class				
Service class 2	−.01	.06	−.13*	−.07
Routine manual	.02	.15	−.12	−.13**
Skilled manual	−.10	−.11	−.26***	−.22***
Unskilled manual	−.09	−.03	−.34***	−.13*
Self-employed	−.17	.02	.02	.05
Gender				
Woman	−.24***	−.10*	−.07*	.02
Constant	.81***	.47***	.82	.27
R^2	.08	.06	.08	.07
N	1631	1249	2331	2019

(*continued*)

TABLE 5.A1 (*continued*)

Dependent variable: Political action index (0–4)

	Liberal regimes	
	Great Britain	Ireland
Welfare state dissatisfaction (0–10)	.03***	.03**
Education (1–7)	.15***	.08***
Age		
Age 30–49	.14**	−.01
Age 50–65	.22***	.06
Age over 65	.19***	−.19**
Left–right ideology (0–10)	−.03**	−.05***
Class		
Service class 2	.06	−.01
Routine manual	.07	−.00
Skilled manual	−.02	−.05
Unskilled manual	−.08	−.03
Self-employed	.09	.07
Gender		
Woman	−.00	−.13**
Constant	.07	.78***
R^2	.07	.05
N	1758	1465

Dependent variable: Political action index (0–4)

	Mediterranean regimes			
	Greece	Italy	Portugal	Spain
Welfare state dissatisfaction (0–10)	.01	.04*	.00	.05***
Education (1–7)	.05**	.21***	.07**	.13***
Age				
Age 30–49	.06	.17*	−.09	.01
Age 50–65	.08	.06	−.01	−.05
Age over 65	.01	−.01	−.18*	−.17
Left–right ideology (0–10)	−.02*	−.03**	−.03**	−.03*
Class				
Service class 2	−.17	.51***	−.03	.01
Routine manual	−.05	.45***	−.16	−.04
Skilled manual	−.07	.22	−.23	−.22
Unskilled manual	−.15	.33**	−.22	−.30
Self-employed	.02	.36**	−.21	−.13
Gender				
Woman	−.02	−.22***	−.13**	−.16**
Constant	.38**	−.18	.77***	.71***
R^2	.03	.13	.07	.12
N	1487	747	1030	1061

Table 5.A1 *(continued)*

| | *Dependent variable: Political action index (0–4)* | | | |
| | *Social democratic regimes* | | | |
	Denmark	*Finland*	*Norway*	*Sweden*
Welfare state dissatisfaction (0–10)	.01	.03**	.03*	.02**
Education (1–7)	.10***	.07***	.13***	.03**
Age				
Age 30–49	−.08	−.04	.07	−.08
Age 50–65	−.08	−.00	.07	−.06
Age over 65	−.27***	−.13**	−.18**	−.20***
Left–right ideology (0–10)	−.07***	−.02**	−.07***	−.05***
Class				
Service class 2	−.10	−.03	.05	.10
Routine manual	−.14	−.14**	.02	−.10
Skilled manual	−.17*	−.24***	−.13	−.24**
Unskilled manual	−.07	−.29***	−.11	−.15
Self-employed	−.08	.02	.05	.28**
Gender				
Woman	.03	.03	−.04	−.02
Constant	.80***	.54***	.64***	.90***
R^2	.06	.07	.08	.06
N	1280	1787	1842	1730

COMMENT: ***$p \leq .01$ **$p \leq .05$ *$p \leq .10$. See Table 5.1 for information on the political action index, the welfare state dissatisfaction index, and regression technique. The *Education* variable ranges between 1 and 7, where 1 is Not completed primary education and 7 is Second stage of tertiary. Four *age dummies* were made to measure the impact of age on political action. The category with respondents of age 29 and younger was chosen as the reference category. *Left–right placement* is a question measuring ideology, and the respondent chooses a number between 1 (left) and 10 (right). Class has been recoded using the Erikson-Goldthorpe scheme (Erikson & Goldthorpe 1992). Industrial worker has been chosen as reference category.

SOURCE: European Social Survey (ESS) 2002.

NOTES

* Several people have read and commented on this chapter during its various life stages. In addition to the ISP-group and the commentators at the Cadenabbia sessions, I would especially like to thank Stefan Dahlberg, Christina Ribbhagen, and Jan Teorell for reading earlier drafts and providing me with useful comments.

1. Mau (2003, pages 58–60) provides a good overview on the criticism of the regime typology.

2. The authors' measure of policy dissatisfaction consisted of an index taking account both of government performance and perceived importance (salience) of 10 policy areas. The authors also used an index of protest and conventional participation. The protest potential index included actions such as petitions, demonstrations, boycotts, occupations, rent strikes, blockades, and unofficial strikes. Conventional participation consisted of reading about politics in newspapers, discussing politics with friends, working on community problems, contacting

politicians or public officials, convincing friends to vote, participating in election campaigns, and attending political meetings.

3. In the well-known American studies of political participation (two examples are Verba & Nie 1972; Verba et al. 1995), the theoretical and empirical concerns have included questions of modes of participation, types of participants, and motivations for participation. The Civic Voluntarism model developed by Verba, Schlozman, and Brady (1995) proves a good example. Little can be found that actually connects evaluations of government output and political participation. In general, the primary interest of these studies is political participation in itself whereas my study aims to explore a *relationship* that includes political participation (or political action as I prefer to label it) as a dependent variable. Although the differences might seem small, the research questions I ask are entirely different from the questions posed by researchers interested in explaining political participation alone.

4. See Jonas Edlund's chapter in this volume for a more through discussion on characteristics of welfare regimes.

5 Since ESS were conducted before the 2004 enlargement of the European Union, the empirical analyses are restricted to Austria, Belgium, Germany, Denmark, Finland, Great Britain, Greece, Ireland, Italy, the Netherlands, Portugal, Spain, Sweden, and the non-EU member Norway.

6. See earlier discussion on definition of political action in this chapter.

7. ESS data show that 59 percent of Swedish respondents have taken some form of political action. In the 2004 Swedish SOM (Society, Opinion and Media) survey, the corresponding number—asking about roughly the same question types, but in relation to five different welfare institutions—is 11 percent. Although these two datasets are not entirely comparable, this nicely illustrates the point that citizens take political action for a number of reasons—the welfare issue is just one.

8. See Staffan Kumlin's chapter in this volume for a discussion on a similar index construction.

9. Since the regression coefficients indicate such weak relationships between welfare state dissatisfaction and political action in all countries, a number of controls were set up to investigate whether this could be an effect of a nonlinear relationship. These controls were performed using dummy variables for every possible value in the welfare state dissatisfaction index. The index ranges from 0 to 10, but has 21 values (0, 0,5, 1, 1,5 and so on). The dummy variable of the value 0 was the reference category. The results are somewhat mixed. First, in Greece, Ireland, and the Netherlands, there are basically no significant differences between the 20 dummy variables entered in the regression and the reference category, value 0. This indicates that there is no difference between a satisfied and a dissatisfied citizen concerning level of political action. Second, in a majority of countries, significant effects can be found in around two-thirds of the entered dummy

variables, but there are variations as to which variables are significantly different from the reference category. In Belgium, Germany, Great Britain, Italy, Norway, Portugal, and Sweden we found significant effects on political action, compared to the reference category, in 15–18 out of 20 entered dummy variables. Taking the size of the effects into account, the picture becomes more complex. In these countries, where a large majority of the variables included in the regression were significantly different from the reference category, there is no general tendency of growing effects on political action as we move along the spectrum toward more dissatisfied citizens. Instead, the effects do not differ much or are very mixed. In Great Britain and Italy and to some extent also Norway, a small tendency to a curvilinear pattern can be found. In these three cases, both the most satisfied and the most dissatisfied are more inclined to take political action, compared to citizens with more lukewarm attitudes. In Germany and Portugal, the effects on political action, compared to the reference category, are quite similar, irrespective of value on the welfare state dissatisfaction index. In Belgium and Sweden, there is a small tendency of increasing effects, or to be more correct, on stronger effects of dissatisfaction of political action than of satisfaction.

10. Complete tables are included in Appendix Table 5.A1.

11. I use the term "public good" to emphasize one special dimension of universalism of public service. This term is commonly used within economics to refer to goods such as water and clean air. Education and health care are of course not public goods in that respect, but the term is still useful for the purposes here to distinguish between different degrees of universalism.

12. Independent schools did not exist in 18 out of 50 municipalities, which was equivalent to 16 percent of the users in the survey. These calculations used statistics on independent schools from the Swedish National Agency of Education (Skolverket 2001).

13. These figures can be nuanced by the fact that 80 percent of private doctors in primary care follow a national system of patient fees, which means that to see a private doctor does not have to cost more than visiting a public doctor (SKL 2005).

14. The research institute of Society, Opinion and Mass Media (SOM) is a cooperation among the Department of Political Science, the Department of Mass Media and Journalism, and the School of Public Administration at Göteborg University, Sweden. A national survey has been conducted annually since 1986, and a regional survey of western Sweden since 1992. The year 2000 survey of western Sweden consisted of two partly parallel questionnaires sent out to 3000 respondents each. The net response rate was 66 percent (Nilsson 2002). Western Sweden is generally considered to be a "mini-Sweden." Comparisons that have been made between the national survey and the western Sweden survey show similar results (Holtti 2004: 517). The western Sweden survey of Society, Opinion and Mass Media always includes a heavy number of welfare state–related questions.

15. There are, of course, some differences in how these variables are measured. Education is a four-graded variable (low education, medium-low education, medium-high education, and high education). These four categories are based on a seven-graded question on education running from public school (6–9 years, depending on when the respondent went to school) to university degree. The age variable is divided into four dummies corresponding to the same age categories as ESS, i.e., 15–29, 30–49, 50–64, 65–85 years of age. Left–right placement is a five-graded question, and the respondent chooses between Far to the left, Somewhat to the left, Neither left nor right, Somewhat to the right, and Far to the right. The class variable is an objective measure based on the respondent's own occupation. The coding scheme was developed by the Swedish election study and is fairly similar to the Erikson-Goldthorpe scheme (see Erikson & Goldthorpe 1992). Seven class categories are usually distinguished: industrial workers, other workers, white-collar lower, white-collar middle, white-collar professional, self-employed, and farmers.

16. When Model 4 is run without the interaction term, the direct effect of dissatisfaction with public schools on political action remains significant. The control variables are unaffected.

REFERENCES

Andree, Lasse. 2005–02–03. "Anmälningar mot vården ökar." *Göteborgs-Posten*, p. 6
Bahri, Kristin. 2004–04–08. "Allt svårare fall hos patientnämnderna." *Landstingsvärlden*, pp. 6–7
Bonoli, Giuliano. 1997. "Classifying Welfare States: A Two-Dimension Approach." *Journal of Social Policy* 26:3:351–372.
Brady, Henry E. 1999. "Political Participation." In *Measures of Political Attitudes: Volume 2 in Measures of Social Psychological Attitudes Series*, edited by John P. Robinson, Philip R. Shaver, & Lawrence S. Wrightsman, San Diego, CA: Academic Press.
Campbell, Andrea Louise. 2003. *How Policies Make Citizens: Senior Political Activism and the American Welfare State*. Princeton, NJ: Princeton University Press.
Dalton, Russel J. 2002. *Citizen Politics: Public Opinion and Political Parties in Advanced Industrial Democracies*. Chatham, NJ: Chatham House.
Erikson, Robert, and John H. Goldthorpe. 1992. *The Constant Flux: A Study of Class Mobility in Industrial Societies*. Oxford: Clarendon Press.
Esping-Andersen, Gøsta. 1990. *The Three Worlds of Welfare Capitalism*. Cambridge: Polity Press.
Farah, Barbara G., Samuel H. Barnes, & Felix Heunks. 1979. "Political Dissatisfaction." In *Political Action: Mass Participation in Five Western Democra-*

cies, edited by Samuel H. Barnes & Max Kaase, et al. Beverly Hills, CA: Sage.

Goul Andersen, Jørgen, & Jens Hoff. 2001. *Democracy and Citizenship in Scandinavia*. New York: Palgrave.

Goul Andersen, Jørgen, Lars Torpe, & Johannes Andersen. 2000. *Hvad folket magter: Demokrati, magt og afmagt*. København: Jurist- og Økonomforbundets Forlag.

Gustavsson, Ingela. 2005–02–02. "Klagomålen har inte minskat." *Borås Tidning*, p. 4

Hirschman, Albert O. 1970. *Exit, Voice, and Loyalty: Responses to Decline in Firms, Organizations, and States*. Cambridge, MA: Harvard University Press.

Hoff, Jens. 1993. "Medborgerskab, brukerrolle og magt." In *Medborgerskab: Demokrati og politiskt deltagelse*, edited by Johannes Andersen, Ann-Dorte Christensen, Kamma Langberg, Birte Siim, & Lars Torpe. Viborg: Systeme.

Holmberg, Sören. 1999. "Down and Down We Go: Political Trust in Sweden." In *Critical Citizens: Global Support for Democratic Governance*, edited by Pippa Norris. Oxford: Oxford University Press.

Holmberg, Sören, & Henrik Oscarsson. 2004. *Väljare: Svenskt väljarbeteende under 50 år*. Stockholm: Norstedts Juridik.

Holmberg, Sören, & Lennart Weibull. 2005a. "Rimligt förtroende?" In *Lyckan kommer, lyckan går. SOM-rapport nr. 35*, edited by Sören Holmberg & Lennart Weibull. Göteborgs universitet: SOM-institutet.

Holmberg, Sören, & Lennart Weibull (eds.). 2005b. *Swedish Trends 1986–2004*. Göteborg University: SOM Institute.

Holtti, David. 2004. "Samhälle Opinion Massmedia Västra Götaland 2003." In *Svensk samhällsorganisation i förändring. Västsverige vid millennieskiftet*, edited by Lennart Nilsson. Göteborgs universitet: SOM-institutet.

Huseby, Beate M. 2000. *Government Performance and Political Support: A Study of How Evaluations of Economic Performance, Social Policy and Environmental Protection Influence Popular Assessments of the Political System*. Trondheim: Institutt for sosiologi og statsvitenskap, Norges teknisk-naturvitenskapelige universitet (NTNU).

Jarl, Maria. 2001. "Erfarenheter av ett utbrett brukarinflytande. En utredning om brukarinflytandet i Sverige." In *Ökade möjligheter till brukarinflytande*, Ds 2001:34. Stockholm: Fritzes.

Jarl, Maria. 2005. "Making User-boards a School in Democracy? Studying Swedish Local Governments." *Scandinavian Political Studies* 28:3:277–293.

Karlsson, Lars. 2003. *Konflikt eller harmoni? Individuella rättigheter och ansvarsutkrävande i svensk och brittisk sjukvård*. Göteborg: Göteborgs universitet, Statsvetenskapliga institutionen.

Kinder, Donald R., & D. Roderick Kiewiet. 1981. "Sociotropic Politics: The American Case." *British Journal of Political Science* 11:129–161.

Kumlin, Staffan. 2004. *The Personal and the Political: How Personal Welfare State Experiences Affect Political Trust and Ideology*. New York: Palgrave Macmillan.

Kumlin, Staffan, & Bo Rothstein. 2004. "Making and Breaking Social Capital: The Impact of Welfare State Institutions." *Comparative Political Studies* 38:4:339–365.

Leibfried, Stephan. 1992. "Towards a European Welfare State? On Integrating Poverty Regimes into the European Community." In *Social Policy in a Changing Europe*, edited by Zsuzsa Ferge & Jon Eivind Kolberg. Boulder, CO: Westview Press.

Lewis-Beck, Michael S. 1988. *Economics and Elections: The Major Western Democracies*. Ann Arbor: University of Michigan Press.

Lindskog, Anna-Lena. 2004–07–26. "Allt fler klagar på sjukvården i länet." *Västerbottens-Kuriren*, p. 5.

Listhaug, Ola. 1995. "The Dynamics of Trust in Politicians." In *Citizens and the State*, edited by Hans-Dieter Klingemann & Dieter Fuchs. Oxford: Oxford University Press.

Lyons, William E., & David Lowery. 1989. "Citizen Responses to Dissatisfaction in Urban Communities: A Partial Test of a General Model." *Journal of Politics* 51:4: 841–868.

Mau, Steffen. 2003. *The Moral Economy of Welfare States: Britain and Germany Compared*. London: Routledge.

McAllister, Ian. 1999. "The Economic Performance of Governments." In *Critical Citizens: Global Support for Democratic Governance*, edited by Pippa Norris. Oxford: Oxford University Press.

Mettler, Suzanne. 2002a. "Bringing the State Back into Civic Engagement: Policy Feedback Effects of the G.I. Bill for World War II Veterans." *American Political Science Review* 96:2:351–365.

Mettler, Suzanne. 2002b. "Policy Feedback for Collective Action: Lessons from Veterans Programs." Unpublished manuscript, Draft, May 13.

Mettler, Suzanne, & Joe Soss. 2004. "The Consequences of Public Policy for Democratic Citizenship: Bridging Policy Studies and Mass Politics." *Perspectives on Politics* 2:1: 55–73.

National Board on Health and Welfare. 2002. "Yearbook of Health and Medical Care 2002 (Hälso- och sjukvårdsstatistisk årsbok 2002)." Stockholm: Socialstyrelsen.

Nilsson, Åsa. 2002. "Samhälle Opinion Massmedia Västra Götaland 2000." In *Flernivådemokrati i förändring*, edited by Lennart Nilsson. Göteborg: Göteborgs universitet, SOM-institutet.

Norris, Pippa. 2002. *Democratic Phoenix: Reinventing Political Activism*. Cambridge: Cambridge University Press.

Östersunds-Posten. 2004–06–17. "Ökat tryck på patientnämnden." *Östersunds-Posten*, p. 3.

Pateman, Carole. 1970. *Participation and Democratic Theory*. Cambridge: Cambridge University Press.

Petersson, Olof, Jörgen Hermansson, Michele Micheletti, Jan Teorell, & Anders Westholm. 1998. *Demokratirådets rapport 1998: Demokrati och medborgarskap*. Stockholm: SNS Förlag.

Petersson, Olof, Sören Holmberg, Leif Lewin, & Hanne Marthe Narud. 2002. *Demokratirådets rapport 2002: Demokrati utan ansvar*. Stockholm: SNS Förlag.

Petersson, Olof, Anders Westholm, & Göran Blomberg. 1989. *Medborgarnas makt*. Stockholm: Carlsson Bokförlag.

Pettersson, Maria, & Christina Ribbhagen. 2003. "Förutsättningar för ett brett medborgerligt deltagande." In *Demokratitrender: SOM-rapport nr 32*, edited by Henrik Oscarsson. Göteborg: Göteborgs universitet, SOM-institutet.

Pierson, Paul. 1993. "When Effect Becomes Cause: Policy Feedback and Political Change." *World Politics* 45:4:595–628.

Rothstein, Bo. 1996. "Political Institutions—An Overview." In *A New Handbook of Political Science*, edited by Robert E. Goodin & Hans-Dieter Klingemann. Cambridge: Cambridge University Press.

Schneider, Anne, & Helen Ingram. 1993. "Social Construction of Target Populations: Implications for Politics and Policy." *American Political Science Review* 87:2:334–347.

Schneider, Larason Anne, & Helen Ingram. 1997. *Policy Design for Democracy*. Lawrence: University Press of Kansas.

Skollag (1985:1100).

Skolverket. 2001. "Barnomsorg, skola och vuxenutbildning. Jämförelsetal för huvudmän. Del 1 2001. Organisation—Personal—Resultat. Rapport nr. 196." Stockholm: Skolverket.

Skolverket. 2005. "http://www.skolverket.se/sb/d/238", 2005.

Socialstyrelsen. 2004. "Nationell handlingsplan för hälso- och sjukvården: årsrapport 2004." Stockholm: Socialstyrelsen.

Soss, Joe. 1999. "Lessons of Welfare: Policy Design, Political Learning, and Political Action." *American Political Science Review* 93:2:363–380.

Soss, Joe. 2002 *Unwanted Claims: The Politics of Participation in the U.S. Welfare System*. Ann Arbor: University of Michigan Press.

Svallfors, Stefan. 2002. "Political Trust and Support for the Welfare State: Unpacking a Supposed Relationship." In *Restructuring the Welfare State: Political Institutions and Policy Change*, edited by Bo Rothstein & Sven Steinmo. New York: Palgrave Macmillan.

Svallfors, Stefan. 2003. "Welfare Regimes and Welfare Opinions: A Comparison of Eight Western Countries." *Social Indicators Research* 64:495–520.

Svallfors, Stefan. 2004. *Klassamhällets kollektiva medvetande*. Umeå: Boréa.

Sveriges kommuner och landsting (SKL). 2004. "Statistik om hälso- och sjukvård

samt regional utveckling—Verksamhet och ekonomi i landsting och re-
gioner." Stockholm: Sveriges kommuner och landsting.

Svenska kommuner och landsting (SKL). 2005. "Privata läkare och sjukgymnaster i öppen vård med ersättning enligt nationell taxa 2004: Sammanställning
av uppgifter avseende läkare och sjukgymnaster med ersättning enligt lag om
läkarvårdsersättning respektive lag om ersättning för sjukgymnastik." Stockholm: Sveriges kommuner och landsting.

Taylor, Michaell A. 2000. "Channeling Frustrations: Institutions, Economic Fluctuations, and Political Behavior." *European Journal of Political Research*
38:1:95–134.

Teorell, Jan. 2003. "Demokrati och deltagande." In *Demokratins mekanismer*,
edited by Mikael Gilljam & Jörgen Hermansson. Malmö: Liber.

Togeby, Lise, Jørgen Goul Andersen, Peter Munk Christiansen, Torben Jørgensen
Beck, & Signild Vallgårda. 2003. *Magt og demokrati i Danmark: Hovedre-
sultater fra Magtudredningen.* århus: Aarhus Universitetsforlag.

Vårdbarometern. 2002. http://www.vardbarometern.nu/1/resultat.
asp?id=54&index=39.

Verba, Sidney, & Norman H. Nie. 1972. *Participation in America: Political Democracy and Social Equality.* New York: Harper & Row.

Verba, Sidney, Kay Lehman Schlozman, & Henry E. Brady. 1995. *Voice and
Equality: Civic Voluntarism in American Politics.* Cambridge, MA: Harvard
University Press.

CHAPTER SIX

Class and Attitudes to Market Inequality
A Comparison of Sweden, Britain, Germany, and the United States

Stefan Svallfors

While the previous chapters have all dealt with welfare state institutions and their correlates in the form of orientations, this chapter broadens the institutional perspective to include attitudes toward the market.* The institutional framework in advanced political economies extends beyond the political sphere in a narrow sense. It also includes the industrial relations system, where the presence or absence of an organizationally coordinated wage setting is one important element. This makes it pertinent to ask whether attitudes not only toward the welfare state but also toward the market are affected by the institutional framework in which actors are embedded.

As a general point of departure, we might expect people with stronger market position to display more favorable attitudes to market principles and distributions. This puts *class* squarely at the center of our analysis. Market transactions seldom take place between players whose resources and power are matched. Instead, the labor market is characterized by power imbalances between those who buy and those who sell labor, or between those whose traits or skills are in great demand and those whose qualities are in excess supply. Just as consumer markets behave differently for those with plentiful resources and those with scant resources, so capital markets differ for those with knowledge and capital and those bereft of such assets.

Consequently our working assumption could be that people who by virtue of their greater assets are the market winners will look upon the market's transactions as more legitimate and be less inclined to redress market distributions than those who wield less power on the market. This means that we can expect groups with higher class positions to be more positive than workers toward the market.

This is, however, a sweeping assumption that ignores several complicating factors. First, attitudes are not created out of self-interest alone, as was maintained in Chapter 1. They are the product of a more complex and composite "moral economy" that centers on notions of reasonableness and justice in different social settings (Svallfors 1996: 17–20; Mau 2003: Ch. 3). Attitudes to the market and the way it operates are naturally no exception to this; the disprivileged can also accept a certain measure of distribution if it is seen as a reasonable outcome of fair procedures.

Second, there is the argument that the operational nature and distributive properties of the market breed much less discontent and attitudinal differences than politics. Lane (1986) maintains that we often see market distribution as something that "just happens" without holding anyone responsible. We tend, argues Lane, to take the market's distribution as a given, unchallengeable phenomenon; the market apportions its resources in an arbitrary and automatic manner, and if we are unhappy with our lot, there is no authority to which we can complain. In politics, however, things work differently: we choose representatives whom we can hold accountable and with whom we can express dissatisfaction if they fail to stick to their promises or conduct themselves inappropriately.[1] Lane argues that we tend to see market distribution as an expression of individual input and personal credit. The social forces behind it are quite simply not as visible as they are in politics.

If Lane is correct, we might not expect to see any major differences between the classes in how they view the market. Market fatalism would eradicate any differences in class interests, leaving the distribution of the market to enjoy abiding legitimacy. Class differences might then arise only on matters of state redistribution (the subject of other chapters in this volume), and perhaps not even then if the original market distribution gains sufficiently widespread acceptance.

A third complication of relevance to the relationship between class and attitudes toward the market is that the institutional framing of national markets differs considerably from one country to another. Self-regulating markets have never been anything but a liberal utopia, as all real markets need a vast institutional framework to avoid being subverted by their own internal dynamics (Polanyi 1944; Granovetter 1985; Fligstein 2001). For instance, if market transactions are to operate properly, there needs to be a legal framework (laws, courts, police, etc.) through which ownership rights are regulated and contracts sanctioned.

However, over and above the legal framework which each market needs to function, there are other ways in which markets become institutionally embedded, and it is here where different kinds of political economy clearly diverge. They include the extent to which work conditions and pay levels are legally regulated; whether wage bargaining is institutionalized through negotiations between organized parties or determined in private between the individual buyers and sellers of labor; and the nature of relations between unions and employers.

Such institutional conditions are often loosely integrated in configurations or "regimes" (Hall and Soskice 2001) depending on the internal connections between these different aspects. It is, for instance, hard to imagine a system for centralized negotiations on pay and other working conditions without a high degree of organization of both the employees and the employers. Any agreements reached centrally would then impinge only lightly on the actual market transactions as they would concern only some companies and particular workers.

One attempt to define these institutional dissimilarities between advanced market economies is to place them on a "coordinated" versus "liberal" axis (Soskice 1999; Hall and Soskice 2001). In coordinated market economies, we find relatively regulated labor markets, financial systems that allow far-sighted planning, and advanced cooperation and negotiation systems between businesses as well as between unions and employers (Soskice 1999: 106–107). Liberal market economies on the other hand are typified by a lower degree of labor market regulation, financial systems preoccupied with immediate gains and stock market prices, competition-based relations between companies and weak systems for collective bargaining (Soskice 1999: 110–111).

In this chapter, class differences in attitudes are compared among four Western countries: Sweden, Britain, Germany,[2] and the United States. These countries represent the span of institutional and political-economic configuration that exists in the West. The United States, but also to an increasing extent Britain as well, are examples of liberal regimes in which the processes of distribution are heavily dominated by different kinds of markets. Sweden and Germany, on the other hand, are examples of market economies in which politics and institutions are based on, and apply, relatively radical modifications of the market game. The reason for choosing these four countries is that they represent the variation we find within the advanced capitalist countries while being fundamentally similar enough not to preclude meaningful comparisons. An even more pragmatic reason for this selection is that the comparative attitude data available is comprehensive and of acceptable quality.

The four countries of concern can be arranged along the axis from "coordinated" to "liberal" market economies, with Sweden and Germany being textbook examples of "coordinated" market economies, and Britain and, even more so, the United States being instances of "liberal" ones. Such a dichotomy is particularly salient when we consider the wage bargaining systems that are in place in these countries (Rueda and Pontusson 2000; Pontusson et al. 2002). In Sweden and Germany, we find well-developed, centralized employer-employee negotiation systems for pay and other work conditions; in the United States and Britain, such systems are almost totally absent.

There is also a marked difference in the status of the labor unions between the liberal and coordinated market economies. In Sweden and Germany (albeit less so in the latter), the unions participate much more in the decision-making process at both a corporate and societal level than in Britain and the United States (see the relevant chapters in Hyman and Ferner 1998). In the case of Sweden, this is combined with a high degree of labor organization; the United States, on the other hand, has the lowest union membership of all wealthy Western economies (Western 1997; Kjellberg 1998).

The presence of wage bargaining institutions and the organization and strength of the workforce are critical factors in determining current pay discrepancies and their development over time (Rueda and Pontusson 2000; Pontusson et al. 2002). A comparison of the pay levels of full-time employees illustrates this. In the mid-1990s, people in the 90th percentile of the income distribution in each country earned approximately 4.6 times (US), 3.4 times (Britain), 2.8 times (Germany), and 2.2 times (Sweden) as much those in the 10th percentile. Of all the developed countries, the United States has the greatest pay spread, while Sweden and the other Nordic countries have the smallest. Wage and salary differentials have widened in all four countries since the early mid-1980s, but much more so in Britain and the United States than in Sweden and Germany (Rueda and Pontusson 2000: 354–356).

If we broaden our scope to cover differences in disposable household income, we also have the effects of household composition, labor force participation, self-employment, capital income, and taxation and transfer systems to take into account. In the mid-1990s, the disposable household income of the 90th percentile in each country was 5.6 times (US), 4.6 times (Britain), 3.2 times (Germany), and 2.6 times (Sweden) higher than that of the 10th percentile. In this respect, the United States and Sweden are polar opposites in the industrialized world (we have to look to Latin America to find greater income gaps than in the United States) (Smeeding 2002: 185). By the same measure, inequalities have also increased in all four countries since the early mid-1980s, and in this respect too they have grown more sharply in Britain and the United States than in Sweden and Germany (Smeeding 2002: 195).

One question we can therefore ask is how attitudes to income distribution are affected by these institutional and distributory differences between countries. Or more specifically: How will class differences in attitudes to income distribution manifest themselves in each of the four countries? Two possible and diametrically opposed hypotheses can be applied here. Since income distribution is very much the object of discussion and negotiation in the coordinated market economies, it is here that we will find the most salient class differences. We can hardly expect to find Lane's "market fatalism" (1986) in countries where income distribution is as politicized as it is in the coordinated market economies. On the other hand, it might possibly be stronger in countries such as Britain and the United States, where wage levels are the result of (ostensibly) impersonally operative market forces.

The opposing hypothesis is that since actual income gaps are much wider and have grown much more quickly in Britain and the United States than in Sweden and Germany, they are much more likely to trigger class antagonisms in these liberal market economies. Put rather crassly, the workers have more to gain and the upper nonmanuals more to lose from redistribution in countries where inequality is greater. If this is one of the instruments behind the formation of attitudes toward income distribution, we would also expect to find greater class differences in the Britain and the United States than in Sweden and Germany.

Another issue of interest for this chapter is how class differences in attitudes toward the market change over time. As we have noted, pay and income differentials have gradually increased in all four countries, particularly so in Britain and the United States; does this also mean that class polarizations in attitudes toward income differentials have become more entrenched as time has passed, and mostly so in these two countries? Or do we find instead that the countries gradually start to resemble one another?

We can also question the general assumption that a lower position on the class hierarchy engenders a more skeptical view of market distribution, by noting that attitudes in this area are multidimensional. Believing something about pay differentials between different occupations is not the same as having ideas about income distribution or the causes of inequality. Class patterns need not be identical in all areas, not even within one and the same attitudinal domain.

So which aspects of attitudes toward the market are we to compare? The first issue we will examine is how wide a pay/income disparity is considered reasonable in all four countries. To do this, we will construct indices of legitimate income differentials on the basis of responses to questions concerning what specific occupations should earn, which we will then compare by country and class and over time.

The second area of inquiry concerns attitudes toward income distribution. To what extent do people consider income differentials excessive and redistribution necessary? Are there any national and class differences in this regard, and do these opinions change over time?

The third issue concerns the perceived causes of inequality. Is inequality primarily the outcome of distributive conflicts or of the need to create incentives for personal development and hard work? And to what extent are these explanations mutually exclusive: can whoever sees inequality as the result of distributional conflict also consider it motivating?

Fourth, we will examine one or two points relating to people's views on the ideal compass of the market. What do the different classes in each country believe that money should buy? Is it fair that people on high incomes use their greater wealth to purchase better health care or better schooling for their children?

Last, we will analyze how different ideas about inequality fit together. Not only levels and class patterns of attitudes, but also the integration of attitudes into a coherent whole is something that might be affected by the institutional environment in which people are embedded. Are those who entertain certain ideas about the causes of inequality also inclined to believe certain things about ideal income spreads or what money should be able to buy? Do these "mental packages" vary between countries and classes?

There are, of course, other opinions about the market that could be examined, such as opinions about its efficiency and the level and targets of consumption, but comparable data on these areas are lacking. Instead, the concerns of this chapter are confined to aspects that focus on the distribution of income and other resources.

DATA AND VARIABLES

The data analyzed in this chapter are taken from the 1992 and 1999 ISSP surveys on *Social Inequality* (see the introductory chapter for a general description of the ISSP).[3] These data allow the first three aspects to be examined as a function of time; only the 1999 survey provides data for the fourth.

All four countries in this study use random sampling methods to survey the adult population. The gross sample size is approximately 2,000 individuals (considerably more in the case of Germany in 1992). In Sweden, the ISSP surveys are conducted by postal questionnaire with regular reminders; in the other countries, they are included as a supplement to national surveys in which the questionnaires are delivered to the sample individuals ("drop off").

The non-response rate for countries varies and is sometimes alarmingly high. Non-response rates range from 26% (the U.S. in 1992) to 57% (Germany in 1999), and typically hovers around 40%.[4] Just what effect these dropout rates have on the results is difficult to ascertain. On the whole, the gender and age composition of the respondents differs little from that of the total population; what may disrupt their representativeness, however, is that the respondents may deviate attitudinally from the rest of the population, and there is no reliable way of determining whether this is the case. A qualified guess (based on what we have learned from fieldwork organizations) is that those who are interested in the subject of the survey will be overrepresented among the respondents. We may therefore assume that if we would also manage to canvass the uninterested, the responses of the "Don't know" or "Neither agree nor disagree" type would increase in number, probably with little impact on attitudinal trends and balance measures. It should also be noted that in an analysis on class differences in attitudes there is a slight underrepresentation of groups without tertiary or even upper-secondary education; that is, workers and lower nonmanuals are probably slightly underrepresented in the achieved samples.

Class—the main independent variable in the analysis—is indicated by the class schema devised by Erikson and Goldthorpe. This perspective views classes as constituted by *employment relations* (Erikson and Goldthorpe 1992: Ch. 2; Goldthorpe 2000). According to this perspective, classes are aggregations of positions within labor markets and production units and can be operationalized through a combination of occupation title and employment status. The schema exists in several versions; in this paper, the occupational codes used in the countries in question are recoded into six classes: unskilled workers, skilled workers, routine nonmanual employees, Service class II (lower-level controllers and administrators), Service class I (higher-level controllers and administrators), and the self-employed.[5]

WHO SHOULD EARN WHAT?—LEGITIMATE
INCOME DIFFERENTIALS

What do the different classes consider to be legitimate income differentials between groups? One way to examine this, as was applied in the ISSP surveys, is simply to ask how much people with a particular occupation should earn (after asking how much they think they actually earn). An almost infinite number of indices can be constructed from this information, each highlighting a particular aspect of what is considered a reasonable income span. Table 6.1 shows the occupations that were included in the 1992 and 1999 surveys and that form the basis of the composite indices that we have constructed and then analyzed.[6]

In Table 6.1, all occupations have been placed in relation to what people in each of the four countries consider an unskilled factory worker should earn. A number of composite indices may be constructed from the indicators in the table. The one provided at the bottom of Table 6.1, the "pay spread index," gives the average relation between the six highest-paying occupations and the three lowest in the table.[7]

As we can see, the differences between the four countries are considerable, Sweden occupying a unique position. The average person in Sweden believes that top business executives should earn about 3 times as much as

TABLE 6.1
Legitimate income differences in Sweden, Britain, Germany, and the United States, 1992 and 1999.

What do you think people in these jobs ought to be paid?	SWEDEN		BRITAIN		GERMANY[a]		US	
	1992	1999	1992	1999	1992	1999	1992	1999
An unskilled worker in a factory?	100	100	100	100	100	100	100	100
A shop assistant?	105[b]	105	98	116	112	115	105	114
A skilled worker in a factory?	121	120	155	152	146	147	186	167
A doctor in general practice?	195	199	366	370	384	386	614	576
A lawyer?	240[b]	236	401	386	382	413	566	520
A cabinet minister in the national government?	226	244	466	470	446	455	500	448
A judge in [country's highest court]?	276[b]	273	584	604	418	479	627	580
A chairman of a large national company?	239	326	843	886	711	875	1114	1052
The owner-manager of a large factory?	301[b]	328	585	686	977	940	934	799
Pay Spread Index	224	245	454	477	465	488	551	516
(n-min)	(752)	(947)	(885)	(603)	(1858)	(700)	(1066)	(924)

[a] refers to Western Germany   [b] created value

unskilled workers, in the United States almost 10 times. In Sweden, people think that the high-paying occupations should award an average remuneration 2.5 times that of the low-paying occupations, in the United States over 5 times. In both cases, Britain and Germany end up nearer the American end of the scale than the Swedish. Given that the legitimate pay spread is growing in Europe and shrinking slightly in the United States, there was a certain tendency toward convergence in the 1990s; despite this, Sweden shows no signs of approaching British or German attitudes in this respect. The mutual differences are much smaller regarding what people believe low-paid workers should earn, and it is around the subject of high-paying occupations that the major disparities arise (cf. Kelley and Evans 1993).

Figure 6.1 shows how the class differences on the "pay spread index" differ by country and year.[8] Notwithstanding the expected tendencies (e.g., that the *Service class* looks more favorably on large pay differences than the workers do), what is interesting are the many exceptions and small class differences. While it may be true that the upper nonmanual group advocates large pay differentials to a much greater extent than any other group, differences in attitude among the other classes are small and not fully consistent. The unskilled workers usually place themselves at the other end of the scale, but apart from that, any deviation from the attitudes of the other classes is minimal. Compared with many other attitudinal dimensions (Svallfors 2006), opinions regarding desired income differences seem to vary only slightly between the classes.[9]

Does this mean that class differences in attitudes toward the (re)distribution of income would also be negligible? Table 6.2 shows two statements from the surveys relating to income distribution in each country. In both cases, there is a five-point response scale from "agree strongly" to "disagree strongly" (with "neither agree nor disagree" being the mid-point). To obtain the mean, the responses have been recoded so that "disagree strongly" scores 0 and "agree strongly" scores 4, and the other response options 1 to 3 accordingly. The "class differential" is calculated by subtracting the mean value of the upper nonmanuals (the class that with only a few isolated exceptions returned the lowest value) from that for the unskilled workers (the class that with only a few isolated exceptions returned the highest value) for each of the statements.

As can be seen from Table 6.2, people in all four countries believe that income differentials are excessive. Moreover, the three European countries

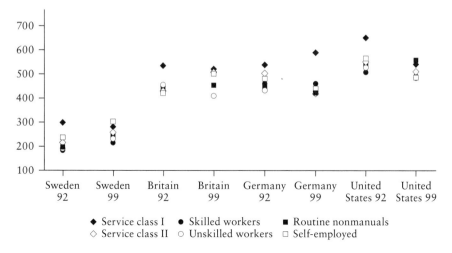

Figure 6.1. Pay Spread Index, 1992–1999.

converged in this respect during the 1990s, since in 1999 more Swedes had this opinion than at the start of the decade, and fewer Germans. In the United States, however, the number of people believing that pay differentials were too large declined, and in 1999 the number was lower than in the three other countries even though, as discussed earlier, actual income differences are greater here than elsewhere.

The United States also stands apart on two other points in the table: the number of people who believe that political measures should be taken to redress income distribution is much lower, and class opinions are more homogenous than in the three European countries. Sweden, closely followed by Germany, exhibits the greatest class differences, while Britain leans toward the United States, as class differences on this issue seem to have waned during the decade. This is also true of Sweden, while in Germany the classes were attitudinally entrenched, if not even more divergent.

To create a composite measure of attitudes toward income differentials, both indicators have been aggregated into one index, which has then been divided by its maximum value and multiplied by 100. The index then ranges between 0 and 100, the higher values denoting a more critical view of income disparity. Figure 6.2 shows the class differences by country and the trends during the 1990s.

TABLE 6.2

Class differences in attitudes to income redistribution in Sweden, Britain, Germany, and the United States, 1992 and 1999.

		SWEDEN		BRITAIN		GERMANY[a]		US	
		1992	1999	1992	1999	1992	1999	1992	1999
Differences in income in [COUNTRY] are too large.	% Agree	61	71	81	81	84	72	77	66
	Scale mean	2.63	2.87	3.08	3.05	3.07	2.85	2.92	2.76
	Class difference	1.24	0.80	0.58	0.31ns	0.58	0.66	0.26	0.34
It is the responsibility of the government to reduce the differences in income between people with high incomes and those with low incomes.	% Agree	54	60	65	68	66	47	38	35
	Scale mean	2.31	2.59	2.67	2.69	2.60	2.29	1.93	1.92
	Class difference	1.32	0.78	1.00	0.71	0.83	1.17	0.80	0.52

[a] refers to Western Germany   ns = class differences not significant at the 0.05 level

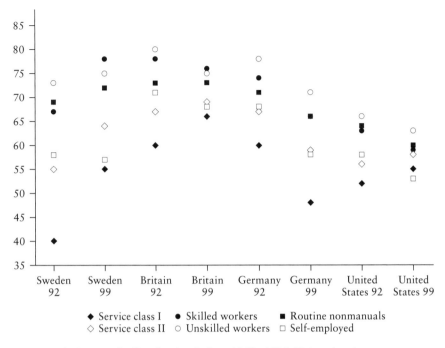

Figure 6.2. Income Redistribution Index, 1992–1999. Values by class.

One observation here is that the two market liberal countries (the United States and Britain) display the smallest class differences in attitudes toward income distribution. Moreover, in both cases these differences narrowed during the 1990s, something that we also notice in Sweden. It is also interesting that the only country in which the class differences remained stable, Germany, is also the only country in which wage bargaining institutions have not inclined toward market liberalism over the past few decades. There will be reason to return to this observation later.

WHAT CAUSES INEQUALITY?

Let us now take a step back in the process of income distribution and ask how the different classes tend to account for the causes of inequality. Such accounts may be of two diametrically opposed kinds. One sees inequality as the result of intergroup conflict and power imbalances; the fact that some people have more than others, the argument goes, is because certain groups have managed to appropriate more of what society has to offer than others. The second line of reasoning adopts a functionalist take on inequality, which it considers a necessary result of the higher remuneration warranted by certain levels of position and responsibility that either command particular authority or require specialist in-demand skills or competencies.

Naturally our job here is not to examine which of these two models has the greatest empirical backing or to judge how much they conflict with or complement each other. It is to investigate the extent to which the different classes in each country subscribe to them. It would be tempting to assume in advance that groups that are less favored by the market's distribution are more likely to see inequality as the result of power struggles than of any functional demands.

Such an expectation assumes that attitudes toward the causes of inequality are one-dimensional, in that whoever advocates the one will reject the other. This cannot, however, by any means be taken for granted. First, the two hypotheses are not mutually exclusive. Second, we cannot simply expect 100 percent consistency in the way people think; indeed, people can often hold contradictory and inconsistent views. Consequently, the extent to which explanations are one-dimensional or composite has to be an empirical issue.

The 1992 and 1999 ISSP surveys contain a collection of statements on the causes of inequality, which are reproduced in Table 6.3 along with the mean values and the class differentials. As can be seen, some of the statements used in the 1992 survey were not repeated in the 1999 survey. The mean value for each item has been calculated by recoding the responses on a 0–4 scale, on which the lower values, throughout, denote the more "inequality-friendly." Thus, whoever agrees with statements 1 and 3 in the table scores high, while whoever agrees with the other three statements scores low. The class differential has been calculated by subtracting the value for a member of Service class I from that for an unskilled worker.

We can make a number of surprising observations from Table 6.3. First, we can see that the countries vary only slightly in their opinions, and that any differences that are discernible are not at all what we might have expected. For instance, the Americans are less inclined than the Europeans to agree with the statements dealing with the necessity of inequality for raising the incentive for self-improvement and responsibility (statements 2, 4, and 5). The Swedes are remarkably prone to agree that inequality is

TABLE 6.3
Class differences in explanations for inequality in Sweden, Britain, Germany, and the United States, 1992 and 1999.

		SWEDEN		BRITAIN		GERMANY[a]		US	
		1992	1999	1992	1999	1992	1999	1992	1999
Inequality continues to exist because it benefits the rich and powerful.	% Agree	53	61	64	62	75	69	58	50
	Scale mean	2.46	2.58	2.68	2.59	2.88	2.77	2.49	2.36
	Class difference	0.85	0.71	0.66	0.29	0.63	0.45	0.35	0.32
No one would study for years to become a lawyer or doctor unless they expected to earn a lot more than ordinary workers.	% Agree	72	71	71	69	88	87	70	62
	Scale mean	1.20	1.24	1.25	1.39	0.78	0.74	1.27	1.43
	Class difference	-0.49	-0.22	-0.39	-0.41	-0.36	-0.30	-0.25	-0.32
Inequality continues to exist because ordinary people don't join together to get rid of it.	% Agree	36	39	41	37	47	43	49	47
	Scale mean	2.05	2.15	2.09	2.03	2.20	2.26	2.25	2.26
	Class difference	0.82	0.62	0.69	0.69	0.79	0.79	0.36	0.36
People would not want to take extra responsibility at work unless they were paid for it.	% Agree	76	—	78	—	72	—	66	—
	Scale mean	1.20	—	1.17	—	1.29	—	1.44	—
	Class difference	-0.06ns	—	-0.49	—	-0.23	—	-0.37	—
Workers would not bother to get skills and qualifications unless they were paid extra for having them.	% Agree	70	—	64	—	77	—	55	—
	Scale mean	1.32	—	1.43	—	1.17	—	1.71	—
	Class difference	-0.24ns	—	-0.43	—	-0.27	—	-0.39	—

[a] refers to Western Germany

ns = class differences not significant at the 0.05 level

needed to create incentives, and there are no signs that the long-standing dominance of social democracy has established any critical stance on the roots of inequality in this particular respect. It should be noted, however, that the items in question do not give any clear indication about the *magnitude* of inequality that respondents feel is necessary to create incentives. It could well be that respondents in Sweden have in mind a much smaller amount of inequality than respondents in the United States.

Another quite unexpected result is that class patterning are "inverted" on items touching on the incentive-generating effects of inequality. It is more common in all four countries for the workers to agree with these statements than the upper nonmanuals. Indeed, the class differences may not be as great here as they were for the conflict statements, but they are nonetheless statistically significant (except on one occasion—statement 4 in Sweden).

In other words, the adoption of a power and conflict perspective on inequality, as reflected in statements 1 and 3, does not necessarily imply the rejection of explanations that stress the incentive aspects of inequality. Manual workers are simultaneously more inclined to see inequality as the outcome of power and conflict and yet more inclined to believe in its powers as an incentive.

The finding that the conflict and incentive perspectives are actually two separate dimensions is also substantiated by correlation and dimension analyses of the statements. The first and third form one dimension, the others a second.[10] We can then, with good theoretical and empirical backing, consider these two dimensions as separate and sensitive in their own ways to class differences.

Against this backdrop, two composite indices were constructed by adding the values for 1 and 3, dividing the result by the maximum value for the index and multiplying by 100 to create a "conflict index." Similarly, an "incentive index" was formed using the same procedures for the other statements.[11] The indices are thus designed so that the higher values denote more "leftist" responses (i.e., those who score high on the "conflict index" and who therefore attribute inequality more to power differences, and those who score high on the "incentive index" and who thus believe *less* in the necessity of inequality for generating incentive). Given that the relevant statements for the "incentive index" were used only in 1992, we can study the class and country differences only for that year.

Figure 6.3 shows the results for the "conflict index." The national class

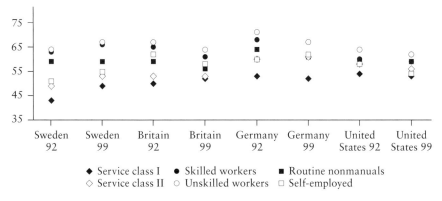

Figure 6.3. Conflict Index, 1992–1999. Values by class.

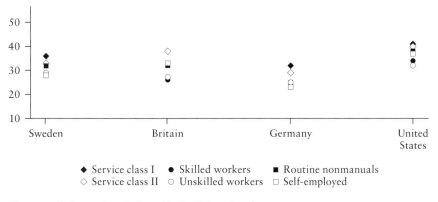

Figure 6.4. Incentives Index, 1992. Values by class.

differences are as we would have expected, with the highest index values among the unskilled workers (in Sweden we find largely the same index values among the skilled workers) and the lowest among the upper nonmanuals. The lower nonmanuals and the self-employed are placed somewhere between the workers and the service class. The class differences are slightly larger in Sweden than in the other European countries, and the lowest are in the United States.[12] Moreover, the gap closes slightly in all countries between 1992 and 1999, something that is particularly noticeable in Britain. Any intercountry differences are insignificant.

Figure 6.4 shows the pattern of class differences for the 1992 "incentive index." As could already be seen in Table 6.3, it was "inverted" in that we find the most "rightist" opinions among the working class, with the upper nonmanuals believing less in the necessity of inequality for creating incentive. The self-employed in Sweden and Germany score similarly to the workers, while in Britain and the United States they fall somewhere between the workers and Service class I.

We cannot overemphasize the importance of the results given in this section. The complexity of the class-attitude nexus is manifested in the way that the demarcators between classes and their relation to politics depend on which aspect of the causes of inequality we are considering. If it is inequality as the product of some need for incentive, the workers take a "rightist" position; this is possibly because university-educated people believe that there are incentives *other* than a higher income for entering higher education, something that may be less obvious to those without similar experiences. A related possibility is that the "incentive environment" in which the upper nonmanuals work differs from that of the workers, the latter offering fewer inherent rewards and incentive that is more purely pecuniary than the former.[13]

However, if our focus of inquiry is inequality as the result of power and conflict, the workers tend toward a "leftist" position. We can note here that the statements used to highlight this aspect of inequality have a rather "radically populist" wording (see Table 6.3). A more "reformist" approach would have been desirable, with the focus instead on the opportunities of redressing inequality through piecemeal political reform, but unfortunately no such data are available. It is not inconceivable that national differences on this point would have been greater if such questions had been studied instead.

WHAT SHOULD MONEY BUY?

Instead of taking a step back, as we did in the previous section, to examine which explanations of inequality are favored by the different classes, we can take a step *forward* and ask what they believe money should be able to buy. What do people see as the acceptable scope of inequality? How far can resource inequality affect different spheres of life without becoming unjust?

These issues are anchored in Walzer's (1983) theory of justice. Walzer dismisses what he refers to as a "simple equality" principle, which advocates equality within all spheres of life. Instead, he advances a "complex equality" principle, according to which different spheres of society can and should be characterized by different forms of equal treatment, whereby a high degree of inequality within any one sphere may be considered fair, provided that it does not become unduly dominant by spreading to other spheres. An unequal distribution of income need not be unjust if it has no impact, say, on people's chances of survival. A cardinal point in Walzer's thesis is therefore the importance of having "blocked exchanges" to prevent the inequality of one sphere spilling over into others. For example, all democracies embody rules that prevent the buying and selling of votes, and all welfare states have regulations preventing trade in human organs.

Our purpose here is not to discuss the practical possibilities of maintaining these boundaries between spheres, even less to debate Walzer's theory of justice and the criticism it has provoked (see, e.g., Rothstein 1998: 39–44). Our intention is to compare classes in the four countries and their opinions on the extent to which income differentials should impinge on societal spheres other than the economy. More precisely, we are interested in studying whether people believe it is fair for such differentials to show through in the ability to purchase better health care and education. Health and education can be considered staple resources, and so it would be interesting to see to what extent people feel that income differentials should be allowed to affect the quality of these services.

The 1999 ISSP survey contained two questions about this very issue; these are reproduced in Table 6.4, which also gives the percentage of people who considered it "just" (either "very" or "somewhat") that high incomes can be used to gain access to better health care/education, along with the mean value and the class difference. The mean value is recoded so that the response "very just" scores 0, "somewhat just" scores 1, "neither just nor unjust" scores 2, "somewhat unjust" scores 3, and "very unjust" scores 4. As in the earlier section, the class difference expresses the difference between the value for an unskilled manual worker and that for a member of the upper nonmanuals.

As we can see, the intercountry differences are considerable, while the interclass differences are not. Only about 10 percent of Swedes and Germans consider it fair that high-earners should be able to buy better health care or education. In Britain, it is 40 percent. While Britain and Sweden/Germany differ by more than one scale point in mean value for both questions, the corresponding differences between unskilled workers and Service class I are less than half a scale point in Sweden and Germany. Class differences are

TABLE 6.4

Class differences in attitudes to what money should buy in Sweden, Britain, Germany, and the United States, 1992 and 1999.

Is it just or unjust — right or wrong — that people with higher incomes can...		Sweden	Britain	Germany[a]	US
Buy better health care than people with lower incomes?	% "Just"	10	41	12	28
	Scale mean	3.14	1.94	2.87	2.36
	Class difference	0.39	−0.24ns	0.40ns	−0.08ns
Buy better education for their children than people with lower incomes?	% "Just"	11	44	12	32
	Scale mean	3.11	1.88	2.86	2.30
	Class difference	0.49	−0.14ns	0.34ns	−0.04ns

[a] refers to Western Germany   ns = class differences not significant at the 0.05 level

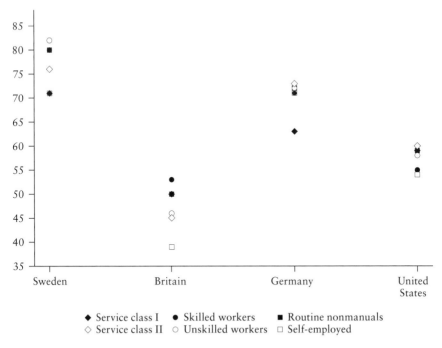

Figure 6.5. Welfare Purchase Index, 1999. Values by class.

even less marked in Britain and the United States and are even inverted, in that the upper nonmanuals are less inclined than the unskilled workers to believe in the fairness of this income/welfare purchase relationship.

Both questions have been combined into a "welfare purchase index" by being added together, divided by the maximum value for the index and multiplied by 100. This gives an index that, like all the indices published here, ranges between 0 and 100,[14] with the values being directly proportional to the belief in the unfairness of this relationship. Figure 6.5 shows the class and national differences.

Here, the marked intercountry differences and the modest interclass differences show up clearly. If we study the class patternings more closely, we find that only Sweden displays the expected class patterns, with the upper nonmanuals and self-employed being the least skeptical toward the fairness of what money can buy and the workers and lower nonmanuals most so. In Germany, it is only the upper nonmanuals who differ, while in the United States, the class differences are nonexistent (i.e., not even statistically significant at the 0.05 level). A puzzling pattern emerges in Britain, where the only distinct difference in attitude is found among the self-employed, who are the strongest advocates of the fairness of this income/welfare purchase relationship.

The results presented in this section are in many ways fascinating from a class perspective. The two liberal market economies (the United States and Britain) have a much greater acceptance of the ability of money to buy health care and education, and display nonexistent or unexpected class differences in this respect; in the coordinated market economies of Sweden and Germany, however, the patternings are completely different. This suggests that the national institutional configurations profoundly shape people's views of what money should be able to buy or, to put it another way, of the legitimate compass of the market. It also suggests that there is an inverse correlation in this regard between the accepted legitimacy of market principles and class differences.

The fact that aggregated country differences are so substantial between the coordinated and the liberal market economies both confirms and contradicts the perspective set out in Chapter 1. Public policies tend, as pointed out in the introduction, to create feelings of entitlements among ordinary citizens. The fact that the more wide-ranging and encompassing welfare states in Sweden and Germany tend to be followed by more skeptical views on the fairness of market criteria in health care and education is therefore not surprising. Less expected, however, are the more accepting views of market criteria among Britons than among Americans. One would have expected that the more private character of American health and education, contrasted with the long-standing existence of the NHS in Britain, would have created the opposite patterns. It is also noteworthy that we find little difference between the fields of health and education, even though private education has been historically widespread in Britain, while private health care has been virtually nonexistent. The findings in this regard are clearly in need of further interpretation.

WHAT IS THE RELATIONSHIP BETWEEN DIFFERENT ASPECTS OF ATTITUDES TOWARD INEQUALITY?

So far, our analyses have "taken one thing at a time" and examined class differences for each aspect or dimension separately. There is more to the issue, however, than that. It is just as interesting to see how views on various aspects of the market and inequality combine to form "mental packages."

It is not difficult to imagine that the different attitudes toward inequality would perhaps be related to one another; so that those who advocate small pay differences would also tend (a) to be critical of current income differences and in favor of redistribution, (b) to argue that inequality is created by power and conflict and is not a necessary incentive, and (c) to want to limit the ability of money to improve other aspects of life. Conversely, those who favor large pay differences should (a) have a more skeptical view of redistribution, (b) see inequality as a necessary incentive rather than the product of power struggle, and (c) consider it self-evident that money should affect other domains of life. However, is this what we actually observe among the different classes and countries?

One simple way to illustrate how different aspects of market and inequality relate is to correlate all the composite indices that have been constructed in this chapter and compare by class and country the nature of the patterns that thus emerge. Table 6.5 provides such a correlation matrix, in part by country and in part for unskilled workers and the upper nonmanuals separately. To keep the numbers manageable, we have reproduced only the results for Sweden and the United States; in most respects discussed below, the other two countries adopt a midway position along this axis. When correlation data for both 1992 and 1999 have been available, we have chosen those relating to the latter year. This has no impact on the results.

Table 6.5 yields some interesting information. If we start by considering the upper part of the table, it would seem that attitude patterns in Sweden are more ideally related than they are in the United States. Correlations are generally higher in Sweden than in the United States, indicating a more integrated attitude spectrum.[15]

At first glance, it might appear that Sweden's more integrated attitudinal pattern would not apply to the correlation between the "incentive index" and the other aspects. However, it is important to remember that the manner of its construction (i.e., the higher the value, the *less* the adherence to the "incentive" rationale) means that higher values represent more "leftist" responses. Bearing this in mind, the moderately strong *negative* correlations that we see between this index and the "redistribution" and "conflict" indices in the United States should be viewed rather as somewhat inconsistent, or at least an indication of a low degree of attitudinal integration.

TABLE 6.5

Correlations between indices among unskilled workers and Service class I in Sweden and the United States, Pearson's R × 100.

	Pay spread	Redistribution	Conflict	Incentive	Welfare purchase
Whole sample					
Sweden					
Pay spread					
Redistribution	−35**				
Conflict	−18**	56**			
Incentive	−05	−01	−09*		
Welfare purchase	−16**	35**	25**	—	
US					
Pay spread					
Redistribution	−16**				
Conflict	−15**	46**			
Incentive	−01	−19**	−30*		
Welfare purchase	−13**	24**	13**	—	
Service Class I				*Unskilled workers*	
Sweden					
Pay spread		−39**	−15**	−13	−11
Redistribution	−46**		47**	−07	28**
Conflict	−35**	57**		−22**	23**
Incentive	−16	29**	05		—
Welfare purchase	−12	35**	30**	—	
US					
Pay spread		−08	−05	07	−12
Redistribution	−32**		37**	−21**	20**
Conflict	−32**	53**		−30**	00
Incentive	03	−15*	−24**		—
Welfare purchase	−25**	33**	17*	—	

** = significant at 0.01 level; * = significant at 0.05 level.

Comparing the indices correlations with each other, we find a very close match between the "conflict index" and the "redistribution index." This means that those who consider inequality the product of power and conflict are more likely to consider income differentials excessive and in need of redistribution.[16] There is also a close relationship between the "redistribution index" and the "welfare purchase index," suggesting that those who believe in income redistribution are also less inclined to accept that money should buy better health care and education. Using Walzer's terminology, we could say that proponents of a "simple equality" principle in the domain of income distribution also tend to support a "complex equality" principle regarding the scope of monetary power.

In the lower part of the table, we can compare attitudinal integration among the upper nonmanuals (the lower-left trilateral for each country) with that among the unskilled workers (the upper-right trilateral). Doing this, we find that the relationship between indices, with a few exceptions, is stronger among the upper nonmanuals than the workers.[17] Notions of inequality are somewhat more integrated in the former group than in the latter.[18]

For instance, it is more common for the workers to agree that inequality is the product of power and conflict, *and* that it is necessary to generate incentive, *and* again that incomes should be more equally distributed. Only among the Swedish upper nonmanuals do we find the expected correlation: that adherents to the "power/conflict" rationale of inequality also tend to dismiss its "incentive" claims. This tendency is, however, weak (Pearson's R = 0.05, not sign).

The class differences in attitudinal integration are more salient in the United States than in Sweden. When we compare the American and Swedish upper nonmanuals, we find that these differences are not so great; however, if we compare the American and Swedish working classes, they become highly conspicuous. In other words, we find that the class differences in correlational patterns in Sweden are not as strong as they are in the United States.

CONCLUSION

Do class differences on the market also create class differences in attitudes toward the market and its distribution? Or is Lane (1986) correct in proclaiming the dominance of market fatalism and in his contention that market distribution generates only a small measure of dissatisfaction? If so, is this manifested by a tendency for all classes, regardless of their relative strength on the market, to have the same attitudes toward inequality and distribution? The answers to these questions must be both qualified and ambiguous.

Lane's theory is substantiated by our findings that class differences are often remarkably small and that groups that can hardly be counted among the market's winners also accept an appreciable spread of income and recognize the legitimacy of market principles. This is particularly the case in the liberal market economies of Britain and the United States, where the working class's acceptance of money's ability to buy health care and education in the former and of large income gaps in the latter is astonishing.

Lane is also backed up by the finding that attitudes toward income disparity as a necessary incentive are not only widespread in all four countries but also favored by the working classes more than any other. It could of course be debated whether believing in the need of income differences for propagating responsibility and improvement is tantamount to accepting the principles of market legitimacy. To some extent it is rather a "meritocratic" belief that hard work and effort need to be rewarded, a belief that is in harmony with many different conceptions of justice. It is, however, highly consistent with prevailing legitimizing principles for market distributions, and from that point of view it is interesting to see that workers to a larger extent than higher nonmanuals tend to accept that inequality is necessary to induce effort.

However, it should be noted that in most respects the coordinated economies of Sweden and Germany evince more distinct class differences than the liberal market economies. This suggests that the greater the politicization of market distribution, the sharper the class differences tend to be. One possible interpretation of this is that when principles of distribution are politically articulated, people are more likely to think of themselves as members of a collective with certain interests and standards rather than as atomized market actors. National variations of this kind never appear in Lane's rationale since it lacks an institutional and comparative focus.

The economy that has undergone the most radical transformation toward "more market" or, in the terms of this volume (see Chapter 1), has been recommodified most rapidly—that of Britain—also seems to be the

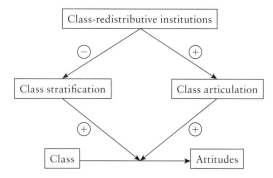

Figure 6.6. Institutions, class stratification, and class articulation.

clearest example of how class differences in attitudes to market distribution narrowed during the 1990s. This is yet another indication of how more clear-cut market distributions, paradoxically enough, tend to be accompanied by smaller class differences in attitudes. The reduced class differences in attitudes toward income distribution that we found in all countries except Germany (see Figure 6.6) are also of interest in this context, as they suggest that the only country where wage-bargaining institutions have remained unchanged over the past decade is also the one with the most stable class differences.

This is probably because such institutions, like those of a more pronounced welfare-state nature, act as focal points for distributive conflicts, with clearly drawn battle lines and conspicuously normative choices (cf. Edlund's chapter in this volume). In more out-and-out market situations, class conflicts tend to become atomized and Lane's "market fatalism" comes into play.

Figure 6.6 is a schematic representation of our line of reasoning.[19] As can be seen, the "class-redistributive institutions" (by which I mean welfare states, collective wage bargaining systems, etc.) impact the class/attitude nexus in two ways. On the one hand, they tend to mitigate the actual class stratification of society by modifying and redistributing the market's allocated resources. All else constant, this would help to undermine the class-attitude structure since a strong class stratification tends to build strong links between class and attitudes. But all else is far from constant. The class-redistributive institutions, we must remember, also help to empower class political articulation, which in turn *enhances* the links between class and attitudes. Our findings as reproduced in this chapter suggest that it is this latter effect that is the more dominant.

At the same time we should be drawing attention to the national differences in the nature of the class/attitude nexus, we should remember that they display considerable homogeneity from one country to the next. The interclass ranking on different attitudinal indices is often strikingly identical, as are the relative intraclass distances. It is clear that at work here are common underlying mechanisms that rest on the different risks and resources with which each class happens to be endowed and that tend to create similar class differences in attitudes in highly disparate institutional and political environments (cf. Wright 1985: Ch 7; 1997: Part IV).

The significance of bringing institutions and political articulation into consideration also becomes obvious when we endeavor to understand the results in the last part of this chapter. Here we showed that attitudinal integration was more apparent in Sweden than in the United States, and more distinct among the upper nonmanuals than among the workers. Differences between classes regarding the integration of attitudinal patternings were thus larger in the United States, where the working class displays a high degree of attitudinal fragmentation.

One way to interpret such differences is to see them as the outcome of political organization and articulation. Granberg and Holmberg (1988) find, as we do, that Swedish attitudes are more integrated than American attitudes; they also find that Swedes are more inclined to vote in accordance with these attitudes than are Americans. The principal explanation for this, they argue, is to be found in the differences in party systems between the countries. They also note that education seems to have a more profound effect on the degree of convergence between ideology and voting behavior in the United States than in Sweden, a finding that concurs with the class differences reported here.

However, the institutional framework and political articulation extend far beyond the compass of the party system, and it is this broader perspective that we have applied here. In a country such as the United States, with its feeble labor market institutions, weak union organization, lack of left-wing party, and virtually market-controlled media exposure, it is perhaps hardly surprising that the attitudinal integration among the working class is anything but tight. In a way, it is more interesting that class patternings emerge at all *in spite of* this lack of political articulation. In all these respects, the Swedish situation is different and, in terms of the ideological integration of the working class, is much more favorable.

In many respects, it is much easier for the upper nonmanuals to achieve ideological integration. Their higher education, positions of power and responsibility, and generally more resource-rich networks, make it easier for them to interlink specific attitudes and to register any contradictions that may arise. The upper nonmanual who entertains fundamentally right-wing political beliefs also has such values confirmed and embedded in a political context through the many editorials and commentaries published/broadcast in the privately owned mass media. This is, of course, particularly marked in the United States, where alternative publicity channels are few and far between, but it is also a salient feature of the otherwise socially democratic Sweden. This is of fundamental importance, since the integration of opinions into coherent ideologies, or even programs of action, is just as important as the standpoints adopted within specific attitudinal dimensions. Thinking that remains fragmented and incoherent is hardly a solid platform for successful action.

NOTES

* The chapter is a revised and extended version of chapter 4 in Stefan Svallfors *The Moral Economy of Class*, Stanford University Press, 2006. The text also includes some sections from the concluding chapter of that book.

1. At least this is what, in theory, can and should happen in politics. In reality, things are not so straightforward. It can, for example, be difficult to locate where in the political machine responsibility should lie, and who should be punished for our displeasure. In such situations, displeasure can undermine faith in politics *per se* rather than in individual political acts or actors (Kumlin 2003).

2. The empirical analyses in the chapter concern only Western Germany, i.e., the *Bundesländer* that formed West Germany before 1990. Analyzing data from Eastern Germany as well will complicate the institutional perspective applied since the formative institutional experiences in East Germany were of a completely different kind during much of the postwar period.

3. This survey was also conducted in 1987, but at the time Sweden was not a member of ISSP and the occupational data registered were not sufficiently detailed to allow the same class categorizations as in later years.

4. Further information on samples and nonresponses can be obtained from the data archive website www.gesis.org/en/data_service/issp/ (under "Data and documentation").

5. The class variable is based on the occupation of the individual. Individuals who are not currently working are classified according to their most recent occupation (if any). Individuals who have never worked but whose spouse works or has worked are classified according their spouses' occupations. For Germany, the United States, and the Swedish and British 1999 samples, recodings were made from the International Standard Classification of Occupations (ISCO). The recodings from 1992 build on ISCO68, while the ones from 1999 build on the updated and revised ISCO88. The logic and procedures for reclassifying ISCO into Goldthorpe classes are adapted from Ganzeboom and Treiman (1996; 2003). Minor deviations between their recodings and the ones used here occur due to national deviations from the standard ISCO classification. In Britain for 1992, recodings were based on the British Standard Occupational Classification (SOC, 3-digit level) and Employment Status Variables, following a scheme provided by John Goldthorpe and Anthony Heath (Goldthorpe and Heath 1992). The data for this reclassification were supplied by the National Centre for Social Research, since the ISSP archive data file included only SOC at the two-digit level. The Swedish 1992 data use the Socio-economic Classification (SEI) and the Nordic Occupational Classification (NYK). The former occupation schema is very similar to the Goldthorpe schema, while the latter is a national adaptation of ISCO68. The reclassification from the Swedish occupational classifications was adapted from Robert Erikson, Janne Jonsson, and Michael Tåhlin at the Swedish Institute for Social Research. The classification used here is not as detailed as theirs, since some of the relevant information is missing from the Swedish ISSP data. Files of recodings may be obtained from the author.

6. The first *Social Inequality* survey was actually conducted in Sweden in 1991, before the country was a member of ISSP. This was effectively a replication of the 1987 survey on the same theme, and includes a list of occupations that differs in part from that of the 1992 survey. Values have been created for the missing occupations (compared with the other countries) by placing them in relation to similar occupations and then making the assumption that the differences between them would have been just as much in 1992 as they proved to be in 1999. In practice, this means that Legitimate income for a shop assistant = Legitimate income for unskilled factory worker $\times$ 1.05; Legitimate income for a lawyer = Legitimate income for a doctor $\times$ 1.23; Legitimate income for a company director = Legitimate income for a chairman $\times$ 1.26; and the Legitimate income for a judge = Legitimate income for a minister $\times$ 1.22.

7. Alternative pay spread indices were tested (cf. Svallfors 2006: Ch. 4). The "top pay index" gives the relation between chairman and director on the one hand and both worker categories on the other. The "high pay index" shows how much people think the six high-paying occupations should earn in relation to what they *believe* an unskilled worker earns, while the "low pay index" gives the corresponding relationships for the three lowest paying occupations in the

table. The class differences for the first two indices are consistent with those for the "pay spread index," while class differences for the "low pay index" are small across the board.

8. The point estimates that are displayed in the figures throughout the chapter were subjected to two kinds of statistical significance testing. First, class differences within countries were tested to determine whether they were statistically significant (0.05 level). In the (few) cases where this was not the case for the indices in question, this is reported in the text. Second, the statistical significance was checked for the differences between countries in the class-attitudes association. This was done by calculating confidence intervals for the point estimates for the highest and the lowest class estimate for each country, and then checking whether the confidence intervals for the entire span overlapped between countries. In the cases where these confidence intervals did not overlap between countries, it was concluded that the class-attitudes association actually differed between countries. The significance level for these checks was set at the 0.05 level. The detailed results of these checks of statistical significance are not reported in the text but can be obtained from the author. Whenever claims are made in conjunction with figures that class differences differ between countries, these intercountry differences are statistically significant (0.05 level).

9. An indication of this is that the Eta correlation ratio varies between 0.08 and 0.18 for seven of the eight parameters in Figure 6.1, which is fairly weak though significant. The fact that the Eta value for Sweden in 1992 is no less than 0.36, denoting a rather strong correlation, is probably due to the artificial generation of a number of occupational values and the effect this had on narrowing the spread of income groups.

10. Factor analyses of the 1992 dataset (principal components, Varimax rotation) show that two factors are distinguished in all countries except the United States when the criterion Eigenvalue > 1 is applied to determine the number of factors. The other factor in the United States falls just "below the line" (Eigenvalue $= 0.99$). When a two-factor solution is applied in the United States, we obtain exactly the same pattern as in the other countries.

11. The reliability of the "conflict index" is worryingly poor, especially in the United States and Britain. For the United States, the Cronbach's alpha reliability coefficient is only 0.36 for 1992 and 0.45 for 1999; for Britain the corresponding values are 0.45 and 0.37. This suggests that in both these countries, the index's substatements measure partially different things. The values are somewhat better for Germany and Sweden (0.50 – 0.58) but are still not fully satisfactory. The results of this index should therefore be interpreted with great caution. However, Table 6.3 shows that the class differences on the two substatements are similar. The "incentive index" is consistently more reliable (0.65 – 0.71) and appears less problematic.

12. We could have attributed this to the poor reliability of the index in the

United States (see previous footnote), but as we can see in Table 6.3, the class differences are smaller in the United States on both statements of the index.

13. My thanks to Åsa Gustafson, who suggested this interpretation.

14. The two statements in the index have extremely high correlations (>0.7), and the Cronbach's alpha reliability coefficient is therefore >0.9 in all four countries. This suggests that people do not differentiate between health and education in their responses but tend to give similar answers to both.

15. The differences between Sweden and the United States are statistically significant (0.05 level) for six out of nine of the coefficients.

16. In a previous paper (Svallfors 1993) I even treated all these subissues as indicators of "Redistribution," which would now appear to have been a dubious procedure to adopt.

17. Tests of statistical significance of the differences in coefficients between workers and higher nonmanuals produce mixed results, something which also is the case for the Sweden–United States comparison within particular classes. Only a handful of these are statistically significant, since the small (*n*)s tend to result in large standard errors, rendering even large nominal differences statistically nonsignificant. The results in these respects must therefore be seen as indicative rather than conclusive.

18. It might seem perplexing that the correlation among the upper nonmanuals *and* the workers is lower or higher on certain matters than the correlation for the entire sample. All this means, however, is that it is in *other* classes we find higher or lower correlations.

19. Thanks to Staffan Kumlin for providing the idea behind the figure.

REFERENCES

Erikson, R., and Goldthorpe, J. H. 1992. *The Constant Flux: A Study of Class Mobility in Industrial Societies.* Oxford: Clarendon Press.

Fligstein, N. 2001. *The Architecture of Markets: An Economic Sociology of Twenty-first Century Capitalist Societies.* Princeton, N.J.: Princeton University Press.

Ganzeboom, H. B. G., and Treiman, D. J. 1996. Internationally Comparable Measures of Occupational Status for the 1988 International Standard Classification of Occupations. *Social Science Research*, 25, 201–239.

Ganzeboom, H. B. G., and Treiman, D. J. 2003. Three Internationally Standardised Measures for Comparative Research on Occupational Status. In *Advances in Cross-National Comparison*, edited by J. H. P. Hoffmeyer-Zlotnik and C. Wolf. New York: Kluwer, pp. 159–193.

Goldthorpe, J. H. 2000. Social Class and the Differentiation of Employment Contracts. In *On Sociology: Numbers, Narratives and the Integration of Research and Theory*, edited by J. H. Goldthorpe. Oxford: Clarendon Press, pp. 206–229.

Goldthorpe, J. H., and Heath, A. 1992. *Revised Class Schema 1992*, Joint Unit for the Study of Social Trends. Oxford: Nuffield College.

Granberg, D., and Holmberg, S. 1988. *The Political System Matters: Social Psychology and Voting Behavior in Sweden and the United States.* Cambridge: Cambridge University Press.

Granovetter, M. 1985. Economic Action and Social Structures: The Problem of Embeddedness. *American Journal of Sociology*, 91, 481–510.

Hall, P. A., and Soskice, D. W. 2001. *Varieties of Capitalism: The Institutional Foundations of Comparative Advantage.* Oxford: Oxford University Press.

Hyman, R., and Ferner, A. 1998. *Changing Industrial Relations in Europe.* Oxford: Blackwell.

Kelley, J., and Evans, M. D. 1993. The Legitimation of Inequality—Occupational Earnings in 9 Nations. *American Journal of Sociology*, 99, 75–125.

Kjellberg, A. 1998. Sweden: Restoring the Model? In *Changing Industrial Relations in Europe* (2nd ed.), edited by R. Hyman and A. Ferner. Oxford: Blackwell, pp. 74–117.

Kumlin, S. 2003. Snedvridet ansvarsutkrävande? In *Demokratitrender*, edited by H. Oscarsson. Göteborg: SOM-institutet Göteborgs universitet, pp. 31–53.

Lane, R. E. 1986. Market Justice, Political Justice. *American Political Science Review*, 80, 383–402.

Mau, S. 2003. *The Moral Economy of Welfare States. Britain and Germany Compared.* London: Routledge.

Polanyi, K. 1944. *The Great Transformation.* New York: Farrar & Rinehart.

Pontusson, J., Rueda, D., and Way, C. R. 2002. Comparative Political Economy of Wage Distribution: The Role of Partisanship and Labour Market Institutions. *British Journal of Political Science*, 32, 281–308.

Rothstein, B. 1998. *Just Institutions Matter: The Moral and Political Logic of the Universal Welfare State.* Cambridge: Cambridge University Press.

Rueda, D., and Pontusson, J. 2000. Wage Inequality and Varieties of Capitalism. *World Politics*, 52, 350–383.

Smeeding, T. M. 2002. Globalization, Inequality and the Rich Countries of the G-20: Evidence from the Luxembourg Income Study (LIS). In *Globalisation, Living Standards, and Inequality: Recent Progresses and Continuing Challenges*, edited by D. Gruen, T. O'Brien, and J. Lawson. Sydney: MacMillan, pp. 179–206.

Soskice, D. W. 1999. Divergent Production Regimes: Coordinated and Uncoordinated Market Economies in the 1980s and 1990s. In *Continuity and Change in Contemporary Capitalism*, edited by H. Kitschelt, P. Lange, G. Marks, and J. D. Stephens. Cambridge: Cambridge University Press, pp. 101–134.

Svallfors, S. 1993. Dimensions of Inequality: A Comparison of Attitudes in Sweden and Britain. *European Sociological Review*, 9, 267–287.

Svallfors, S. 1996. *Välfärdsstatens moraliska ekonomi: välfärdsopinionen i 90-talets Sverige.* Umeå: Boréa.

Svallfors, S. 2006. *The Moral Economy of Class. Class and Attitudes in Comparative Perspective*. Stanford, Calif: Stanford University Press.

Walzer, M. 1983. *Spheres of Justice: A Defense of Pluralism and Equality*. New York: Basic Books.

Western, B. 1997. *Between Class and Market: Postwar Unionization in the Capitalist Democracies*. Princeton, N.J.: Princeton University Press.

Wright, E. O. 1985. *Classes*. London: Verso.

Wright, E. O. 1997. *Class Counts: Comparative Studies in Class Analysis*. Cambridge: Cambridge University Press.

CHAPTER SEVEN

Are We the People?

National Sentiments in a Changing Political Landscape

Mikael Hjerm

We have seen that differences among welfare state regimes affect the structure of class differences in attitudes. We have also seen how experiences with institutions and welfare state programs affect trust, political alienation, and general welfare state support. Institutions matter for people's preferences and actions, which in turn matter for the existence of institutions. However, this does not tell the whole story of institutions and their possibilities and limitations. Alesina and Glaeser (2004) conclude in their comparison of poverty in Europe and the United States that different institutions explain differences in the actions taken to remedy poverty. The emergence and existence of these institutions is a result of differences in ethnic and cultural homogeneity between Europe and the United States. This shows that the limitations as well as possibilities, at present and in the future, of what the state can and cannot do are dependent on the people making up the political entity, that is, the *demos*. Lord Acton formulated this over 150 years ago when he said, "The great importance of nationality in the State consists in the fact that it is the basis for political capacity. The character of a nation determines in great measure the form and vitality of the State" (Acton, 1996 [1862], p. 36). This position is of as immediate interest today as it was 150 years ago. If we do not understand the character of the nation, how can we understand the possibilities and limitations of the nation-state?

This question becomes even more important today in times of shifts in the decision-making process, the formation of new groups of solidarity across state borders, increasing migratory movements, and so on. In other words, the solidarity binding the *demos* together is under pressure. The question is whether the basis for political capacity founded in the nation-state is withering away with diminishing solidarity among the members of the *demos*. In seeking the answer, we set out to examine possible changes in various forms of national attachment, or sentiment, in seven countries. We will examine whether such sentiments have changed in strength, substance, and effect over the period 1995–2003.

In a world of presumed nation-states, the nation is the primary collective identity for the legitimization of political and social institutions. The need for the nation as the sole provider of collective identity is questionable as there clearly are other forms of collectivity. The need for, at least, a minimum form of collective identity for sustaining a *demos* is, however, unquestionable (Cederman, 2001; Dahl, 1989; Weiler, 1999). Cederman captures this well in his definition of *demos* as "a group of people the vast majority of which feels sufficiently attached to each other to be willing to engage in democratic discourse and binding decision-making" (p. 144). This understanding gives rise to two important questions: First, how large is the "vast majority"? and second, what does this "attachment" consist of?

The first question, of how vast the majority needs to be, is beyond the scope of this chapter. All people in any given society need to adhere to at least a minimum form of constitutional attachment and affiliation. Democracy theorists often seem to overlook that attachment, and identities are never solely based upon such thin political unity. They simply do not account for the institutionalization of cultural aspects in the political sphere. The story of all nation-states is the story of cultural pluralism uniting under the banner of "We the People." This is a group of people, or a community of faith, that creates and sustains institutions that can govern for them. We cannot measure the degree of homogeneity needed for this to function,[1] but once in effect, the construction and preservation of homogeneity becomes institutionalized. This implies that the answer to the first question becomes highly dependent on the second question—namely, that how vast the majority needs to be depends on what the majority is.

The second question is very often taken for granted in that political theorists almost axiomatically assume that the *demos* needs to coincide with the *etnos* for functional political institutions to be possible (e.g., Lijphart, 1977; e.g., Scharpf, 1999). This line of reasoning is also put forward by liberal nationalists (Kymlicka, 1995; Miller, 1995; Moore, 2001; Tamir, 1993; Young, 1990). The latter do it from a somewhat different perspective in focusing on the question of equality in a plural society. They also assume, as do the political theorists, that some form of collective culture is intrinsic for national institutions to be functional. The liberal nationalists have not made the substance of such collective culture clear. Moreover, the liberal nationalists have also included an axiomatic understanding of human nature in assuming that *individuals* need a specific collective identity in order to be "free." The commonality between the two, partly different, strands of research is the assumption that a thick form of attachment needs to be the foundation for the *demos*.

North American research on racism and prejudice indirectly supports the idea that institutions function better in a culturally homogenous environment. The lack of cultural or ethnic attachments and sameness makes redistribution of common resources extremely difficult. Realistic group threat theory (e.g., Bobo, 1983; Sears and Jessor, 1996) shows that people (white in this case) oppose redistribution of resources to people (blacks) with whom they do not identify. Sears and Citrin (Citrin et al., 1997; Sears and Citrin, 1985) show that the unwillingness to spend money on various welfare state programs relates to racism. They show that self-interest cannot explain support for public spending on areas like schools, welfare, and health care or the preferred size of government, whereas racism can explain such attitudes (see also Gilens, 1999). The explanation is that racist whites believe that redistribution is more beneficial for blacks. Similar results have also been suggested by McLaren (2002), who shows that the opposition toward the EU springs from racist or xenophobic attitudes. These attitudes are transformed into political realities, as exemplified by Alesina and Glaeser (2004; see also Luttmer, 2001), who show that state redistribution increases with ethnic homogeneity across countries (as well as across the U.S. states).

The gist of the matter is that the present attachment or lack of such between members of the society affects what the state can and cannot do. It affects the political possibilities. It cannot be extrapolated from this that the early liberals' conclusion is correct—namely, that the existence of free institutions is not possible in a country with ethnic heterogeneity (Mill, 1975). Liberal nationalist as well as many political theorists are still claiming this indirectly under the flag of trust. Some even claim that multiculturalism— read: lack of homogeneity—undermines political stability (Salins, 1997). The claim is that the nation *ought to be* interchangeable with the *demos*.

Regardless of the theoretical arguments against this, we can simply note that all societies are ethnically and culturally plural, and the stronger the ethnic and cultural attachments, the greater the risk for exclusion of minority groups.[2]

Not all agree about the thick version of attachment; a thinner version can be found in the ideas of civic patriotism as advocated by Habermas (1992) and Viroli (1995), where the collective identity is based on a common binding to the procedures of the civic society and recognition of others as honoring such agreements. In practice, this position comes close to what Scharpf (1997, 1999) calls "governing for the people" or an output-oriented democracy. In other words, this is a situation where attachments are weak, and the ones that exist do so only to secure the delivery of some particular output. Regardless of the need or not for thick and thin forms of attachments, it is clear that some kind of attachment is fundamental for the constitution of *demos* and, in the end, for the possibilities and limitations of national institutions. National attachments are not static but constantly renegotiated in relation to external and internal transformations.

CHANGING CIRCUMSTANCES, CHANGING SENTIMENTS?

The introductory chapter of this book outlined important transformations like changes in the decision-making process and patterns of stratification. Four important transformations stand out when put into the context of *demos* and national sentiments.

A vertical shift in the decision-making structure is the first factor. The introductory chapter discussed both an upward as well as a downward shift in responsibilities. The latter can possibly affect national sentiments, but it is primarily the former that is of importance in this case. The grand example is of course the European Union (EU). The rapid emergence of supranational political entities like the EU, which supersede the nation as the primary source of political power, undermines the principles of nationality and people's identification with the nation. People view the EU as a threat to the nation-state (e.g., Taggart, 1998).

Political legitimization founded upon national solidarity risks becoming increasingly more difficult to sustain, and this threatens both the common denominator needed for a functional liberal democracy and the chance of leaving people in a vacuum that impedes their understanding of who they are. This implies the possibility that *national sentiments have changed in strength*. Both weakened and strengthened sentiments are possible. Perhaps national sentiments will erode in relation to the transcendence of the nation-state (Guéhenno, 1996; Hall, 1992; Richmond, 1984; van der Veer, 2003). It will be increasingly difficult to uphold political practices based on a homogenous nation-state, which leads to the erosion of national sentiment. However, the historical embeddedness of the nation-state and the strong fundaments upon which it rests make it clear that the opposite is possible—namely, that national sentiment will not erode or be replaced by other forms of attachment in the near future (Schnapper, 1995; Smith, 1991, 2001). We must not forget that the EU draws its legitimacy from the existing nation-state and that any transcendence of this principle may instigate a revival of nationalist sentiments as a backlash. The functionality of the principle of nationality makes it far from obsolete.

Second, a horizontal shift in the decision-making structure is taking place. This includes the formation of new political, grassroots, cross-country allegiances; the increasing power of multinational corporations; formation of elite organizations; general changes in people's relation to the economic and political systems;[3] and so on. It is possible to question the extent to which our time is really one of a global economy (Hirst and Thompson, 1996; Wade, 1996). It is nonetheless often assumed that an increasingly international market, in a broad sense, will smooth out cultural differences. This process could render the principles of nationality obsolete while making national identification increasingly meaningless. The increasing mobility of goods, services, and, perhaps foremost, of people can lead to the decay of national sentiments. Following from this is the possibility that other forms of identification based on, for example, collegial, or interest solidarity will increasingly replace national identification (Barber, 1995; Giddens, 1991). Not only can this affect the strength of national sentiments, but it is also often assumed that it can lead to a situation where *national sentiments change in substance*. Hobsbawm (1990) claims that increased cultural, political, and economic influences from abroad strengthen the ethnic dimension of national sentiments because of a perceived sense of insecurity. The claim is that post-industrialism does not put nationalism in the dustbin but instead refurnishes it under strengthened ethnic banners (e.g., Melucci, 1989; e.g., Richmond, 1984; Schlesinger, 1987). New divisions of labor, the weakening of classic political allegiances, and the diffusion of the political power make ethnic national sentiments the only cohesive national sentiments left. A shift in *demos* from one that, more or less, coincides with national boundaries to one that is increasingly transnational (e.g., European) and/or cross-national means that the sentiments left within the state boundaries are the thick ethnic sentiments.

The increasing diversity within the nation-states is the third transformation that can affect national sentiments. Rokkan's (1970) class-based political parties founded in a unitary *demos* are threatened by new allegiances, which do not always have a place within a unitary *demos*. Internal changes in the form of increasing pluralism risk to undermine and diminish the "vast majority" to include fewer and fewer people (Anderson, 2002). The modern nation-states are perhaps not able to handle increasing diversity (cf. Parekh, 2002).[4] Not only can de facto increasing pluralism be a problem but also reactionary attempts to draw sharp boundaries against "others." Right-wing populist parties in many European countries, like Denmark and Austria, claim outright that immigrants threaten stability (MigrationNews, 2002). These are parties that no longer occupy a political vacuum without influence or power; nor is theirs a view that is restricted to just this breed of political party. The Spanish government expressed its concern that "uncontrolled migration" fueled xenophobia, while introducing its new bill on illegal immigration (MigrationNews, 2000). A staggering 39 percent of Europeans believe that tension between ethnic groups will decrease if immigration is stemmed.[5] Regardless of actual or perceived strains to an all-inclusive conception of identification, it is obvious that the emphasis on the issue, as expressed in the strength of right-wing populism in Europe, risks contributing to a situation where the majority comprises fewer and fewer people. The *demos* is seen as being diluted by outsiders. This transformation means that it is possible that *the effect of national sentiments has changed*—for example, that the relation between sentiments and xenophobia is strengthened. Changes in effect are possible even though there is stability in strength and substance. It is possible that the civic part of society is being increasingly ethnicized but that this is discursively hidden under the veil of civic neutrality. This could lead to a situation where civic national sentiments become more and more antagonistic. It is also possible that the overt focus on the so-called downsides of immigration and multiculturalism around Europe as well as the resurgence of right-wing populism contribute to a shift in the understanding of the nation from external to internal points of references, which could lead to changing effects of national sentiments.

The fourth possible transformation is a change in patterns of stratification where individuals have become increasingly dependent on market forces for their life changes. Breen (1997) calls this process "recommodification." Regardless of the universality of this process, it is clear that not all groups of individuals in all countries are "recommodified" to the same extent. In line with the argument of horizontal shifts in the decision-making process, it means that it is possible that *changes in national sentiments vary between different groups.* The logic behind this is that "the less the dependency on the state, the less the need for a binding solidarity with other people in my country." Gabel (1998) shows similarly that people are more or less supportive of European integration, depending on their economic interests. The views of people in highly developed welfare states differ from the views of people in less-developed welfare states. This is one thing, but more important is the possibility that sentiments vary among smaller aggregates of people. This is because there are group differences within a certain welfare state or country as to the effect of recommodification. It is possible that national sentiment is withering away for the upper classes, but that different processes are under way among the lower classes. It is also possible that this varies between countries in relation to how far the process of recommodification has gone.

It is obvious that we have simplified the case somewhat, in that a vertical shift in the decision-making structure can also have an effect on the substance of national sentiments. It is also likely that increasing heterogeneity within the states influences not only the outcome of national sentiments but also the effect and the substance of them. Still, we are dealing with four possible ways in how national sentiments can change; *strength, substance, effect, and intergroup variation.*

THE COMPARATIVE PERSPECTIVE

A number of factors may directly affect national sentiments as well as how such sentiments may change. The story is, however, more complex than this: it is possible that there is variability across countries, given that the internal changes we have outlined vary across countries. To enable us to control for these effects, we have drawn data from eight countries, specifically

Britain, Germany, and Sweden; Australia, Canada, and the United States; Hungary and the Czech Republic.

We have two reasons for this choice and grouping of countries. The first is that these countries represent differences in changing political responsibility. In this study we are mainly concerned with the upward shift of responsibility, and specifically, with its upward shift from the countries to the European Union. Monet and Schumann realized the importance of this shift in assuming that such an upward shift would lay the foundation for a new emerging European identity. The latter still has a long way to go, but it is nonetheless obvious that the political institutions affect sentiments. National attachments are stronger in non-federal countries, whereas regional attachments are stronger in federal countries (Hooghe and Marks, 2001). The nation-state is under threat from supranational juridical institutions (Alesina and Spolaore, 2003). This condition implies that national sentiments ought to be under more pressure in EU countries where European institutions are replacing national ones. National sentiments will not necessarily diminish with the emergence of supranational institutions. It is possible, moreover, that such a shift in power induces stronger national sentiments, especially as a first reaction. Müller-Peters (1998) shows in this respect that attitudes toward European institutions relate negatively to nationalist sentiments.

The groupings of the eight selected countries are straightforward. Britain, Germany, and Sweden have by now been members of the EU for a longer time, although at the time of the first ISSP survey Sweden had just become an EU member. The two eastern European countries of Hungary and the Czech Republic have only recently joined the Union. The European countries offer contrasts with the three non-European countries, Australia, Canada, and the United States.

The second reason for choosing these countries is that they embody three different types of nation formation. There are the countries from the New World: Australia, Canada, and the United States. Australia and Canada were founded on immigration with a history of monoculturalism (or biculturalism in the case of Canada) that was replaced by official policies of multiculturalism in the early 1970s. These are policies that strive toward downplaying the importance of sameness in society while stressing equality for all, regardless of ethnic belonging. The United States was also founded on immigration, but multiculturalism has been a part of the country from the beginning. The United States, like Australia and Canada, is highly pluralistic, but the social contract is at the same time much thinner and foremost civic, which makes it a country that is unique in its realization of civic nationalism (Greenfeld, 1992).

Britain, Germany, and Sweden are older political entities and have had a longer tradition of nation formation. There are large differences between these countries, for example, in immigration regimes. Britain is usually seen as a specific case with its colonial background (Castles and Miller, 1993). Sweden, on the other hand, comes closer to the countries of the New World in adopting multiculturalism and relatively generous immigration politics (Hjerm, 1998a), whereas Germany embodies the classic ethnic country with its diversified citizenship laws dependent on ethnic belonging.

The countries of Eastern Europe—the Czech Republic and Hungary— have much in common with other Eastern European countries in nation formation. This commonality has been claimed to demonstrate in these states a striving to create a national unity based on ethnic homogeneity. Kohn (1945) showed in his early study of nationalism that there are two different types of nationalism: an "Eastern" type that is based on common descent or ethnicity, and a "Western type" based on the civil society. This heritage from Kohn has later been adopted, developed, and supported from different vantage points by many (Ignatieff, 1993; Lovell, 1999; Smith, 1986, 1991; Sugar, 1969; White, 2000). There are voices raised against the classic division of Eastern and Western nationalism (Hjerm, 2003; Kuzio, 2001, 2002), but there are still differences that could be expressed in the sentiments examined here. This is not a story of national sentiments per se; it is a story of *changing* national sentiments. This notwithstanding, there are reasons to consider the cross-country differences. We claimed earlier that four overarching trends could cause national sentiments to change. The third was "the nation-state's ability to handle diversity," which is related in an obvious way to nation-formation and its relation to immigration and integration regimes. For example, each of these countries handles the diversity "problem" differently, which may cause different changes in national sentiments across countries.

Any classification of countries into a limited number of ideal types based on the institutionalization of nationality, into overt regimes, is a blunt instrument and a gross simplification. However, the countries in this study differ in their institutionalized concepts of the nation, as expressed in their citizenship and immigration regimes. They also differ in the degree to which they are subject to a shift in the decision-making process, as exemplified by the European Union. These factors combined make it reasonable to assume that the selected countries cover the range of possible cross-country variation.

DATA AND METHOD

To answer the foregoing questions, we need a dataset that fulfills three criteria. First, it has to be cross-country comparable. Second, it has to focus on issues such as national sentiments in a nontrivial way, and third, it has to be able to measure national sentiments as a function of time. The 1995 and 2003 ISSP (see the introductory chapter for a general description of the ISSP) surveys are the only datasets that fulfill these criteria today.

The ISSP surveys "Aspects of National Identity" from 1995 and 2003 deal with topics like national identity, nationalism, patriotism, globalism, and xenophobia. The 2003 survey is to a large extent a replication of the 1995 survey. Some items were omitted and some were added between 1995 and 2003, but the majority of the items were asked in exactly the same way on both occasions. Moreover, none of the important items was omitted in 2003.

Problems we had to contend with were differences in sampling, data collection, and response rates.[6] All countries used probability sampling procedures with different forms of stratification. Sweden and Britain used standard probability sampling in 1995, whereas Australia used both an old panel and probability sampling for the whole population. Moreover, the Eastern European countries used face-to-face interviews, whereas the other selected countries used self-completion methods. The response rates were somewhat low, but the respondents were comparable to national census data on variables such as age, gender, and unemployment. The respondents were weighted whenever this was not the case. Overall, it is possible to assume that the samples were representative for the populations in each of the eight countries.

Noncitizens, or so-called denizens (cf. Hammar, 1990), and people with an immigrant background are included in the analysis. It may be reasonable to exclude people who have not had time to obtain any form of national sentiment toward the country they reside in now, but where should the cutoff be made? Should we exclude all noncitizens or merely all people with some form of immigrant background, or perhaps people who have lived in the country for less than, say, 10 years? The solution to this problem is not obvious, regardless of demarcation. Most important, the focus of the study is on changes in national sentiments, and one of the possible explanations is internal change. This means that excluding certain groups could be misleading. The choice is therefore to keep the full samples in order to keep the populations representative.

We use two forms of national sentiments to scrutinize the stated possibilities of change. These are *nationalist sentiments* and *patriotism*.[7] We need both types of sentiments to test the strength as well as the effect of the sentiments. The question of whether the substance of the sentiments has changed is tested only in terms of patriotism, for reasons that will soon become clear. These sentiments need to be observed at different times for possible changes to be measured over the period between 1995 and 2003. The relatively short period of eight years is limiting for the analysis, especially as national sentiments are strong forms of attachments that are relatively stable. It may be a contradiction in terms to try to measure changes over such a short time span. However, the actual magnitude of change is not the focus of investigation—only whether there are changes.

There are reasons to believe that there have been changes. People's relation to the nation is affected by threats to the nation's political and social existence (Bokaszanski, 2000). The EU is an example of a threat against the political existence of a nation. Some of the countries in the study have recently joined the EU, while others have been members for a longer time. An example of a threat against the social existence of a nation is an increasingly heterogeneous population. Factors that have a propensity to affect national sentiments are clearly present, and it should at least be possible to discern a tendency, if one is present. Moreover, the articulation of nationalism can change very swiftly. The developments in the former Yugoslavia after the death of Tito is an example of such change, where Serbian and Croatian nationalism began to flourish within an extremely short period.

STRENGTH OF NATIONAL SENTIMENTS

We will start our examination of the thesis that national sentiments have changed in strength by investigating nationalist sentiments in the selected countries. The notion of nationalism covers partly different phenomena. Modernists like Anderson (1983; 1998), Gellner (1983), and Hobsbawm (1990) try to explain the emergence and the role of nationalism in the origin of modern societies. Others, like Billig (1995; see also Calhoun, 1997), refer to the ideological habits and discourse that contribute to reproducing societies through everyday practices. Treanor (1997) argues that it is a functional world order that minimizes the divergence within states and determines the number of states in the world. The different understandings of nationalism often boil down to the level of analysis. Breuilly's distinction among nationalism as a doctrine, sentiments, and politics sums up such differences well (Breuilly, 1982; 1996).

The focus here is on nationalist sentiments or attitudes of nationalism that people from a specific nation have toward their nation or national belonging. Such sentiments, however, always relate to the political side of nationalism. There are different ways to understand the political side of nationalism, but one thing is clear: nationalism has its roots in historical experiences (e.g., Calhoun, 1995; 1997; Smith, 1995) that have shaped nationalism into a thick form of attachment. Nationalism is a doctrine of national self-determination where ethnicity continues to play a substantial part (Brown, 2000; Gellner, 1983). In the words of Smith: "Yet in practice, these types frequently overlap, and a given national state will often display ethnic as well as civic components in its form of nationalism, sometimes in a historical layering, or its nationalism may move some way from one type to another and back" (1998, p. 212). Regardless of all the classic Janus-face divisions (liberal–illiberal, eastern–western, civic–ethnic, new–old, evaluational–project, etc.), the problem with the nationalist discourse is how to define the "other" in a nonexclusionist way (cf. Spencer and Wollman, 2002). Nationalist sentiments derive from political and ideological ideas that include both the myth of common ancestry, or ethnocultural belonging, and the idea of a common homeland. Nationalist sentiments spring from its base in this ideology of unity among certain members of a society and, for the same reason, exclusion of "others" not defined as belonging to the nation, irrespective of whether those "others" are situated within or outside the state borders.

Nationalist sentiment is operationalized as a form of belonging based in both civic and ethnic aspects by using four statements.[8] It is, of course difficult to operationalize the nationalist sentiment. Regardless of how the operationalization is done, it will, by definition, not completely cover the entire multidimensional spectrum of nationalism, but it may be seen as an indicator that can help to understand the nationalistic belief system. The question and statements are as follows:

> How much do you agree or disagree with the following statements?
>
> 1. I would rather be a citizen of [Country] than of any other country in the world.
> 2. The world would be a better place if people from other countries were more like [Country].
> 3. [Country] is a better country than most other countries.
> 4. When my country does well in international sports, it makes me proud to be [Country].

The possible answers range from "agree strongly" to "disagree strongly" on a five-point scale. The statements have been reliability tested with Cronbach's alpha. The results are 0.71 (1995) and 0.70 (2003) for the pooled data for the two examined years.[9] An addition of the statements results in a scale that ranges, after transformation, from 0 to 100 with higher values indicating a stronger nationalist sentiment. We have chosen to flag all changes that exceed five units. A rule of thumb for all the displayed means, in all the tables, is that a difference of more than 2.5 percent is statistically significant at the 95 percent level. Still, this does not mean that such a change has any analytical meaning. A 6.25 percent change in the nationalist sentiment index is equivalent to a change of one unit on the original additive scale, so anything less than this is in practice not worth considering. To be somewhat lenient, we have chosen to flag all changes that exceed 5 percent.

Table 7.1 shows that the strength of nationalist sentiment has not changed at all in the selected countries. Large changes were not expected, regardless of whether one supported the death or the revival of nationalism hypothesis. Neither in the older EU member states, nor in the Eastern European ones, nor in the countries of the New World is it possible to discern any changes. Nationalist sentiments are not easily replaced, since such sentiments are as prevalent now as in 1995. It seems that we can refute the shift-in-the-strength-of-national-sentiments thesis, but before doing this rather prematurely, the other form of national sentiment must be examined.

TABLE 7.1
Nationalist sentiment, average index value (0–100).

	1995	2003	Direction of change
Britain	66.2	64.9	↔
Germany	54.1	54.4	↔
Sweden	62.2	60.2	↔
Australia	75.7	75.0	↔
Canada	73.1	75.9	↔
United States	74.9	75.8	↔
Hungary	64.7	66.5	↔
Czech Republic	61.0	62.9	↔
Pooled data	67.5	68.1	↔

NOTE: Changes of 5% or more are flagged.

SUBSTANCE OF NATIONAL SENTIMENTS

To be able to examine the substance of national sentiments we need to introduce a form of sentiment that actually can take different forms, namely patriotism. Patriotism comprises individual sentiments of pride toward the nation-state. Nationalist sentiment, understood as an attitude of national superiority, comes close to patriotism but is nonetheless different (Billig, 1995; Kedourie, 1993; Smith, 1994). Billig (1995) rightly argues against the common distinction between nationalism and patriotism, giving the former negative and the latter positive connotations. Patriotism comprises individual sentiments of allegiance toward the nation, whereas nationalist sentiment operates on different levels and is associated with both belonging to a nation and with views of national superiority.

Two things separate the two concepts. First, patriotism need not be ideological. Nationalism as a sentiment is not a clear-cut ideology, but the imagined ethnic foundations and national self-determination that it rests upon comprise the nationalist understanding of the nation. Viroli (1995) even claims that nationalism is a twisted form of civic patriotism that changes the meaning of "love of country" from the love of civic virtues to the love of cultural homogeneity. There is a thick notion of belonging built into nationalist sentiment, which is not the case with patriotism.

Second, nationalism as a sentiment has negative connotations (Hjerm, 1998b; Keane, 1994; Nairn, 1988). This is not automatically the case with patriotism since it is perfectly compatible with both cosmopolitanism and chauvinism. Patriotism can be a "love of country" based upon critical understanding (Levinson, 1950/1982).

It seems clear that patriotism can assume different dimensions. A diversity of factors makes up such dimensions, but it is possible to identify two overarching notions that contain this diversity: political and cultural patriotism. Political patriotism relates to the civic side of a society or the political institutions, the economy, and the social security system. Cultural patriotism comprises the people's history, cultural practices, and achievements. This division comes close to the classic division of civic and ethnic national identity, but it does not cover all aspects of that division; therefore the choice has been to use different and somewhat narrower notions. Moreover, patriotism differs from national identity in the depth of the attachment. National identity is an awareness of affiliation with the nation that gives people a sense of who they are in relation to others or infuses them with a sense of purpose that makes them feel at home, whereas patriotism is the love of one's nation. National identity is both a macro and a micro phenomenon simultaneously. It can represent the attributes of a nation as well as individuals' self-definition of belonging to a larger community. This is not the case with patriotism, which is foremost individuals' relationship with their nation. Nonetheless, it is possible to examine patriotism on an aggregate level, even though patriotism is more open to current political and structural changes in a given nation. This means that it is possible that patriotism varies over time more than does national identity. Thus, if the strength and substance have changed, there are strong reasons to suspect this to be visible in people's patriotism. We use nine items to operationalize and assess patriotism:

How proud are you of [Country] in each of the following?

1. The way democracy works.
2. Its political influence in the world.
3. [Country's] economic achievements.
4. Its social security system.
5. Its fair and equal treatment of all groups in society.
6. Its scientific and technological achievements.
7. Its achievements in sports.
8. Its achievements in the arts and literature.
9. Its history.

The possible answers range from "very proud" to "not proud at all" on a four-point scale. A first glance suggests that the included variables in fact measure different dimensions of patriotism. Pride in the way democracy works, political influence, economic achievements, the social security system, and equal treatment of different groups of people relate to the state or the polity of the country, that is, to the political dimension of patriotism. Pride in sports, science, literary achievements, and history on the other hand come closer to a cultural understanding. It seems justifiable to see the last four variables as the same dimension—the cultural.

A factor analysis shows that the different statements constitute two different dimensions.[10] There is a clear two-factor solution in all countries for both years, where the first five items load high on one factor and the last four on another factor. The only deviation from the patterns is that "its history" in Britain (in 2003), in the United States for both years[11] and "scientific achievements" in Britain (in 1995) load almost similarly on both factors. These exceptions are minor and do not change the manifest overall pattern. The first five variables are combined into a political dimension index, and the last four variables are combined into a cultural index.

The two indexes can vary between 0 and 100, where higher values indicate a stronger sense of patriotism.

Table 7.2 shows that there are changes in the strength of political patriotism in four of the eight countries. Only in the Czech Republic do we see a decline in political patriotism. The change in the "pride over economic achievements" indicator explains almost the whole change of index value in Britain. A decline in this item explains also part of the general decline of political patriotism in the Czech Republic, where there has also been a decrease in the pride over the country's political influence in the world. The failure to negotiate the final wording of the constitution during the republic's EU negotiations can possibly explain this. There has been a more general across-the-line increase in patriotism in Hungary and Australia. It is not easy to account for the general increase in Hungarian patriotism. One possibility is that joining the EU had a positive influence on people's apprehension of their country, but this does not explain why nationalist sentiments have not increased. Given the extremely low figures for political patriotism in Hungary in 1995, even in comparison to other countries not included here, we cannot totally dismiss poor data quality.

As for cultural patriotism (see Table 7.3), only in Hungary and the United States is it possible to discern an increase. The situation in Hun-

TABLE 7.2
Political patriotism, average index value (0–100).

	1995	2003	Direction of change
Britain	50.9	56.6	↑
Germany	54.8	50.4	↔
Sweden	46.7	49.5	↔
Australia	54.2	60.5	↑
Canada	66.0	65.3	↔
United States	62.5	66.8	↔
Hungary	28.7	40.4	↑
Czech Republic	37.8	32.7	↓
Pooled data	52.5	53.9	↔

NOTE: Changes of 5% or more are flagged.

TABLE 7.3
Cultural patriotism, average index value (0–100).

	1995	2003	Direction of change
Britain	70.6	69.0	↔
Germany	57.4	58.3	↔
Sweden	66.6	65.9	↔
Australia	74.3	77.1	↔
Canada	74.5	74.3	↔
United States	72.8	81.6	↑
Hungary	70.8	75.9	↑
Czech Republic	67.5	68.8	↔
Pooled data	70.1	72.3	↔

NOTE: Changes of 5% or more are flagged.

gary coincides with an increasing focus on the rights of ethnic Hungarians outside of Hungary. Hungary granted special status to the approximately 2.5 million ethnic Hungarians living outside of Hungary prior to the country's joining the EU. There is a substantial increase of cultural patriotism in the United States. The latter is not surprising, given the growing focus on the United States as not only the economic and military superpower but also in the country's capacity as the cultural and moral world leader during the Bush administration.

The lack of overall change in strength corroborates the result we found regarding nationalist sentiments and clearly refutes the idea that national sentiments are under pressure. Moreover, there is no overall increase in cultural patriotism nor a decrease in political patriotism. This means that

TABLE 7.4
Percentage with only one form of patriotism.

	1995		2003	
	Political	*Cultural*	*Political*	*Cultural*
Britain	0.9	28.4	2.2	18.3
Germany	6.1	9.3	6.8	18.7
Sweden	1.9	32.5	3.6	28.8
Australia	0.7	30.1	1.0	17.7
Canada	2.4	7.7	2.2	10.4
United States	0.9	14.8	0.3	10.7
Hungary	0.6	60.0	0.6	50.0
Czech Republic	0.6	47.5	0.9	55.9
Pooled data	2.6	27.5	2.1	25.4

the claim that the post-industrial world is one where ethnic sentiments are likely to proliferate seems to be faulty.

Let us examine that last point in somewhat more detail. Individuals can be, and are, both cultural and political patriots at the same time. However, there are, and should be, people who demonstrate only one of the two attributes. The criterion to be a political patriot is a score *above* 50 on the political index and *below* 50 on the cultural index, and vice versa for cultural patriotism.

Table 7.4 shows that a clear-cut political patriotism is not very common in any of the countries whereas a clear-cut cultural patriotism exists. Between 50 percent and 60 percent of Hungarians are cultural patriots, but only around 10 percent of Canadians.[12] There has been a decline in the proportion of people with an exclusive cultural patriotism in most of the selected countries. Germany and the Czech Republic are the exceptions in this regard; this springs from the general decline of political patriotism in the two countries. There has been little or no change in Canada, but the starting point was so small that any decrease was almost impossible. It is clear that we cannot discern any EU versus non-EU tendency or any region- or country-specific changes in political responsibility. The proportion of people having a distinct political patriotism is very small, which means that interpreting changes is not meaningful. These figures are highly dependent on where the cut-off line is drawn, but it is obvious that the relation has stayed approximately the same over the period. Thus there is no reason to suspect that the substance of the national sentiments has been affected, and there is clearly no support for the idea that national sentiments are becoming increasingly ethnic.

THE EFFECTS OF NATIONAL SENTIMENTS

National sentiments have proven to be surprisingly stable, but that does not necessarily imply that the effects of such sentiments are likewise stable. National sentiments relate to two different targets. National sentiments can be internal, aimed at preserving the national unity at the expense of others living within the territory. They can also be external, for example, related to the preservation of the nation-state against external threats or pressures. An example of the former is the attitude toward newcomers to the territory. It is possible that a change in national sentiment will affect the spread of xenophobia (Triandafyllidou, 2001). An example of the latter is antipathy toward the European Union or the urge to protect domestic goods and services. We therefore look at the correlation of patriotism and nationalist sentiment with xenophobia as well as with protectionism in order to examine possible differences in connotation between 1995 and 2003. Xenophobia relates to internal national sentiments and protectionism to external ones.

Xenophobia is defined as a negative attitude toward, or fear of, individuals or groups of individuals who are in some sense different (real or imagined) from oneself or the group one belongs to. In this case, only attitudes toward immigrants are considered. The following question and four statements operationalize xenophobia. The answers range from "agree strongly" to "disagree strongly" on a five-point scale:

> There are different opinions about immigrants from other countries living in [Country]. (By "immigrants" we mean people who come to settle in [Country].) How much do you agree or disagree with each of the following statements?
>
> 1. Immigrants increase crime rates.
> 2. Immigrants are generally good for [Country's] economy.
> 3. Immigrants take jobs away from people who were born in [Country].
> 4. Immigrants make [Country] more open to new ideas and cultures.

The statements have been combined into an index that can vary between 0 and 100 (100 being the most xenophobic). An internal reliability analysis shows that the statements measure the same dimension as the alpha scores vary between 0.60 (the Czech Republic in 2003) and 0.81 (Australia

TABLE 7.5
Correlations between national sentiment and xenophobia (Pearson's R).

	NATIONALIST SENTIMENT		PATRIOTISM, POLITICAL		PATRIOTISM, CULTURAL	
	1995	2003	1995	2003	1995	2003
Britain	.38	.40	−.12	−.17	.07	.07
Germany	.49	.35	0	−.17	.27	.14
Sweden	.47	.39	−.23	−.19	0	0
Australia	.28	.37	−.12	.06	.12	.14
Canada	.16	.06	−.14	−.24	0	−.10
United States	.31	.34	−.07	−.05	0	.0
Hungary	.16	.16	−.18	−.14	−.12	−.06
Czech Republic	.14	.12	−.23	−.29	0	.06
Pooled data	.22	.20	−.24	−.30	0	0

NOTE: Values indicate $p < 0.05$.

in 2003) for the single countries. Alpha scores for the pooled data are 0.78 in 1995 and 0.79 in 2003. The actual level of xenophobia is not what is in focus here, but it is nonetheless good news that the overall levels have not deteriorated—this is in spite of the new heyday of European right-wing populism and stricter rules for immigrants and asylum seekers that have been launched during the period. Correlating xenophobia with national sentiments produces the results in Table 7.5.

Table 7.5 shows that nationalist sentiment is clearly negative in that it relates strongly to xenophobia. Kedourie (1993) argues that the disastrous idea that "self-government" is better than "good government" is built into the fabric of nationalism. There is little reason to dispute his very negative understanding of nationalism. Still, there are differences between the selected countries in that the correlations are much stronger in Britain, Germany, Sweden, Australia, and the United States than in the other three countries. The reason for this is not evident, but it relates to the classic idea of different forms of nationalism found in different countries. One way to express this is in terms of reference points, where in newer democracies nationalism is related to external points of reference and in older democracies to internal points of reference. Such is also the case in Canada (cf. Rex, 1996). Matic (1999) argues along this line regarding recent changes in Eastern Europe in claiming that nationalism had a positive role in bringing down communism and opening the field for democracy in Eastern Europe. She also realizes that nationalism is a doubled-edged sword as it also threatens democracy.

Political patriotism and xenophobia correlate negatively, with similar strength, in both 1995 and 2003. This means that the more patriotic people feel over the political side of society, the *less* is the risk that they are xenophobic (see also Blank and Schmidt, 2003; see also Hjerm, 2003). This negative correlation is still manifest even if the "fair and equal treatment of all groups in society" statement is omitted from the index, thus refuting the possible objection that this correlation is a tautology. The virtue of civic patriotism is obvious. The cultural dimension of patriotism does not, except for a few cases, correlate with xenophobia. Germany is the only exception to this. White (2000) shows that Hungarian identity was not a romantic construct built on a common language but on an imperial territorial legacy. This could be the reason for the lack of negative connotations in Hungarian cultural patriotism. The finding that political patriotism in Australia correlates positively with xenophobia in 2003 could be a reason for concern—that is, that the multicultural concept built into the fabric of Australian society is losing out to the old "white Australia" policy.[13] A change in sign in two of the items in the scale, pride in the social security system and democracy, explains the general shift in attitude. Cutbacks in the Australian welfare states, combined with more austere asylum policies, make it possible that people who are proud of the social security system as well as democracy are so for the reason that those systems nowadays simply exclude more immigrants, that is, the majority take more pride in a system that is not as generous to others. We should not emphasize this too much, but bear it in mind for the future. In spite of the small deviance, it is obvious that very little change has taken place and that the meaning of the national sentiments has prevailed. This is, however, only in relation to internal points of reference.

We must also relate national sentiments to external points of reference, which in this case relate to protectionism. Protectionism is measured by collapsing four items, which range from "agree strongly" to "disagree strongly" on a five-point scale, into an index. The index varies, as before, between 0 and 100, where higher values indicate a stronger sense of protectionism. The items included in the index are these:

1. [Country] should limit imports to protect economy.
2. [Country] should follow its own interests even if it leads to conflict.
3. Foreigners should not be allowed to buy land in [Country].
4. Television should give preference to [Country] programs.

TABLE 7.6
Correlations between national sentiment and protectionism (Pearson's R).

	NATIONALIST SENTIMENT		PATRIOTISM, POLITICAL		PATRIOTISM, CULTURAL	
	1995	*2003*	*1995*	*2003*	*1995*	*2003*
Britain	.52	.49	.15	0	.19	.22
Germany	.61	.40	.18	−.17	.41	.16
Sweden	.51	.50	0	0	.13	.09
Australia	.33	.38	.09	.08	.24	.22
Canada	.22	.28	0	0	.14	.14
United States	.46	.44	.12	.14	.13	.12
Hungary	.35	.30	0	0	0	.09
Czech Republic	.34	.33	−.08	0	.08	.17
Pooled data	.45	.40	0	0	.27	.22

NOTE: Values indicate $p < 0.05$.

There has been a slight decrease in protectionism in Australia and Sweden, whereas the other countries display stability. The latter is also the case for the relation between national sentiments and protectionism (see Table 7.6).

As in the case with national sentiments and xenophobia, clearly there has been no change in the outcome of those sentiments. Nationalists are, not surprisingly, very inclined to be protectionist as well. John Hall is certainly wrong in claiming that the "stable geopolitical settlement has broken the link between nationalism and protectionism" (2000, p. 77). This goes for those with a high sense of cultural patriotism too, whereas political patriotism does not correlate with protectionism in general. There are exceptions to his rule, but the general conclusion is that there are no correlations, and this is corroborated by the lack of correlation in the pooled data set.[14] There is no evidence that national sentiments in the selected countries have become either increasingly external or internal. This does not refute our earlier discussion about points of reference; it only shows that both internal and external points of reference are a part of the nationalist belief system, regardless of place. It also means that the effects of national sentiments remain the same over the period in the countries examined in this study.

INTERGROUP VARIATION OF NATIONAL SENTIMENTS

In spite of the marginal changes in national sentiments, it is still possible that national sentiments have changed in different ways across different groups of people. It is possible, for instance, that external and internal change in the contemporary world could affect particular groups of people in different ways. Recommodification has already been mentioned as one factor. For example, it is a reasonable assumption that national sentiments have decreased in strength among highly educated, affluent people, whereas they have increased among the less educated, less affluent. It is also possible that this kind of group-specific change is not a universal process, but country-specific.

We examine only nationalism as the dependent variable in this analysis. The reasons for this approach are simplification and that nationalism entails the properties of both types of patriotism. We have seen that the relation between nationalism and xenophobia is manifest in all the selected countries. This means that we can make inferences from research on racism and prejudice about the independent variables that are of importance.

Class is included in the analysis because of its clear relation to the recommodification process. If this process contributes to a situation where national sentiments are becoming increasingly diversified, it should be most apparent between classes. Occupational codings have been recoded into the following EGP classes: workers (unskilled and skilled workers have been merged), routine nonmanual employees, Service Class II (low-level controllers, administrators, etc.), Service Class I (higher-level controllers, administrators, etc.), and self-employed.[15]

Education has been shown repeatedly across space and time to have a positive effect on anti-immigrant attitudes (e.g., Coenders and Scheepers, 2003; Hello et al., 2004; Hjerm, 2001; Smith, 1981).[16] The liberalizing effect of education is often said to explain this relationship. Education can also be seen in terms of recommodification, where it is predicted that the less affluent are those who are more exposed to recommodification, which means that there are reasons to believe that there have been diverging changes in different educational groups. Education is measured in three categories: primary, secondary, and university education.

The effect of age on anti-immigrant attitudes has been demonstrated in cross-comparative research (Hjerm, 2001) as well as in the United States

(Case et al., 1989), wherein older people generally display higher levels of anti-immigrant attitudes. The reasons for this are not conclusive owing to the lack of studies able to separate life cycle from cohort effects. It could be that age is a proxy variable for general liberalization, or that age in fact measures changes in an individual's psychological makeup over a life cycle. This study cannot solve this issue beyond the consideration of age as a factor.

Few but the classic studies (Adorno et al., 1982 [1950]) have tried to explain why gender should have an effect on the attitudes examined here. Many studies simply conclude that it is of some importance (Hjerm, 2001; Quillian, 1995) or of no importance (Scheepers et al., 2002) in explaining anti-immigrant attitudes. As with age, it is beyond the scope of this analysis to explain the underlying reasons for any causality. Another important factor to include in the analysis is whether a person has an immigrant background. We use citizenship as an indicator of the latter.

We use multilevel modeling (see Hox, 2002; Singer, 1998; see Snijders and Bosker, 1999) to test whether any effect of the structural variables has changed and whether such changes vary across countries. Multilevel modeling assumes that individuals interact with the social context to which they belong; it is an empirical way to understand the relationship between the structure and the individual. In this case, we do not have any macro-level variables except for country in itself. This means that we do not have any problems with the small number of countries. Still, we can take advantage of multilevel modeling as it enables us to test whether effects are the same across countries. The use of this modeling has an empirical advantage over regression analysis as it does not underestimate standard errors, which would be the case if macro-level variables were to be included in an OLS regression analysis, owing to the lack of variability between countries.

We first need to examine whether there is any cross-country variation in the structural variable. Comparing a random effects model with a fixed effects model will do this. In other words, we are comparing two models where the effect of, for example, education varies across countries and one where education has the same effect in all countries. Using a random model instead of a fixed model does not significantly improve the overall model fit. The decrease in unexplained variance is only 1.5 percent and 1.8 percent for the two years, showing that the included variables in general do have very similar effects in all countries. Therefore, we use a hierarchical linear model, which is effectively a multiple regression analysis that can handle

TABLE 7.7
Regression coefficients (multilevel structure) for nationalist sentiment.

	1995		2003	
	I	II	I	II
Class				
Self-employed	3.7*	1.0	3.0*	0.9
Manual	7.8*	3.0*	4.7*	1.3
Routine nonmanual	5.5*	2.1*	3.2*	0.7
Service Class II (Service Class I				
reference category)	2.2*	0.6	−0.3	−1.0
Women	−2.0*	−1.9*	−1.3*	−1.4*
Non-citizen	−11.6*	−11.3*	−9.8*	−9.6*
Age				
16–29	−10.3*	−8.8*	−6.4*	−5.4*
30–39	−9.3*	−8.0*	−5.2*	−4.3*
40–49	−8.0*	−6.9*	−4.9*	−4.2*
50–59 (60+ ref. category)	−4.7*	−3.9*	−3.1*	−2.8*
Education				
Primary		8.9*		7.7*
Secondary (University ref.				
category)		3.3*		3.6*

*p < 0.05

nested sources of variability, like individuals in countries. This means, in practice, that eight regression analyses are squeezed into one output for each year.

Table 7.7 shows that there are no real changes between groups and years. Recommodification or not, it is obvious that this has not caused any increased diversity in nationalist sentiments across classes. Workers are clearly more nationalistic in 1995 and 2003 than Service Class I. The effect of class substantially diminishes in 1995 and disappears completely in 2003 as education is introduced into the model (Model II). It is, in other words, not the employment status that is decisive but the educational part of one's class position.

Education is by itself an important factor, for there are large differences between citizens and noncitizens. The elderly display the strongest nationalist sentiment, whereas there are small differences between men and women. The similarity between the years is obvious even though the effect of age has become somewhat smaller. Overall, it is clear that there are no real changes across groups. This includes country-specific changes as well as across-country differences.

CONCLUDING DISCUSSION

National sentiments have not increased or decreased in strength nor have they changed in substance or effect during the 1995–2003 period of this study. It is impossible to prophesy about possible changes to come based on the presented results. Yes, eight years is a relatively short period, but how long is needed? The fact that it is impossible to falsify the "death of the nation" thesis at any given time makes it somewhat problematic. It is always possible for its proponents to claim that "we are not there yet."

Falsification or not, it is at least obvious that national sentiments were extremely stable over the period. The stability also means that Castells's (1997) claim, that the age of globalization is the age of nationalism and focus on the nation, is very much an exaggerated description of reality.

Turner claims that "cosmopolitanism is a normative standard of public conduct, but empirically the social order is breaking up into antagonistic, ethnic, and regional and national identities" (2001, p. 199). Antagonistic tendencies and secessionist movements do exist, but there is little reason to suspect that this is the case in democracies founded on the nation-state. It is obvious that the 1995–2003 period of this study is short in relation to the time that has elapsed since the rise of the modern nation-state. Still, some changes that have taken place in the selected countries have a potential to affect the makeup of the nation-state as well as people's sentiments toward it. We are thinking about changes both in terms of vertical and horizontal shifts in the decision-making structure and the degree of homogeneity and the focus on the latter. The Czech Republic and Hungary have wandered down the road toward membership in the European Union, and Sweden has been a member during the period of study. There has also been an increasing focus on issues of immigration and in the end what constitutes "them" and "us" in the majority of the selected countries. Fundamental changes were not to be expected in strength or substance, but it seems clear that the framework for at least minor changes are there.

The fundament for the collective identity necessary to legitimate the liberal democracy does not seem to be under imminent threat. On the downside, the thicker ethnic sentiments that make up this identity are not on the way of being replaced by the thinner civic sentiments, even though the overall decrease in the proportion of people displaying an exclusive cultural patriotism has decreased somewhat. The proponents of a thick concept of *demos* could, of course, interpret the latter as something negative—something that diminishes the possibilities for a functional democracy. This is not the place to recapitulate the debate that runs back to Hobbes, Locke, and Mill on one side and Rousseau and Hegel on the other. We only note that this argument has little empirical support. Thomas (2001) makes an interesting point when claiming that thick and thin attachments, or civic and ethnic identities, should be seen as a zero-sum game where a decrease in one form corresponds to an increase in the other. Thomas's position would clearly thwart the argument that a decreasing thick concept of *demos* is problematic. Moreover, the ethnic types of sentiments relate to excluding attitudes, such as xenophobia and protectionism, which implies that such sentiments cannot be unproblematic as heterogeneity increases within the nation-state.

The introductory chapter raised the question about what would follow in the footsteps of changing forms of governance. Are we witnessing a democratic dystopia or a democratic utopia? This chapter cannot provide the answer to this question other than stating that we are yet to witness the death of the nation as foundation for identity. As long as this is not the case, we will not witness the disintegration of *demos* (Delanty and O'Mahony, 2002). The political landscape is changing to meet new external and internal demands. If political possibilities are limited and restrained by who "We the People" are, then it is clear that such limitations at least are not larger than they were yesterday.

The claim of the imminent death of the nation, as well as the prophecy of the liberal democracy under threat, is built on a misconception. Greenfeld (1992) claims that "democracy was born with a sense of nationality" (p. 10).[17] This does not imply that the model is static, or as Magala (1994) claims, that the modern nation-state has produced its own ruin by allowing other agencies to compete over the socialization of its citizens. The proponents of "post"-something are perhaps correct that the political landscape is changing in certain ways, but from this we cannot argue that communities of faith are evaporating and that government is rapidly being replaced by governance (e.g., Taylor, 2002). The strong relation between a geographically bounded political landscape and a unitary community of faith may well be under pressure, but it does not mean that the foundations are crumbling. It only means that "We the People" will be renegotiated, as it always has since the founding of the national liberal democracy.

This process does not always run smoothly. The real threat in the near future is the increase in heterogeneity. This development is perhaps not a serious challenge for the nation-state or the liberal democracy per se, but it could nonetheless be a strain on the welfare state. The ethnic part of national sentiment is not diminishing, which means that immigrants are likely to be excluded from "the People." The larger and/or more visible these groups become, the less likely it is that citizens will sustain an encompassing welfare state, a welfare state that supports non-nationals. Alesina and Glaeser's (2004) research, dealing with the relation between ethnic heterogeneity and redistribution, clearly supports the argument that there is such a risk. The challenge of integrating newcomers into society is not only related to individual and group quality but is also critical to future opportunities to diminish inequality.

NOTES

1. This is often overlooked in the study of European integration (Hooghe and Marks, 2001). It is claimed that Europe lacks a profound cultural or ethnic unity, which is assumed to have been much greater during the formation of the modern nation-states. The latter is an interesting possibility but far from a proven empirical reality.

2. This, without mentioning things like the risk of stagnation in extremely homogenous environments or the external disasters that the emphasis on national homogeneity had during the twentieth century under the banners of fascism and Nazism. Moreover, it is also possible to argue that with less emphasis on white Christianity as the uniting form of solidarity in the United States there would be a lower risk of exclusion of others. Thus, it is not more homogeneity that is needed but a shift in what constitutes such homogeneity.

3. For example, increasing or decreasing dependencies due to a shift in the structure of the labor market.

4. See Riggs (2002) for a discussion of what types of democratic organization forms are best suited to handle diversity.

5. Figure from the European Social Survey 2002.

6. Britain had 61 percent, the Czech Republic 70 percent, and data for the other countries fell between those figures in 1995.

7. The ISSP-familiar reader will notice that national identity is not used although question batteries were constructed to measure it. This was because the batteries were not comparable between the years, since the measure used in 1995 did not include any good indicators of ethnic national identity.

8. Three more statements in this battery were included in the questionnaire. One was phrased in only the 2003 survey and could thus not be used. Another was excluded since it did not measure the same dimension as the others when tested with Cronbach's alpha. The last item (*"People should support their country even if the country is in the wrong"*) was excluded so that all statements are in relation to the respondent's own nation/state and not to the general concept of nation/states; the aim was also to keep a more neutral concept. Inclusion of this statement does not change the results in any fundamental way.

9. Cronbach's alpha varies between 0.77 (Britain in 1995) and 0.60 (Hungary in 1995) for the individual countries. The statements also produce a one-factor solution (PCA) for both 1995 and 2003.

10. Results available from the author.

11. This could, of course, be interpreted in line with the United States' acclaimed civic history (Greenfeld, 1992) where its history is related not only to the nation but also to the civic contract.

12. The proportion of people with an exclusive cultural identity in Hungary goes against Cspeli's (1997) claim that Hungarian national identity is dual, with explicit civic and ethnic elements. The point is not to argue whether the old division between Eastern and Western national sentiments is correct; it is to examine change.

13. This interpretation seems to be faulty as the same proportion of people agree/disagree in two statements about multiculturalism: "It is impossible for people who do not share Australia's traditions to become fully Australian" and whether immigrants should "maintain their distinct customs and traditions" or "adapt and blend into the larger society."

14. The change of direction in Germany is not an empirical error. However, it cannot be interpreted in isolation but should be understood in the context that protectionism and political patriotism in general are not related.

15. Occupational codings have been converted from ISCO88 into EGP classes. This is a straightforward process for 2003 data. In the 1995 data, we first had to convert some of the country data into ISCO88. This includes data from ISCO 68 in Germany and the United States, from the British Standard Occupational Classification (SOC, 2 digits) in Britain, and from the Socio-Economic Classification (SEI) and Nordic Occupational Classification (NYK) in Sweden.

16. Still, there are studies that question the generality of this conclusion in relating education to biased answering (Jackman and Muha, 1984).

17. The importance of nationalism in the creation of the modern nation-state has been put into question (Farrar et al., 1998).

REFERENCES

Acton, John. 1996 (1862). "Nationality." In *Mapping the Nation*, edited by G. Balakrishnan. London: Verso (pp. 17–38).

Adorno, Theodor W., Frenkel-Brunswik, Else, Levinson, Daniel J., and Sanford, Nevitt, R. 1982 (1950). *The Authoritarian Personality*. New York: Norton.

Alesina, Alberto, and Glaeser, Edward L. 2004. *Fighting Poverty in the US and Europe. A World of Difference*. Oxford: Oxford University Press.

Alesina, Alberto, and Spolaore, Enrico. 2003. *The Size of Nations*. Cambridge, Mass.: MIT Press.

Anderson, Benedict. 1983. *Imagined Communities: Reflections on the Origin and Spread of Nationalism*. London: Verso.

Anderson, Benedict. 1998. *The Spectre of Comparisons. Nationalism, Southeast Asia and the World*. London: Verso.

Anderson, James. 2002. "Introduction." In *Transnational Democracy. Political Space and Border Crossings*, edited by J. Anderson. London: Routledge (pp. 1–5).

Barber, Benjamin. 1995. *Jihad vs McWorld*. New York: Times Books.

Billig, Michael. 1995. *Banal Nationalism*. London: Sage.

Blank, Thomas, and Schmidt, Peter. 2003. "National Identity in a United Germany: Nationalism or Patriotism? An Empirical Test with Representative Data." *Political Psychology*, 24(2): 289–311.

Bobo, Lawrence. 1983. "Whites' Opposition to Busing: Symbolic Racism or Realistic Group Conflict." *Journal of Personality and Social Psychology*, 45: 1196–1210.

Bokaszanski, Zbigniew. 2000. "National Identity in the Perspective of Systemic Changes in Poland." *University of Lodz: Working paper*.

Breen, Richard. 1997. "Risk, Recommodification and Stratification." *Sociology*, 31(3): 473–489.

Breuilly, John. 1982. *Nationalism and the State*. Chicago: University of Chicago Press.

Breuilly, John. 1996. "Approaches to Nationalism." In *Mapping the Nation*, edited by G. Balakrishnan. London: Verso (pp. 146–174).

Brown, David. 2000. *Contemporary Nationalism. Civic, Ethnocultural and Multicultural Politics*. New York: Routledge.

Calhoun, Craig. 1995. *Critical Social Theory*. Cambridge, Mass.: Blackwell.

Calhoun, Craig. 1997. *Nationalism*. Buckingham: Open University Press.

Case, Charles, Greely, Andrew, and Fuchs, Stephen. 1989. "Social Determinants of Racial Prejudice." *Sociological Perspectives*, 32: 469–483.

Castells, Manuel. 1997. *The Power of Identity*. Oxford: Blackwell.

Castles, Stephen, and Miller, Mark J. 1993. *The Age of Migration*. London: MacMillan.

Cederman, Lars-Erik. 2001. "Nationalism and Bounded Integration: What It Would Take to Construct a European Demos." *European Journal of International Relations*, 7(2): 139–174.

Citrin, Jack, Green, Donald P., Muste, Christopher, and Wong, Cara. 1997. "Public Opinion toward Immigration Reform." *Journal of Politics*, 59(3): 858–881.

Coenders, Marcel, and Scheepers, Peer. 2003. "The Effect of Education on Nationalism and Ethnic Exclusionism. An International Comparison." *Political Psychology*, 24(2): 313–343.

Cspeli, Gyorgy. 1997. *National Identity in Contemporary Hungary.* New York: Columbia.

Dahl, Robert A. 1989. *Democracy and Its Critics.* New Haven: Yale University Press.

Delanty, Gerard, and O'Mahony, Patrick. 2002. *Nationalism and Social Theory.* London: Sage.

Farrar, L. L., Jr., McGuire, Kiernan, and Thompson, John E. 1998. "Dog in the Night: The Limits of European Nationalism, 1789–1895." *Nations and Nationalism*, 4(4): 547–568.

Gabel, Matthew J. 1998. *Interest and Integration. Market Liberalization, Public Opinion, and the European Union.* Ann Arbor: Michigan University Press.

Gellner, Ernest. 1983. *Nations and Nationalism.* Oxford: Blackwell.

Giddens, Anthony. 1991. *The Conditions of Modernity.* Cambridge: Polity.

Gilens, Martin. 1999. *Why Americans Hate Welfare.* Chicago: University of Chicago Press.

Greenfeld, Liah. 1992. *Nationalism. Five Roads to Modernity.* Cambridge, Mass.: Harvard University Press.

Guéhenno, Jean-Marie. 1996. *The End of the Nation State.* Minneapolis: University of Minnesota Press.

Habermas, Jürgen. 1992. "Citizenship and National Identity: Some Reflections on the Future of Europe." *Praxis International*, 12(1): 1–19.

Hall, John A. 2000. "Globalization and Nationalism." *Thesis Eleven*, 63(Nov.): 63–79.

Hall, Stuart. 1992. "The Question of Cultural Identity." In *Modernity and Its Features*, edited by S. Hall.

Hammar, Tomas. 1990. *Democracy and the Nation State.* Hants: Avebury.

Hello, Evelyn, Scheepers, Peer, Vermulst, Ad, and Gerris, Jan R. M. 2004. "Association between Educational Attainments and Ethnic Distance in Young Adults." *Acta Sociologica*, 47(3): 253–275.

Hirst, Paul, and Thompson, Grahame. 1996. *Globalisation in Question.* Cambridge: Polity Press.

Hjerm, Mikael. 1998a. "National Identities, National Pride and Xenophobia: A Comparison of Four Western Countries." *Acta Sociologica*, 41(24): 335–347.

Hjerm, Mikael. 1998b. "Reconstructing 'Positive' Nationalism: Evidence from Norway and Sweden." *Sociological Research Online*, 3(2). http://www .socresonline.org.uk/socresonline/3/2/7.html.

Hjerm, Mikael. 2001. "Education, Xenophobia and Nationalism: A Comparative Analysis." *Journal of Ethnic and Migration Studies*, 27(1): 37–60.

Hjerm, Mikael. 2003. "National Sentiments in Eastern and Western Europe." *Nationalities Papers*, 31(4): 413–430.

Hobsbawm, Eric. 1990. *Nations and Nationalism since 1780*. Cambridge: Cambridge University Press.

Hooghe, Liesbet, and Marks, Gary. 2001. *Multi-Level Governance and European Integration*. Lanham: Rowman and Littlefield.

Hox, Joop. 2002. *Multilevel Analysis. Techniques and Applications*. Mahwah, N.J.: LEA.

Ignatieff, Michael. 1993. *Blood and Belonging: Journeys into the New Nationalism*. New York: Farrar.

Jackman, Mary R., and Muha, Michael J. 1984. "Education and Intergroup Attitudes: Moral Enlightment, Superficial Democratic Commitment or Ideological Refinement." *American Sociological Review*, 49: 751–769.

Keane, John. 1994. "Nations, Nationalism and Citizens in Europe." *International Social Science Journal*, 140: 169–184.

Kedourie, Elie. 1993. *Nationalism*. Oxford: Blackwell.

Kohn, Hans. 1945. *The Idea of Nationalism*. New York: Macmillan.

Kuzio, Taras. 2001. "Nationalising States or Nation Building? A Critical Survey of the Theoretical Literature and Empirical Evidence." *Nations and Nationalism*, 7: 135–155.

Kuzio, Taras. 2002. "The Myth of the Civic State: A Critical Survey of Hans Kohn's Framework for Understanding Nationalism." *Ethnic and Racial Studies*, 25: 20–39.

Kymlicka, Will. 1995. *Multicultural Citizenship*. Oxford: Oxford University Press.

Levinson, Daniel J. 1950/1982. "The Study of Ethnocentric Ideology." In *The Authoritarian Personality*, edited by T. W. Adorno et al. New York: Norton (pp. 102–150).

Lijphart, Arend. 1977. *Democracy in Plural Societies*. New Haven: Yale University Press.

Lovell, D. W. 1999. "Nationalism, Civil Society, and the Prospects for Freedom in Eastern Europe." *Australian Journal of Politics and History*, 45(1): 65–77.

Luttmer, Erzo. 2001. "Group Loyalty and the Taste for Redistribution." *Journal of Political Economy*, 109(3): 500–528.

Magala, Slawomir. 1994. "The Threshold of Statehood." In *Nationalism, Ethnicity and Identity. Cross National and Comparative Perspectives*, edited by R. F. Farnen. New Brunswick: Transaction (pp. 177–191).

Matic, Davorka. 1999. "Understanding the Role of Nationalism in New Democracies." *Collegium Antropologicum*, 23(1): 231–247.

McLaren, Lauren M. 2002. "Public Support for the European Union: Cost/ Benefit Analysis or Perceived Cultural Threat?" *Journal of Politics*, 64(2): 551–566.

Melucci, Alberto. 1989. *Nomads of the Present: Social Movements and Individual Needs in Contemporary Society*. London: Hutchinson.

MigrationNews. 2000. 7(11): 11/01/2000.

MigrationNews. 2002. 9(4): 04/01/2002.

Mill, John Stuart. 1975. *Three Essays. Consideration on Representative Government, On Liberty, The Subjection of Women*. Oxford: Oxford University Press.

Miller, David. 1995. *On Nationality*. Oxford: Oxford University Press.

Moore, Margaret. 2001. *The Ethics of Nationalism*. Oxford: Oxford University Press.

Müller-Peters, Anke. 1998. "The Significance of National Pride and National Identity to the Attitude toward the Single European Currency: Europe-Wide Comparison." *Journal of Economic Psychology*, 19: 701–719.

Nairn, Tom. 1988. *The Enchanted Glass: Britain and Its Monarchy*. London: Radius.

Parekh, Bhikhu. 2002. "Reconstituting the Modern State." In *Transnational Democracy. Political Spaces and Border Crossings*, edited by J. Anderson. London: Routledge (pp. 39–55).

Quillian, Lincoln. 1995. "Prejudice as a Response to Perceived Group Threat: Population Composition and Anti Immigrant Racial Prejudice in Europe." *American Sociological Review*, 60(4): 586–611.

Rex, John. 1996. "National Identity in the Democratic Multi-Cultural State." *Sociological Research Online*, 1(2). http://www.socresonline.org.uk/ socresonline/1/2/1.html.

Richmond, Anthony H. 1984. "Ethnic Nationalism and Postindustrialism." *Ethnic and Racial Studies*, 7: 4–18.

Riggs, Fred W. 2002. "Globalization, Ethnic Diversity, and Nationalism: The Challenge for Democracies." *Annals, AAPSS*, 581(May): 35–47.

Rokkan, Stein. 1970. *Citizens, Elections, Parties*. New York: Mckay.

Salins, Peter D. 1997. *Assimilation, American Style*. New York: Basic Books.

Scharpf, Fritz. 1997. *Games Real Acors Play. Actor-Centered Institutionalism in Policy-Research*. Boulder: Westview.

Scharpf, Fritz. 1999. *Governing in Europe. Effective and Democratic*. Oxford: Oxford University Press.

Scheepers, Peer, Gijsbert, Mérove, and Coenders, Marcel. 2002. "Ethnic Exclusionism in European Countries. Public Opposition to Civil Rights for Legal Migrants as a Response to Perceived Ethnic Threat." *European Sociological Review*, 18(1): 17–34.

Schlesinger, Philip. 1987. "On National Identity: Some Conceptions and Misconceptions Criticised." *Social Science Information*, 26(2): 219–264.

Schnapper, Dominique. 1995. "The Idea of Nation." *Qualitative Sociology,* 18(2): 177–187.

Sears, David O., and Citrin, Jack. 1985. *Tax Revolt. Something for Nothing in California.* Cambridge, Mass.: Harvard University Press.

Sears, David O., and Jessor, Tom. 1996. "Whites' Racial Policy Attitudes: The Role of White Racism." *Social Science Quarterly,* 61: 16–53.

Singer, Judith D. 1998. "Using SAS PROC MIXED to Fit Multilevel Models, Hierarchical Models, and Individual Growth Models." *Journal of Educational and Behavioral Statistics,* 24(4): 323–355.

Smith, A. Wade. 1981. "Racial Tolerance as a Function of Group Position." *American Sociological Review,* 46: 558–573.

Smith, Anthony D. 1986. *The Ethnic Origins of Nations.* Oxford: Blackwell.

Smith, Anthony D. 1991. *National Identity.* London: Penguin Books.

Smith, Anthony D. 1994. "The Problem of National Identity: Ancient, Medieval and Modern." *Ethnic and Racial Studies,* 17(3): 375–400.

Smith, Anthony D. 1995. *Nations and Nationalism in a Global Era.* Cambridge: Polity Press.

Smith, Anthony D. 1998. *Nationalism and Modernism.* London: Routledge.

Smith, Anthony D. 2001. *Nationalism.* Cambridge: Polity.

Snijders, Tom A. B., and Bosker, Roel J. 1999. *Multilevel Analysis.* London: Sage.

Spencer, Philip, and Wollman, Philip. 2002. *Nationalism. A Critical Introduction.* London: Sage.

Sugar, Peter F. 1969. "External and Domestic Roots of Eastern European Nationalism." In *Nationalism in Eastern Europe,* edited by P. F. Sugar and I. J. Lederer. Seattle: University of Washington Press (pp. 3–54).

Taggart, Paul. 1998. "A Touchstone of Dissent in Contemporary Western European Party System." *European Journal of Political Research,* 33(5): 363–388.

Tamir, Yael. 1993. *Liberal Nationalism.* Princeton: Princeton University Press.

Taylor, Peter J. 2002. "Relocating the Demos?" In *Transnational Democracy. Political Spaces and Border Crossing,* edited by J. Anderson. London: Routledge (pp. 236–244).

Thomas, Paul. 2001. "Modalities of Consent, Compliance, and Non-Compliance: Exit, Voice and Loyalty Reconsidered." In *Beyond Nationalism?* edited by F. Dallamyr and J. M. Rosales. Lanham: Lexington (pp. 3–18).

Treanor, Paul. 1997. "Structures of Nationalism." *Sociological Research Online,* 2(1). http://www.socresonline.org.uk/socresonline/1/2/1.html.

Triandafyllidou, Anna. 2001. *Immigrants and National Identity in Europe.* London: Routledge.

Turner, Bryan S. 2001. "National Identities and Cosmopolitan Virtues: Citizenship in a Global Age." In *Beyond Nationalism? Sovereignity and Citizenship,* edited by F. Dallamyr and J. M. Rosales. Lanham: Lexington (pp. 199–219).

van der Veer, K. 2003. "The Future of Western Societies: Multicultural Identity or Extreme Nationalism?" *Futures*, 35: 169–187.

Viroli, Maurizio. 1995. *For Love of Country. An Essay on Patriotism and Nationalism*. Oxford: Clarendon Press.

Wade, Robert. 1996. "Globalisation and Its Limits." In *National Diversity and Global Capitalism*, edited by S. Berger and R. Dore. London: Routledge (pp. 60–68).

Weiler, J-H. H. 1999. *The Constitution of Europe. Do the New Clothes Have an Emperor?* Cambridge: Cambridge University Press.

White, George W. 2000. *Nationalism and Territory. Constructing Group Identity in Southeastern Europe*. Lanham: Rowman & Littlefield.

Young, Iris Marion. 1990. *Justice and the Politics of Difference*. Princeton, N.J.: Princeton University Press.

CHAPTER EIGHT

Conclusion

The Past and Future of Political Sociology

Stefan Svallfors

To place the contributions of this book in context, we need first to briefly outline the main contours of development of the field of survey-based political sociology.[1] The contributions of the volume may be seen as part of a "fourth generation" of scholarship in the field, where feedback effects of institutions and public policies are analyzed in a comparative perspective. To understand the specific contributions of this generation of scholars, we have to know something about the scholarly generations that preceded them.

What we would today conceive of as political sociology is a child of the 1940s. If a particular birthplace should be chosen, it would be New York City, at Columbia University's Bureau of Applied Social Research, under the intellectual leadership of Paul Lazarsfeld. Although the theoretical antecedents to political sociology could probably be traced back as far as anyone started to think about political matters, and although the first social surveys had appeared already in the late nineteenth century (Bulmer et al. 1991: 235), a number of contributions made by the "Columbia School" and in particular by Lazarsfeld were formative for the research field.[2]

Methodologically, Lazarsfeld and his colleagues introduced the theoretically guided survey among university scholars, making opinion polling a key social scientific tool instead of something mainly of interest to social reformers, market researchers, and political pundits (Converse 1987: Ch. 9). As for methods of analysis, Lazarsfeld pioneered the analysis of latent structures. The importance of this way of thinking lies in the notion that manifest indicators of various sorts represent information about latent structures, which are themselves not directly accessible. Many of the contemporary uses of scaling, index construction, and various analytical techniques build on foundations laid by Lazarsfeld.

Substantively, the Columbia School made the first rigorous and systematic attempts to analyze the social influences on voting. The famous, but sometimes over-interpreted quote, "A person thinks, politically, as he is, socially. Social characteristics determine political preference" (Lazarsfeld et al. 1944: 27), is a summary of the basic findings in this respect. Lazarsfeld and colleagues found that knowledge about a set of individual social characteristics could be used to predict voting with a fair degree of certainty.

Another major substantive contribution was the analysis of the effects of political communication and, in particular, mass media effects. Lazarsfeld and his colleagues came to summarize the findings as the "two-step flow" model. Mass media messages did not affect mass publics in any direct fashion, they contended, but their effects were mediated through "opinion leaders" who transmitted and interpreted media messages in local contexts. Through this model, they inaugurated a research tradition that is still highly present in mass media studies.

At a general level, Lazarsfeld and his colleagues were driven by questions rather than by theories or methods. As we shall discuss later, this drive is still something that characterizes the best work within the field of political sociology, and something that the present volume illustrates. Furthermore, they were occupied in finding explanations for social phenomena, not primarily in describing findings in any particular empirical domain. Theories and methods were used for that purpose, not as aims in their own right.

The Columbia School came under contemporary criticism for espousing a "social determinism" in the study of political behavior (summarized in Carmines and Huckfeldt 1996: 228–229). Critics argued that the active role of political parties themselves, and the specific aspects of politics itself, tended to be obscured by the emphasis on social determinants. By far the most important and influential attempts to modify the putative sociological determinism came from the national election studies of the "Michigan School" at the University of Michigan's Survey Research Centre.[3] Their work may be seen as one part of a second generation of postwar political sociology. The study of the "American Voter" (Campbell et al. 1960) introduced a "funnel model" to explain voting, where social determinants were at the "wide end" of the funnel. Closer to the actual voting decision were factors of a social-psychological kind, such as party identification and political attitudes.[4]

The Michigan School came to be particularly connected with the "non-attitudes" thesis. According to Converse, one of the key Michigan scholars, a large part of the electorate did not hold any coherent or stable attitudes in social and political matters (Converse 1964). This could be shown, for example, in the low correlations between individuals' attitudes and the policy positions of their chosen parties, in the low consistency between various attitudinal components, and in the very low stability over time in panel studies. Attitudes did not correspond to votes; they were not constrained by other attitudes in similar matters; and they seemed to fluctuate in an almost random manner over time. These findings led Converse to introduce the "black-and-white model," according to which only a minority of the electorate actually held any attitudes, while a large majority did not have any opinions, but answered survey questions in a basically random fashion.

The non-attitudes thesis attracted immediate flak for using a too restrictive definition of attitudinal constraint and for mistaking measurement problems for the absence of clear attitudes. The discussion of its empirical underpinnings and normative implications is wide-ranging (for a summary of the debate see Kinder 1983). We will return to it later in this chapter.

Another influential extension of the Columbia School model is found in the work of Seymour Martin Lipset, who also must be seen as part of the second generation of scholars and perhaps as the most influential one. In his 1960 book *Political Man*, Lipset investigated the social bases of various political movements (such as communism and fascism), and in particular the class bases of various political parties (Lipset 1960). In the introduction to *Party Systems and Voter Alignments* (1967), Lipset and co-author Stein Rokkan extended the argument into a comparative framework for studying the rise and fortunes of political parties. They argued that the democratic party systems reflected a set of social cleavages (class, land vs. industry, state vs. church, center vs. periphery) in the countries in question. The party systems in the West had acquired a "frozen" form, so that the party structure of the 1960s basically reflected the interwar social cleavage structure. The Lipset/Rokkan focus was thus mainly set on *parties* and the way the party system reflected basic social cleavages rather than on *citizens/voters* as was the case in the early postwar political sociology.

The research program proposed by the Lipset/Rokkan framework could have led to a rising interest in a comparative political sociology of the kind espoused in this book, asking not only about the connections between social cleavages and political parties but more generally about the political translation of social cleavages into sociopolitical orientations and action patterns. Such a "micropolitical" turn, however, was not what occurred in the field of comparative political sociology "post-Lipset/Rokkan," perhaps because of their relative inattention to the output side of politics.

Instead, the main strand of research from the mid-1970s onward came on the one hand to be comparative macro-analyses of welfare states (for a selection of seminal studies, see Rimlinger 1971; Wilensky 1975; Esping-Andersen 1990; Scharpf and Schmidt 2000; Pierson 2001; Huber and Stephens 2001). The turn here was toward macro-comparisons that asked what demographic, political, and institutional factors could account for the different size and structure of the welfare states of the advanced political economies in the postwar era.

On the other hand, the legacy from Lipset/Rokkan also took expression as a number of comparative analyses of electoral systems and their electoral consequences (for a selection of important studies, see Sartori 1976; Bartolini and Mair 1990; Lijphart and Aitkin 1994; Bartolini 2000; Norris 2004). Precisely as with Lipset/Rokkan, the focus in these studies is mainly set on electoral rules and parties' behavior, and less emphasis is put on the microlevel orientations of voters/citizens. Systematic and sustained comparative research came to be largely disconnected from the kinds of issues we have raised in the present volume.

New impetus for analyzing the orientations of mass publics instead came from new thinking in the institutionalist camp, which may be said to constitute a "third generation" of scholarship in the field. In this tradition, researchers came increasingly to focus on "feedback effects" from institutions on the orientations and actions of elites and mass publics (Pierson 1993). This research direction thus shifted the focus from input-centered to output-centered explanations of political orientations and actions (Mettler and Soss 2004). The organizational and distributional effects of public policies,[5] in particular, came to be seen as fundamental in organizing constituencies, forming attitudes, and translating orientations into action. In this way, one could say that the institutionalist thinking came to emphasize the micro-effects (such as individual orientations) of macro-variables (such as institutions and public policies).

The "input-centered" critique of the putative social determinism of the early political sociology, exemplified by the Michigan School and by critics such as Sartori (1969), focused on the active roles of parties in translating social cleavages into political programs and strategies. The new institutionalist thinking replaced this, at least in theory, by an "output-centered" alternative. This alternative introduced a new kind of contingency in the relation between social cleavages and political outcomes, one centered on public policies as the practical outcomes of political institutions and their feedback effects. Doing this, Mettler and Soss argue, set a "political tradition" apart from and alongside sociological, economic, and psychological approaches to political life (Mettler and Soss 2004: 58).

THE STALLED REVOLUTION AND WAYS FORWARD

In spite of the increasing theoretical emphasis on feedback effects on mass publics, little in the way of systematic empirical analysis has yet been provided. Paul Pierson's complaint in the early 1990s, that feedback effects on mass publics "have yet to receive sufficient attention" (Pierson 1993: 597), is echoed by Mettler and Soss a decade later, when they argue that feedback "scholarship still pays insufficient attention to citizens" and that feedback effects "on mass opinion and behavior remain remarkably undertheorized" (Mettler and Soss 2004: 60; see also Weakliem 2005: 244).

Accordingly, the bulk of analyses of mass politics is still fairly input-centered. When Carmines and Huckfeldt eloquently summarized the state of the art in the research field of "political behavior," they were able to put forward what they saw as "a distinctively political model of citizenship" (Carmines and Huckfeldt 1996: 248) without once mentioning institutions or public policies. Social contexts, social networks, media effects, and political heuristics—all typically connected with the input side of politics—were presented as important parts of such a "political model of citizenship," while political institutions and public policies are marked by their absence.[6] A decade later, Weakliem (2005) did include "policy feedback" as one important aspect of recent research on the determinants of political attitudes but noted that Pierson's observation on the paucity of empirical research still applied.

In general, the field of political sociology is still heavily dominated by U.S. scholars,[7] and it is remarkable how little notice is taken of the importance of the political macro-context. Even excellent state-of-the-art papers such as Carmines and Huckfeldt (1996), Sniderman (1993), Brooks and Manza (Brooks et al. 2003; Manza et al. 2005), and Mettler and Soss (2004) take little notice of how specific some of the arguments and findings they present are for the U.S. context. Sometimes authors seem hardly aware that they discuss findings that are, or might be, specific for the United States. The neglect of the macro-context among U.S. scholars then becomes another obstacle to bringing political institutions and public policies systematically into the analysis.

Since so much of existing scholarship in the field is American, and since so little of it takes a comparative perspective into account, it is worth pointing out how different the American polity and cleavage structure is from the European context. First, the level of political and labor market organization is lower than in many European countries. Political parties have never been organized as mass parties with clear roots in the social structure and a strong party discipline, but as loose networks of pressure groups and specific constituencies (Lipset 1996: 39–46). Union density is much lower than in most European countries and has declined considerably in the last decades (Western 1997).

The weakness of political parties and trade unions makes the input side of politics quite different in the United States than in Europe, where organized collectives formulate demands and pursue policies. Such differences may also explain the lower level of attitudinal constraint and higher level of "non-attitudes" among Americans than among Europeans, or at least Scandinavians (Granberg and Holmberg 1988)—something that makes the Michigan School's focus on "non-attitudes" somewhat parochial. The findings in Chapter 6 of this book are also illustrative in pointing to the more coherent attitudes toward inequality found among Swedes than among Americans. Since the organizational structure of politics is much weaker in the United States than in Europe, political articulation becomes feebler, making politics less intelligible and more personalized, and this is probably the main explanation for findings in this respect.

Another most important difference between the American and the European context is the low institutional density of welfare policies in the United States. European citizens encounter the welfare state in many more shapes and to a much greater extent than Americans, thus making also the output side of politics rather different in Europe compared to the United

States. This has important implications for the analysis of feedback effects. For example, the distinction between clients and citizens is less clear-cut in universal systems, since most citizens are also in a sense clients of the welfare state, as parents, as receivers of social insurance benefits, or as receivers of pensions and services for the elderly. This also means that most Europeans have a much greater stake in the welfare state than most Americans. In universal systems, problems of redistribution and organization of services tend not to be about how "we" (the taxpayers) should treat "them" (people in need of the welfare state), but about how "we" (financiers *and* beneficiaries of the welfare state) should solve "our" problems (Svallfors 1996: Ch. 10; Rothstein 1998: Ch. 6).

Arguments such as these clearly call for comparative analysis. From the 1990s onward, an increasing number of studies have tackled issues about how national institutions and policy regimes affect, or are affected by, orientations among mass publics (for a selection of theoretically guided comparisons, see Bonoli 2000; Iversen and Soskice 2001; Andress and Heien 2001; Mau 2003; Svallfors 2003; 2006). Many of these analyses have taken as their departure the "worlds of welfare" framework famously introduced by Esping-Andersen, and analyze whether attitude patterns and conflict patterns correspond to the typology he suggested, and what might explain instances of noncorrespondence (for example, Andress and Heien 2001; Bonoli 2000; Svallfors 2003).

Yet, it has to be said that the ratio between theoretically and methodologically advanced comparative analyses, and papers parading "league tables of distributions showing merely 'gee whiz' national differences" (Jowell 1998: 168), is depressingly small. In the absence of any clear theoretical framework guiding the field, many comparative analyses of orientations among mass publics have tended to be of an ad hoc variety. Although the scholarly community has learned many things from such "single-issue" studies, the cumulation of knowledge in the field has been painstakingly slow.

It seems also that the main research strategy for the theoretically guided comparisons, to take their starting-point in Esping-Andersen's "worlds of welfare" framework, is now somewhat exhausted. We can hope to learn little that is new from yet another comparison of "x number of worlds of welfare" and their adjunct attitudes to the welfare state. However, this does not mean that the "regime" framework is of little value for continuing research. We hope to show in this book that it is now both possible and desirable to take steps beyond the "welfare regime" approach and ask both broader and more specific questions about the relations between cleavages, institutions, and orientations in a comparative perspective.

A precondition for such a "comparative turn" in political sociology has been the creation of new comparative databases, the two most important ones being the ISSP and the ESS, which we have used extensively in this volume.[8] The scope and continuity of the ISSP, the EVS/WVS, and the ESS are impressive and stand in stark contrast to previous attempts in the 1960s and 1970s to create comparative databases for political sociology. They all eventually floundered when the leading scholars retired or lost interest (Scheuch 1990). This points to the importance of the institutionalization of comparative surveys to avoid the death-and-rebirth cycle characteristic of previous attempts.

There are other signs apart from the improved data situation indicating that the field may now be entering a stage of marked progress. For one, progress in terms of data access has been matched by innovations and new directions in the methods applied to such data. These include techniques for analyzing categorical data (for an introduction, see Long 1997), for analyzing latent structures (such as LISREL, see Hoyle 1995; and Latent Class Analysis, see Hagenaars and McCutcheon 2002), and for conducting multilevel analysis (for an introduction, see Hox 2002). These techniques enable researchers to address theoretically pertinent issues with more rigor than allowed by standard regression techniques.[9]

Alongside these improvements in terms of data and methods, new theoretical developments have occurred, mainly within institutionalist theories. Many of these developments formed the core for the theoretical framework presented in Chapter 1, so there is no need to repeat them here. Suffice it to say that concepts and ideas such as feedback effects of institutions and public policies, and the moral economy of welfare states, clearly improve the conceptualization of the relation between institutions, social cleavages, and orientations. The discussion on how to go "beyond welfare regimes" is also clearly improving our opportunities to analyze the impact of changes in institutions and policies on orientations and action patterns.

CONTRIBUTIONS FROM THE ANALYSES

So the ground is prepared for researchers to take important steps ahead. To what extent has the present volume risen to the occasion and provided important contributions to political sociology? Note that the analyses we have conducted within the frame of this volume rest to a large extent on achievements provided by other comparative researchers. From comparative welfare state research we have picked a focus on institutional configurations and typologies ("regimes"). On many points we have criticized or extended existing categorizations and conceptualizations, and suggested other ways to understand the relation between national institutional configurations and individual-level orientations, but we have nevertheless relied extensively on precisely these typologies for framing our own queries.

Similarly, although we are skeptical about much in the sprawling field of comparative attitude studies, clearly few of our analyses could have been conducted without a background of knowledge about attitudinal patterns in comparative perspective. Such a background has been provided by existing research that uses the large-scale comparative databases that we have trawled ourselves.

Another main source of inspiration for our analyses is the extensive electoral research that has been conducted both nationally and in a comparative perspective. From this line of research we have picked a focus on how individuals' connection to parties and politics is conditioned by institutional and situational factors, a common thread in several of our chapters.

As argued by Huckfeldt and Sprague (1993: 299), it is a mistake to believe that small, intimate contexts close to the individual are the most important in affecting individual behavior and orientations. This is a line of thought that we have tried to implement in our analyses through our emphasis on a comparative and institutional perspective. In so doing, we are "bringing politics back in" in a completely different manner from that of the Michigan School and other critics of the "social determinism" that (supposedly) characterized early political sociology. Our route goes via historical institutionalism and comparative analyses, in sharp contrast to the turn toward political psychology that many commentators have suggested as the way forward in analyses of political life (for example, Kinder 1983: 413–416). In doing this, we are adopting a perspective on political life suggested already in 1961 by V. O. Key, when he complained that the growing social psychological influence in the study of public opinion had "abstracted public opinion from its governmental setting," and that the records needed to be rebalanced in that respect (Key 1961: vii). Our focus on the effects of political institutions and public policies clearly follows in that direction. Such programmatic statements aside, how have our chapters actually contributed to the field? This is not the place to summarize key empirical findings from the individual chapters—we attempted to do that in Chapter 1. We would prefer to discuss three more general themes from the analyses, under the headings of *institutional feedback mechanisms*, *political citizenship*, and *comparative European political sociology*.

Institutional Feedback Mechanisms

This first theme relates to the perennial question of what institutions actually do, or more specifically, what kinds of institutional feedback mechanisms are entailed. When discussing such effects, Pierson (1993) summarizes them under the headings of *resource and incentive effects* and *interpretive* effects. He argues that when feedback effects on mass publics are the focus, the resource and incentive effects are mainly manifested as "lock-in" effects, where previous institutional choices and pathways affect material interests so as to make changes difficult, while the interpretive effects are manifested as different degrees of visibility and traceability of policies.

The effects that Pierson points to are certainly important. Based on the results of work described in this volume, it nevertheless seems necessary to add a third feedback mechanism: a *normative* one. A normative feedback mechanism is present where public policies provide citizens with a sense not only of what their material interests are and who is responsible for different political decisions but also of the desirable state of affairs. This conception is clearly linked to the notion of a *moral economy*, which we have put squarely at the center of our analyses. Such normative effects cannot be reduced to "interpretive" effects. The latter, as Pierson points out, work mainly through the informational contents of policies: What do institutions tell citizens about how the world really works? Normative effects work rather through the evaluative aspects of policies: What do institutions tell citizens about what the world ought to look like?

A number of findings from particular chapters indicate that institutions affect normative considerations. For example, the findings that Swedes see smaller income differences as more legitimate than Americans, Britons, and Germans do (Chapter 6), or that there are manifest differences among countries about what money should buy (Chapter 6) and what government ought to do (Chapter 2), are hard to understand other than as normative effects from institutions.

The normative effects of institutions become really visible only when we apply a broad conception of feedback effects—that is, effects that are more than the direct effects of personal experiences with policies. The effects will include the total experience of living in a particular institutional environment, which constantly provides clues on what the desirable state of affairs should be. Such broad and indirect feedback effects demand a comparative framework of analysis to become visible for researchers. As long as one moves within a single national institutional framework, most of these broad and indirect feedback effects become constants and thus impossible to understand properly.

Another point where our arguments and analyses have provided input to the understanding of institutional effects is by emphasizing how institutions work as "focal points" around which political conflicts form and evolve. As Edlund points out in Chapter 2, the most important effects of institutions may be precisely such "second-order" effects. Institutional "guardians" and "challengers" impact the orientations of mass public through political articulation around existing institutions. Edlund's specific example is the existence of class-redistributive institutions in relation to the articulation of class politics, but the argument has a wider application. For many policy domains, the existence of institutions with a specific content tend to structure the interest groups that find it important to mobilize in defense or attack. This, in turn, helps to create and maintain specific orientations and cleavages among the mass publics in question.

Political Citizenship

The contributors to this volume have also provided substantial input into the analysis of political citizenship. We characterize political citizenship as the full inclusion in the polity of all citizens—that is, their inclusion as knowledgeable actors with the rights, the will, and the capacity to pursue their interests in the political arena. The classic treatment of political citizenship is found in T. H. Marshall's characterization of it as "the right to participate in the exercise of political power, as a member of a body invested with political authority or as an elector of the members of such a body" (Marshall 1950: 11). In Marshall's rendition, political citizenship is the second part of a sequence commencing with civil citizenship (granting judicial rights) and completed by social citizenship (granting rights to decent living conditions).

It is probably fair to say that comparative studies of citizenship have been preoccupied mainly with *social* citizenship (for some recent selected examples, see Korpi 1989; Esping-Andersen 1990; Orloff 1993; Korpi and Palme 1998, 2003; O'Connor et al. 1999; Huber and Stephens 2001). In this strand of investigation, researchers have analyzed the extent to which different policy arrangements secure social rights for different parts of the population in different polities and welfare regimes. Studies of political citizenship have been conducted mainly within countries (in particular the United States) or in fairly limited comparisons, although important exceptions can be found (see, in particular, Norris's triptych 2000; 2001; 2002).

Several chapters in this volume show that political citizenship is more complex than Marshall's definition implies. This was probably the case already in Marshall's days but is clearly so to an increasing extent today. For one thing, the issue that Hjerm raises in Chapter 7 is how to define *demos*: Who is considered a legitimate member of the body that is represented politically? Individuals' movements between nation-states, as well as the growth of supra- and subnational political representation, make the delineation of *demos* a more problematic question than in Marshall's days. Hjerm shows that although the nation-state has been challenged to a large extent, people's conception of the nation and their sense of allegiance and belonging are very stable.

An important extension of Marshall's conception of political citizenship may be found in several other chapters—by Kumlin (Chapter 3), Oskarson (Chapter 4), and Pettersson (Chapter 5)—which focus on the relation between public policies and institutional design on the one hand, and participation, (dis)trust, and alienation on the other. What emerges clearly in these chapters is, first, that a contemporary definition of political citizenship cannot focus solely on the formal *rights* to participate in political life but must also include the *real opportunities provided and competencies required*, in the form of interest, information, and efficacy. These chapters show that such things are unevenly distributed between groups within nation-states but also that they have different effects and interrelations in different institutional contexts.

Furthermore, these chapters also point out the importance, when analyzing political citizenship, of focusing not only on the input side but also on the output side of politics. What is missing from Marshall's definition is that people are political subjects in a double sense: they are ultimately the source of political legitimacy, but they are also the recipients of public policies (cf. Pierre 1995). In encompassing welfare states, citizens meet political life much more often in the form of public policies than as voters and political activists. What politics does for citizens in the form of public policies colors their view of themselves as political subjects: "Public policy shapes citizenship just as citizenship shapes public policy" (Hacker et al. 2005: 201).

When discussing what public policies do for citizenship, it is common to assume that universal and encompassing welfare states are always more empowering for citizens. They are therefore, the argument goes, more conducive for fostering substantial citizenship, both in its social and political aspects, than more targeted and circumscribed welfare states. This may well be true. However, the analyses in this book show clearly that encompassing welfare states may also be particularly conducive to disillusionment and alienation, if and when they are unable to keep the social contracts with their citizens (see, in particular, Chapters 3 and 4 by Kumlin and Oskarson, respectively). Here we may also speak of feedback effects of public policies—that is, the normative backlash that may follow when a state that has promised to guarantee living conditions for the whole population proves unable to deliver on its promises. In this respect, too, the notion of a moral economy proves useful for understanding powerful mass resentment about what may, in a comparative perspective, be seen as fairly modest cutbacks in the most encompassing welfare states. It is the feeling that the authorities have broken the tacit social contract that drives resentment, not necessarily the actual hardship imposed by cutbacks.[10]

An important third aspect of the analyses of political citizenship is what might be called the "long arm" of class relations. From Edlund (Chapter 2) and Svallfors (Chapter 6) we can see that class has important, although variable, effects on a host of normative aspects of redistribution and welfare state intervention. What is noted by Kumlin, Oskarson, and Pettersson (Chapters 3 through 5) is that class differences are substantial also when it comes to political discontent and disillusion, and political participation and activism. These findings are noted more in passing by the authors, since their main questions are different and they use class mostly as a control variable, but the findings still show up very clearly. These class differences seem to apply across a wide selection of countries and institutional contexts and point to the importance of not neglecting the impact of social cleavages grounded in the division of labor in explaining variations in political citizenship. Class relations must, according to our fairly restrictive definition of institutions, be seen as extra-institutional. It is important not to become so obsessed with institutional variation and feedback effects that such important extra-institutional factors are rendered invisible. In this sense, we are suggesting that the focus on social determinants, characteristic of early postwar political sociology, are not at all misplaced in contemporary analyses of political life in general and political citizenship in particular.

This is not, of course, to propagate any sociological reductionism in the study of political citizenship. The observation made in comparative electoral research, that the autonomy of the political has to be retained in the analysis of how social cleavages impact voting (Goldthorpe 1999), applies perhaps with even greater force to the study of how institutions affect the relationship between social cleavages and political citizenship.

Toward a Comparative European Political Sociology

The chapters in this volume, furthermore, move toward what might be termed a *comparative European political sociology*. Hjerm (Chapter 7) compares nationalism and patriotism in different countries with differing policy regimes, different relations to the European Union, and different immigration histories, and finds stability in virtually all countries in spite of quite different "baselines" for nationalist sentiments. Kumlin (Chapter 3) compares a large set of European countries to test the relation between dissatisfaction and declining normative support for income redistribution, finding that this effect seems to be particularly pronounced in the social democratic welfare regime of the Scandinavian countries. Oskarson (Chapter 4) compares countries with little welfare state retrenchment and countries with substantial retrenchment, revealing that social risk exposure had a particularly pronounced effect on political alienation in the latter. Pettersson (Chapter 5) compares how political dissatisfaction is translated into political action in different welfare regimes, discovering the effects to be generally weak and without any clear relation to welfare state regimes. It is interesting that while the welfare regime framework reveals interesting patterns in Kumlin's analysis, it has some but no large bearing on Oskar-son's results, and is virtually useless in interpreting Pettersson's findings. It seems different *explananda* are served differently well by using the welfare state regime typology.

Analyses like these, limited though they are, point out that even within a comparatively homogenous institutional environment such as the Euro-pean one, the complexity of institutional arrangements risks overwhelming the analytical tools we possess. The cautionary thoughts of Mayer (2005: 35) in summarizing the state of the art in life course research—that "out-comes are not conditioned on welfare 'regimes' or varieties of political economies, but rather on the concrete specifics of particular institutional rules and incentive systems," and that "aggregating countries therefore must introduce ambiguities which undermine the uses of such schemata in developing causal hypotheses"—applies with perhaps even greater force to comparative political sociology. The challenge is to become specific enough to tease out important institutional differences among countries without becoming overwhelmed by unwieldy variation. The solution, as prescribed by Mayer and practiced in the chapters in question, is to maintain a focus on the mechanisms through which institutions exert their influence. In this way, systematic patterns of association may be detected beneath the speci-ficity of national arrangements.

As Swedes, we cannot help noting that this focus on institutional mech-anisms seems to reveal findings about Sweden that amount to a debunking of persistent myths about how political life in this "model" country works. Edlund and Svallfors show that class differences in attitudes toward wel-fare policies and redistribution are particularly pronounced in Sweden—contrary to pronouncements about the consensual character of Scandinavian polities. Pettersson, Kumlin, and Oskarson in their research on partici-pation, trust, and alienation show patterns and levels to be quite similar in Sweden and in other European countries—contrary to assertions about how ingrained political equality is in the Scandinavian countries compared to elsewhere. Kumlin and Oskarson also show that the risk for "normative backlash" when the welfare state fails to deliver seems to be especially acute in Sweden—contrary to claims about how the universal Swedish welfare state is more or less immune to backlash. Findings such as these should not be read as amounting to a complete overhaul of previous arguments about Sweden's consensualism, equality, participatory polity, and universal support for welfare policies. Much of this is probably true. However, the findings work as necessary qualifications of what has sometimes amounted to hagiographic sagas of the triumphs of the Scandinavian welfare states.

BLIND SPOTS AND WAYS AHEAD

What lies ahead? More specifically, on what topics and aspects should a comparative European political sociology focus in coming years? For a start, we should *not* expect within political sociology in the near future any convergence on a "one best theoretical model." As put by Carmines and Huckfeldt (1996: 235), there is "no official microtheory that is inseparable from the political sociology tradition," and things will probably stay that way. What we can expect rather is the development of a set of issues and ways to tackle them. In this way, political sociology will remain true to the approach of the pioneering Columbia School half a century ago. Research problems and substantive topics are likely to run the field, not theories or methods.

We should also note a couple of substantive issues that are completely missing from our own analyses but clearly deserve attention in a European comparative perspective. One is gender. Our focus has been mainly set on class, but many of the assumptions and analytical strategies we have applied could just as fruitfully be applied to the question of how gender as a social cleavage affects orientations and how this relation is modified by institutions and public policies. An interesting hypothesis to test in this regard would be that the political salience of gender, and attitudinal differences between men and women, are affected less by the real gender differences in different contexts, and more by the political articulation of gender issues.[11]

A second missing aspect is Europeanization itself—that is, the orientation toward the European supra-state machinery and its output. Many of the analyses in this book have compared citizens of European countries in their orientations toward national policies; an important future task would be to apply the same kind of framework and strategies in comparing citizens' orientations toward pan-European issues (cf. Mau 2005). This is especially interesting since many of the problematic aspects we have described about national politics—low visibility, diffuse accountability, little comprehensibility for ordinary citizens—would seem to apply with even greater force at a European level (cf. Schmidt 2005).

Apart from filling up these obvious gaps, it would seem worthwhile to focus more explicitly on the dynamics of orientations than we have done in this volume. Here we have been severely restrained by data access, but this will change in the future when subsequent rounds of the European Social Survey and the International Social Survey Program become available.[12]

Fruitful as these new datasets will doubtlessly prove, the creation of truly longitudinal comparative studies, where the same individuals are followed over a long period, would be even more desirable. As we have shown in several of our chapters, trying to determine causal relations in cross-sectional datasets can result only in suggestive interpretations rather than conclusive statements. Panel data, in contrast to cross-sectional data, if properly produced and analyzed will allow the establishment of the time order of events, making it possible for the analyst to establish causal effects with a greater degree of certainty.

Note also that the comparisons allowed by existing ESS and ISSP data have to be posed at a fairly general level, thus possibly concealing important variations between different institutional settings. Crucially lacking are data specific enough to reveal any possible variations in attitudes between different institutional and cultural environments, yet comparable across countries. Not least, such data could allow comparisons of how personal experiences of different kinds of public policies impact orientations. Important within-country analyses of this kind exist (Soss 1999; 2005; Kumlin 2004), but it seems essential to extend these into comparative analysis. As Pettersson argues in Chapter 5, there are good theoretical reasons to expect the effect of personal experiences on orientations and action patterns to differ both between and within different welfare regimes, but existing data do not allow systematic comparisons on this point.

More extensive contextual data and analyses can also bring our understanding forward. In the chapters of this book, there have certainly been data about the macro-context. These data have supported categorizations of countries, motivated selection of cases, and served as support for explanatory interpretations. One important task for the future would be to more explicitly model the macro-context and bring it in as a set of variables in multilevel analyses. The data, in the form of comparative macro-indicators of all sorts, and methods in the form of various techniques for multilevel modeling already exist, but analyses lag behind.

To summarize: the field of survey-based political sociology has changed considerably since its early postwar inception. It has become explicitly comparative, using country variation as an important tool for understanding the mechanisms of political life, and it has become more attentive to the effects of the output side of politics on orientations and action patterns. The analyses offered in this volume are, of course, but a small contribution to this field. However, as has been pointed out repeatedly in this concluding chapter, there is reason to believe that the field will now once again rise as a very dynamic and scientifically progressive one. Much is done; everything remains.

NOTES

1. In this chapter, I discuss the development of the subfield of political sociology that relates to survey-based research. No attempt is made to write the history of political sociology in general, including topics such as regime transitions, theories of the state, causes of revolutions, social movements, and so on. Given the amount of research, that would be a daunting task and an appropriate topic for a book-length text that to a large extent would fall outside our purview here.

2. The section about the Columbia School draws extensively on Cole (2004) and the works cited there.

3. The section on the Michigan School draws mostly on Manza and Brooks (1999: 14–15) and Kinder (1983).

4. The approach of the Michigan School set an example and a framework for election studies that were inaugurated elsewhere during the 1950s and 1960s—for example, the Swedish election study, which is the most long-standing of such surveys. What information to collect in such surveys was clearly decided by a "Michigan type" model of electoral behavior (Thomassen 2005: 1).

5. The difference between institutions and public policies is not clear-cut. As put by Streeck and Thelen, some public policies "stipulate rules that assign normatively backed rights and responsibilities to actors and provide for the 'public,' that is, third party enforcement," and may therefore be seen as institutions (Streeck and Thelen 2005: 12)

6. Characteristically, political institutions are discussed in other chapters of the same volume, without any particular emphasis on the behavior of mass publics (Rothstein 1996).

7. One indication of this can be found in the 2005 *Handbook of Political Sociology* (Janoski et al. 2005), where only 7 out of 49 contributors were based outside the United States. Of these 7, 3 hold PhD degrees from an American university, a fourth was employed for almost a decade at the University of Wisconsin–Madison, and 2 of the remaining contributors were based in Canada and Mexico. That is, only 1 out of 49 contributors had both his current and previous positions and his degree from Europe.

8. A third important data source is the European/World Values Surveys, which have been conducted in 1981, 1990, 1996, and 1999.

9. The basics of all these statistical innovations have been known for a long time, in some cases several decades, and have been widely used for some time. Their application in routine analytical use requires that appropriate easy-to-use software is available in order to make investment costs less prohibitive. The past couple of decades have seen considerable improvements in this regard.

10. This is a very similar line of reasoning to the one found in Thompson's (1971) original rendering of the term "moral economy." Here he argued that the recurring "bread riots" in eighteenth-century England were driven not mainly by hunger and desperation but by feelings of injustice and betrayal that he explained by the existence of a "moral economy," which summarized the mutual rights and obligations between people and authorities.

11. An interesting development in this respect is the foundation of a new gender-based party (*Feministiskt initiativ*) in Sweden in 2005. This party articulates women's grievances in what is arguably the most gender-equal society in the world and one that has moved rapidly toward gender equality during the postwar period. It demonstrates clearly that *de*creased real stratification may well lead to *in*creased political articulation regarding that issue. It will be interesting to see to what extent this new party affects gender differences in policy attitudes—that so far have been quite muted compared to class differences.

12. Earlier rounds of ISSP than the ones we have used are available—for example, the Role of Government 1986 and 1990 and Social Inequality 1987. Due to the coverage of countries and coding of important variables, they have been of less interest for us.

REFERENCES

Andress, H. J., and Heien, T. 2001. Four Worlds of Welfare State Attitudes? A Comparison of Germany, Norway, and the United States. *European Sociological Review*, 17, 337–56.

Bartolini, S. 2000. *The Political Mobilization of the European Left, 1860–1980: The Class Cleavage*. Cambridge: Cambridge University Press.

Bartolini, S., and Mair, P. 1990. *Identity, Competition and Electoral Availability: The Stabilisation of European Electorates 1885–1985*. Cambridge: Cambridge University Press.

Bonoli, G. 2000. Public Attitudes to Social Protection and Political Economy Traditions in Western Europe. *European Societies*, 2, 431–52.

Brooks, C., Manza, J., and Bolzendahl, C. 2003. Voting Behaviour and Political Sociology: Theories, Debates, and Future Directions. *Research in Political Sociology*, 12, 137–73.

Bulmer, M., Bales, K., and Sklar, K. K. 1991. The Social Survey in Historical Perspective. In *The Social Survey in Historical Perspective 1880–1940*, edited by Bulmer, M., Bales, K., and Sklar, K. K. Cambridge: Cambridge University Press.

Campbell, A., Converse, P. E., Miller, W., and Stokes, D. E. 1960. *The American Voter*. New York: Wiley.

Carmines, E. G., and Huckfeldt, R. 1996. Political Behavior—An Overview. In *A New Handbook of Political Science*, edited by Goodin, R. E., and Klingemann, H.-D. Cambridge: Cambridge University Press, pp. 223–54.

Cole, J. R. 2004. *Paul F. Lazarsfeld: His Scholarly Journey*. Keynote address delivered at "An International Symposium in Honor of Paul Lazarsfeld," June 4–5, 2004, Brussels.

Converse, J. M. 1987. *Survey Research in the United State: Roots and Emergence 1890–1960*. Berkeley: University of California Press.

Converse, P. E. 1964. The Nature of Belief Systems in Mass Publics. In *Ideology and Discontent*, edited by Apter, D. E. New York: Free Press.

Esping-Andersen, G. 1990. *The Three Worlds of Welfare Capitalism*. Cambridge: Polity Press.

Goldthorpe, J. H. 1999. Commentary. In *The End of Class Politics? Class Voting in Comparative Context*, edited by Evans, G. Oxford: Oxford University Press, pp. 318–22.

Granberg, D., and Holmberg, S. 1988. *The Political System Matters: Social Psychology and Voting Behavior in Sweden and the United States*. Cambridge: Cambridge University Press.

Hacker, J. S., Mettler, S., and Pinderhughes, D. 2005. Inequality and Public Policy. In *Inequality and American Democracy: What We Know and What We Need to Learn*. Edited by Jacobs, L., and Skocpol, T. New York: Russell Sage Foundation, pp. 156–213.

Hagenaars, J. A., and McCutcheon, A. L. 2002. *Applied Latent Class Analysis*. New York: Cambridge University Press.

Hox, J. J. 2002. *Multilevel Analysis: Techniques and Applications*. Mahwah, N.J.: Lawrence Erlbaum.

Hoyle, R. H. 1995. *Structural Equation Modeling: Concepts, Issues, and Applications*. Thousand Oaks, Calif.: Sage.

Huber, E., and Stephens, J. D. 2001. *Development and Crisis of the Welfare State: Parties and Policies in Global Markets*. Chicago: University of Chicago Press.

Huckfeldt, R., and Sprague, J. 1993. Citizens, Contexts and Politics. In *Political Science: The State of the Discipline II*, edited by Finifter, A. W. Washington: American Political Science Association, pp. 281–303.

Iversen, T., and Soskice, D. 2001. An Asset Theory of Social Policy Preferences. *American Political Science Review*, 95, 875–93.

Janoski, T., Alford, R., Hicks, A., and Schwartz, M. A., eds. 2005. *The Handbook of Political Sociology: States, Civil Societies, and Globalization*. Cambridge: Cambridge University Press.

Jowell, R. 1998. How Comparative Is Comparative Research? *American Behavioral Scientist*, 42, 168–77.

Key, V. O. 1961. *Public Opinion and American Democracy*. New York: Alfred A Knopf.

Kinder, D. R. 1983. Diversity and Complexity in American Public Opinion. In *Political Science: The State of the Discipline*, edited by Finifter, A. W. Washington: American Political Science Association, pp. 389–425.

Korpi, W. 1989. Power, Politics, and State Autonomy in the Development of Social Citizenship—Social Rights during Sickness in 18 OECD Countries since 1930. *American Sociological Review*, 54, 309–28.

Korpi, W., and Palme, J. 1998. The Paradox of Redistribution and Strategies of Equality: Welfare State Institutions, Inequality, and Poverty in the Western Countries. *American Sociological Review*, 63, 661–87.

Korpi, W., and Palme, J. 2003. New Politics and Class Politics in the Context of Austerity and Globalization: Welfare State Regress in 18 Countries 1975–1995. *American Political Science Review*, 97, 425–46.

Kumlin, S. 2004. *The Personal and the Political: How Personal Welfare State Experiences Affect Political Trust and Ideology*. New York: Palgrave Macmillan.

Lazarsfeld, P. F., Gaudet, H., and Berelson, B. 1944. *The People's Choice: How the Voter Makes Up His Mind in a Presidential Campaign*. New York: Duell Sloan and Pearce.

Lijphart, A., and Aitkin, D. 1994. *Electoral Systems and Party Systems: A Study of Twenty-seven Democracies, 1945–1990*. Oxford: Oxford University Press.

Lipset, S. M. 1960. *Political Man. The Social Bases of Politics*. Baltimore: Johns Hopkins University Press.

Lipset, S. M. 1996. *American Exceptionalism: A Double-edged Sword*. New York: W.W. Norton.

Lipset, S. M., and Rokkan, S. 1967. *Party Systems and Voter Alignments: Cross-national Perspectives*. New York: Free Press.

Long, J. S. 1997. *Regression Models for Categorical and Limited Dependent Variables*. Thousand Oaks, Calif.: Sage.

Manza, J., and Brooks, C. 1999. *Social Cleavages and Political Change: Voter Alignments and U.S. Party Coalitions*. Oxford: Oxford University Press.

Manza, J., Brooks, C., and Sauder, M. 2005. Money, Participation, and Votes: Social Cleavages and Electoral Politics. In *The Handbook of Political Sociology: States, Civil Societies, and Globalization*, edited by Janoski, T., Alford, R., Hicks, A., and Schwartz, M. A. Cambridge: Cambridge University Press, pp. 201–26.

Marshall, T. H. 1950. *Citizenship and Social Class and Other Essays*. Cambridge: Cambridge University Press.

Mau, S. 2003. *The Moral Economy of Welfare States. Britain and Germany Compared*. London: Routledge.

Mau, S. 2005. Democratic Demand for a Social Europe? Preferences of the European Citizenry. *International Journal of Social Welfare*, 14, 76–85.

Mayer, K. U. 2005. Life Courses and Life Chances in a Comparative Perspective. In *Analyzing Inequality. Life Chances and Social Mobility in Comparative Perspective*, edited by Svallfors, S. Stanford, Calif.: Stanford University Press, pp. 17–55.

Mettler, S., and Soss, J. 2004. The Consequences of Public Policy for Democratic Citizenship: Bridging Policy Studies and Mass Politics. *Perspectives on Politics*, 2, 55–73.

Norris, P. 2000. *A Virtuous Circle: Political Communications in Postindustrial Societies*. Cambridge: Cambridge University Press.

Norris, P. 2001. *Digital Divide? Civic Engagement, Information Poverty, and the Internet Worldwide*. Cambridge: Cambridge University Press.

Norris, P. 2002. *Democratic Phoenix: Reinventing Political Activism*. Cambridge: Cambridge University Press.

Norris, P. 2004. *Electoral Engineering: Voting Rules and Political Behavior*. Cambridge: Cambridge University Press.

O'Connor, J. S., Shaver, S., and Orloff, A. S. 1999. *States, Markets, Families: Gender, Liberalism and Social Policy in Australia, Canada, Great Britain and the United States*. Cambridge: Cambridge University Press.

Orloff, A. S. 1993. Gender and the Social Rights of Citizenship—the Comparative Analysis of Gender Relations and Welfare States. *American Sociological Review*, 58, 303–28.

Pierre, J. 1995. The Marketization of the State: Citizens, Consumers, and the Emergence of the Public Market. In *Governance in a Changing Environment*, edited by Peters, B. G. and Savoie, D. J. Montreal: McGill-Queens University Press, pp. 55–81.

Pierson, P. 1993. When Effect Becomes Cause: Policy Feedback and Political Change. *World Politics*, 45, 595–628.

Pierson, P. 2001. *The New Politics of the Welfare State*. Oxford: Oxford University Press.

Rimlinger, G. V. 1971. *Welfare Policy and Industrialization in Europe, America, and Russia*. New York: Wiley.

Rothstein, B. 1996. Political Institutions—An Overview. In *A New Handbook of Political Science*, edited by Goodin, R. E. and Klingemann, H.-D. Cambridge: Cambridge University Press, pp. 133–66.

Rothstein, B. 1998. *Just Institutions Matter: The Moral and Political Logic of the Universal Welfare State*. Cambridge: Cambridge University Press.

Sartori, G. 1969. From the Sociology of Politics to Political Sociology. In *Politcs and the Social Sciences*, edited by Lipset, S. M. New York: Oxford University Press, pp. 65–100.

Sartori, G. 1976. *Parties and Party Systems: A Framework for Analysis*. Cambridge: Cambridge University Press.

Scharpf, F. W., and Schmidt, V. A. 2000. *Welfare and Work in the Open Economy.* Oxford: Oxford University Press.

Scheuch, E. K. 1990. The Development of Comparative Research: Towards Causal Explanations. In *Comparative Methodology*, Vol. 4, edited by Øyen, E. London: Sage, pp. 19–37.

Schmidt, V. A. 2005. Democracy in Europe: The Impact of European Integration. *Perspectives on Politics*, 3, 761–79.

Sniderman, P. M. 1993. The New Look in Public Opinion Research. In *Political Science: The State of the Discipline II*, edited by Finifter, A. W. Washington: American Political Science Association, pp. 219–45.

Soss, J. 1999. Lessons of Welfare: Policy Design, Political Learning, and Political Action. *American Political Science Review*, 93, 363–80.

Soss, J. 2005. Making Clients and Citizens: Welfare Policy as a Source of Status, Belief and Action. In *Deserving and Entitled: Social Constructions and Public Policy*, edited by Schneider, A., and Ingram, H. Stony Brook: State University of New York Press, pp. 291–328.

Streeck, W., and Thelen, K. 2005. Introduction. In *Beyond Continuity. Institutional Change in Advanced Political Economies*, edited by Streeck, W., and Thelen, K. Oxford: Oxford University Press, pp. 1–39.

Svallfors, S. 1996. *Välfärdsstatens moraliska ekonomi: välfärdsopinionen i 90-talets Sverige*, Umeå: Boréa.

Svallfors, S. 2003. Welfare Regimes and Welfare Opinions: A Comparison of Eight Western Countries. *Social Indicators Research*, 64, 495–520.

Svallfors, S. 2006. *The Moral Economy of Class. Class and Attitudes in Comparative Perspective.* Stanford: Stanford University Press.

Thomassen, J. 2005. *The European Voter. A Comparative Study of Modern Democracies.* Oxford: Oxford University Press.

Thompson, E. P. 1971. The Moral Economy of the English Crowd in the Eighteenth Century. *Past & Present*, 50, 71–136.

Weakliem, D. L. 2005. Public Opinion, Political Attitudes, and Ideology. In *The Handbook of Political Sociology: States, Civil Societies, and Globalization*, edited by Janoski, T., Alford, R., Hicks, A., and Schwartz, M. A. Cambridge: Cambridge University Press, pp. 227–47.

Western, B. 1997. *Between Class and Market: Postwar Unionization in the Capitalist Democracies.* Princeton, N.J.: Princeton University Press.

Wilensky, H. L. 1975. *The Welfare State and Equality: Structural and Ideological Roots of Public Expenditures.* Berkeley: University of California Press.

INDEX

(Italic page numbers indicate material in tables or figures)